The White-Collar Crime Explosion

How to Protect Yourself
and Your Company
from Prosecution

Roger J. Magnuson
Dorsey & Whitney
Minneapolis, Minnesota

Foreword by Boris Kostelanetz

McGraw-Hill, Inc.
New York St. Louis San Francisco Auckland Bogotá
Caracas Lisbon London Madrid Mexico Milan
Montreal New Delhi Paris San Juan São Paulo
Singapore Sydney Tokyo Toronto

Library of Congress Cataloging-in-Publication Data

Magnuson, Roger J., date
   The white-collar crime explosion : how to protect yourself and
your company from prosecution / Roger J. Magnuson
      p. cm.
   Includes index.
   ISBN 0-07-039520-9
   1. White collar crime investigation—United States.
2. Corporations—United States—Corrupt practices. 3. Corporation
law—United States—Criminal provisions. I. Title.
HV8079.W47M34 1992
364.1'68'0973—dc20   92-3351
                                                       CIP

1 2 3 4 5 6 7 8 9 0 DOC/DOC 9 8 7 6 5 4 3 2

ISBN   0-07-039520-9

*The sponsoring editor for this book was Betsy N. Brown, the editing supervisor was
Valerie L. Miller, and the production supervisor was Pamela A. Pelton. It was set in
Baskerville by Carol Woolverton, Lexington, Mass.*

Printed and bound by R. R. Donnelley & Sons Company.

To my Mother
who taught me that crime does not pay

About the Author

Roger J. Magnuson is an attorney with the firm of Dorsey &
Whitney, Minneapolis. He has successfully defended both
corporations and individuals who have been prosecuted by
the government for white-collar crimes. Mr. Magnuson also
works in the area of First Amendment litigation, and is the
author of *Shareholder Litigation*.

Contents

CAUTIONARY

generally
larger-set pol.
regardless of
their performance

Foreword

In 56 years (a span of time which exceeds one-fourth of the life of this Republic) in the vocation of a prosecutor some of the time and defense counsel for the most, this lawyer has seen countless books written by lawyers about the law. Volumes have varied in approach from "how-to" books to esoteric studies only for fellow specialists. Indeed, there are even modest memoirs which recount in great detail how their authors won cases that should have been lost, giving but brief view to lost cases which they should have won. Since so much has been written by lawyers, what makes this book special?

For one thing, while the author repeatedly cites Scriptures and classics as authority, this book does not in any way pretend to resemble a tonal replicate of Deuteronomy. On the contrary, it ably provides laymen with the kind of intellectual discourse concerning citizens' rights and obligations that are exchanged regularly among lawyers—however, it does so in laymen's language. Many of the profound observations are written in the first person and represent communications from one person to another.

It is my observation, with a degree of caution, that the growth of recent prosecutions in the prosecutors' "war" on white-collar crime is a reflection of an appropriate reference to recent political history which boasted the aim of "getting Washington off the backs of business." While this goal had an aim properly commendable, one result was less policing and control of tawdry business practices. In some cases, leaving business to police itself created a familiar image as "letting the fox police the chicken coop." Consequently, we can expect that white-collar crime, its prosecution and defense, are here to stay for a considerable time.

This writer believes that *The White-collar Crime Explosion* teaches two major lessons. Firstly, it properly tells the reader that involvement of any kind in a white-collar offense can have the most serious criminal implications. The individual, be that person a chief executive officer or even a lowly bookkeeper, simply cannot handle the legal problems in a legal subspecialty all by himself no more than he could pull a tooth or remove a cataract without professional help. A lawyer working in this area can present a mass of anecdotal evidence of mishandled cases, many of which were beyond repair.

Secondly, this book performs a social service in revealing to the lay reader that our laws and our Constitution have within them the important conception that the obligation of members of society to keep their house in order applies to all except the lawyer of a person professionally involved in a claim of crime. His sole responsibility is to be at his client's side and to secure the client's exoneration within the law. The prescription has been well worded by a lawyer of an earlier generation who practiced in New York and who wrote:

> When I obtained an acquittal in a meritorious case (which did not always mean innocence) I have had the satisfaction of knowing that I helped to prevent an injustice by mitigating the rigors of the law. When I succeeded in enabling a malefactor to escape his just deserts I had the glowing gratification of having accomplished a professional *tour de force.*
>
> This gratification was intensified by the knowledge that I had lived up to my obligation as an officer of the court, had acted in accordance with the codes of legal ethics and centuries of tradition.
>
> 9 Rec. A.B. City N.Y. 218 (1954).

Indeed, our traditions are such that even "the guilty" have rights. As often stated, they have the right to silence, in most instances, the right not to produce records, the right to ask to appear before the grand jury, the right to have the prosecution come to court with clean hands, the right to counsel at trial, the right to trial by jury, the right to prove that the prosecution is wrong, the right to testify or not to testify on their own behalf, the right to have the jury advised of their rights, and most importantly the opportunity to be found innocent.

Boris Kostelanetz

Preface

The newspapers increasingly delight in turning inside out the smudged white collars of corporate executives accused of criminal behavior. There is a "man bites dog" journalistic appeal to stories of the powerful and prestigious sitting forlorn in the dock.

But as common as these stories are, with the recent and astonishing explosion of white-collar crime prosecutions, there are many more potential stories just beneath the surface. The tip of the iceberg is, here as elsewhere, a small portion of the total mass. Thousands of businesses and business executives are threatened, even though no indictment ultimately comes down.

This book contains a variety of accounts both of white-collar criminal investigations and actual prosecutions. Some have come to public attention and are generally known. Some have never come to public attention or have been mentioned only briefly and locally.

For that reason, this book seeks to, in the time-honored phrase, "protect the innocent." While many publicized cases are referred to by name, there are many others in which names have been changed and facts altered, to prevent embarrassment to clients or other parties. For example, names, facts, and circumstances have been changed in the account of "John Fletcher" in Chapter 4 and the other anecdotes in that chapter. Real names have not been used in the accounts of that chapter or for the stories related in Chapters 6 and 9. Any similarity to names of real persons is coincidental. The stories are based on real situations, but the names are fictitious. While the names may be fictional, the risks depicted were, and are, real. And the critical facts are as they have been portrayed.

Roger J. Magnuson

1

The United States versus You

When the phone rang in our suite on the 16th floor of the Kellogg Apartments, directly across from the federal courthouse, Tom Bedell was sitting in an easy chair in the corner, eclipsed from view by *The Wall Street Journal* that he had a death grip on.

The jury had gone out several hours before to deliberate the fate of Berkley and Company, a successful fishing products company conceived by Tom Bedell's father, Berkley Bedell, in his basement, when he had found while yet a teenager that he had a special knack for tying flies. Now, however, the jury was deliberating the fate of both the company and its president, Donald Porter, on 26 counts of alleged federal crimes.

Tom, young, bright, and savvy, a Stanford graduate who had successfully run a number of political campaigns in Washington and had a few months earlier returned to take over the presidency of Berkley, was sitting with me and my colleague, Brian Palmer, after a lengthy trial.

He had been remarkably calm throughout the ordeal. But a single ring of the telephone belied his studied reserve.

As the phone rang its first ring, a possible signal that the jury had reached a verdict, *The Wall Street Journal* ripped down the middle, leaving Tom with half a newspaper in each hand. I recalled the statement of Learned Hand, one of the great federal judges in American history, who said, "After now some dozen years of experience I must say that as a litigant I should dread a lawsuit beyond almost anything else short of sickness and death."

The call was no false alarm. The jury had returned. We walked slowly to the elevators, the quiet broken sporadically by small talk. We strolled

1

across the street and found our way back to the familiar courtroom. Don Porter and his counsel, Alan Cunningham, were already there.

As with all jury verdicts in important cases, the process took forever. At stake was a company, the professional career of its president, the political career of Berkley Bedell, still the substantial owner and chairman of the company's board (and a sitting congressman known as an ethical watchdog in the House of Representatives), and, potentially, the freedom of Mr. Porter.

Judge and jury entered the courtroom. Everyone rose. The suspense-filled dance began.

"Ladies and Gentlemen, have you reached a verdict?" the judge asked.

The foreman rose with a paper in his hand. "Yes we have, your Honor."

"You may give it to the clerk."

The clerk walked slowly toward the foreman, took the verdict, and carried it over to his judge. The judge read through it carefully. Counsel for both sides strained to see any expression on his face that would tip them off as to the contents of what he was reading. The judge's face was expressionless.

The judge then gave the verdict back to the clerk. "You may read the verdict."

The clerk, standing rigid and formal, cleared his throat and began to read.

"United States District Court, District of Minnesota, Fourth Division." The reading of the caption seemed to take minutes.

"United States of America versus Berkley and Company and Donald E. Porter, Defendants." Counsel scanned the faces of the jury to see if there was a smile or disapproving deflected eyes. "We, the jury, find the Defendant Berkley and Company," the clerk paused for dramatic effect, "not guilty as to Count 1 of the indictment." That meant there were 12 more to go with respect to the company, as well as 13 with respect to Mr. Porter. "Not guilty with respect to Count 2. Not guilty with respect to Count 3. Not guilty with respect to Counts 4 through 13." Tom Bedell smiled, making a clenched fist and pumping it. Don Porter and counsel sat stoically at the table waiting for their results.

"We, the jury, find Donald E. Porter . . . not guilty with respect to Counts 1 through 13." Don and his lawyer shook hands. Don looked at the jury and nodded a silent, smiling thank you.

Soon the jury was dismissed after a few words from the judge, and the United States attorney and government agents walked out of the courtroom, the U.S. attorney whispering to his assistant from Customs, "at least maybe you learned something."

There were congratulations all around on the defense side, a call to Congressman Bedell, a press conference in which the congressman expressed gratitude for vindication of his company and its employees, the normal victory laps, the rush that comes with combat successfully concluded.

But I still remembered that ripping *Wall Street Journal*, and the relative rarity of federal acquittals (approximately 10 percent of crimes charged). I thought of how many companies, as honorable as Berkley, and how many individuals, as honest as Don Porter, would continue to find themselves under unimaginable stress in such courtrooms, seeing themselves as they never had before—as criminal defendants. Perhaps many such cases could be prevented if managers about to make an "aggressive" decision could picture themselves sitting in that chair at the Kellogg Apartments, waiting for the phone to ring.

2
The Explosion of White-Collar Crime Prosecutions

(Why Pharisees Get Convicted and Publicans Get Acquitted)

A biblical parable tells the story well. Two men go up to the temple to pray. The one is a highly regarded Pharisee, well dressed and confident, the very model of the respected professional. The other is a publican, a tax collector, an occupation known for fraud and extortion.

The Roman tax system was partly responsible, to be sure, for the publican's peculiar temptations. Publicans were permitted a percentage of the taxes they collected. The incentives created by this contingent fee arrangement were obvious. And most publicans seized this license to steal with both hands.

The business community regarded publicans with the same esteem they regarded common thieves. While the regular tax collectors collected the normal property, income, and poll taxes and were no more popular than the IRS of our day, this *publican* was of an ingenious breed known as the *mokhes*, whose very title has the root meaning of theft and oppression. The publican aggressively collected duties on axles, wheels, pack animals, bridges, roads, pedestrians, quays, licenses, river crossings, and anything else he could think of to exact a 12 to 26 percent *ad valorem* duty on.

4

But the money that the publican swindled was no worse than his vexatious practices in collecting it. The traveler was always being stopped by the wayside, forced to unload his pack animal, open every package or bale, expose every bit of correspondence, and await the verdict of the rapacious mokhes. So bad were the publicans' reputations for corruption that any form of deception against them was explicitly permitted by religious law.

The popular perception, therefore, was well established. As a common folk tale had it, the son of a publican died at the same time as the son of a pious man. Surprisingly, the citizens of the town gave the publican honors at his burial while neglecting to mourn the passing of the pious son. The anomaly had the following explanation. The son of the pious man had committed one sin in his life, while the publican has committed one good deed. Such an extraordinary act of moral supererogation by the publican, in rising above his fellows, merited special distinction at death. It was "man bites dog" news.

Against this backdrop, the Pharisee began to pray first. As he noticed his companion, he could not resist the obvious comparison. "Lord, I thank thee that I am not covetous, unjust, or a swindler like this publican." But the comparisons could not stop there, on a negative note. The Pharisee went on to remind God of the positive virtues he possessed that the publican manifestly did not, the habits of tithing, fasting, and charitable giving. In all these contrasts, this bright young professional felt good about himself and his future.

But while the Pharisee was thanking God for his rectitude, the publican could not even lift up his face toward heaven. He was making no comparisons. He was reciting no virtues. He could only beat his breast and pray, "God be merciful to me a sinner." His visit to the temple was for him a visit to a courtroom. He gave no appearance of feeling good about himself.

But then we are advised of the irony that gives the story its special moral. There is a split verdict. We are advised that the publican went away "justified"—or, as another translation has it, "acquitted." The Pharisee? Guilty as charged.

Why Pharisees Get Convicted: White-Collar Jeopardy

There are many reasons for such surprising convictions. Some will be explored in succeeding chapters. But one is paramount.

The Pharisee never saw the jeopardy he was in, and thus took no steps to protect himself against it.

The Pharisee knew the judge was outraged at the conduct of publicans, as well he should be. They were disloyal and dishonest. What he did not understand was that God's prosecutorial eye was appraising conduct of people like him with equal severity—perhaps *more* severity—of that of the common street criminal. His prosecutor had an eye on the well-dressed professional.

Figure 2-1, taken from a recent FBI report on white-collar crime, suggests how the FBI these days looks at your sophisticated telephone system and office layout.

But the jeopardy of white collars is apparent from more than pictures. Statistics reflect the growing interest of federal and state prosecutors in business crimes. In the recent FBI report, *White-Collar Crime: A Report to the Public,* William S. Sessions, Director of the FBI, opens the report as follows:

> The investigation of white-collar crime remains one of the top national priorities of the Federal Bureau of Investigation (FBI). More FBI resources are dedicated to this crime problem than any other

Figure 2-1. Financial crimes. (*White-Collar Crime: A Report to the Public, Department of Justice, Federal Bureau of Investigation, p. 22.*)

criminal program within our jurisdiction. Approximately 1,600 Special Agents have been tasked to address over 17,000 investigations nationwide . . . During fiscal year 1988, FBI white-collar crime program investigations were funded with approximately $174,563,000.

Such a war chest few corporate legal budgets will match. And the FBI is only one of the cops on the white-collar beat. Other agencies, such as the Postal Service, the Customs Service, the IRS, and the Department of Agriculture, also have their own police force seeking evidence of criminal activity. Consider the following graphs from the FBI (Figs. 2-2 through 2-4), and imagine similar patterns for other federal agencies.

Whether mail fraud, contract fraud, environmental fraud, financial fraud, environmental crime, HUB fraud, veterans administration fraud, or any of a host of other regulatory crimes mentioned in the report, the graphs all point sharply upward to increased jeopardy for the white-collar defendant.

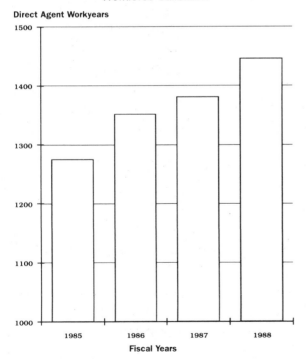

White-Collar Crime Program

Workforce Utilization

Direct Agent Workyears

Figure 2-2. White-collar program: Workforce utilization. (*White-Collar Crime: A Report to the Public, Department of Justice, Federal Bureau of Investigation, p. 31.*)

White-Collar Crime Program

Percentage of Workforce Utilized on Priority Cases

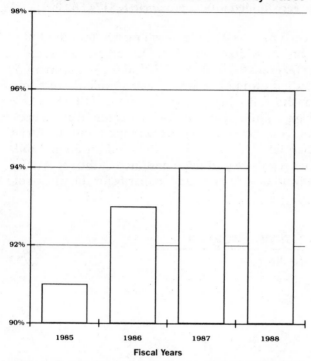

Fiscal Years

Figure 2-3. White-collar crime program: Percentage of work-force utilized on priority cases. (*White-Collar Crime: A Report to the Public, Department of Justice, Federal Bureau of Investigation, p. 31.*)

As *The Washington Post* reported, in March of 1990:

> The indictment earlier this week of Exxon Corp. on charges stemming from the Exxon Valdez oil spill and Northrup Corp.'s guilty plea to 34 criminal fraud charges are the latest in the string of criminal investigations and prosecutions to hit some of the best-known companies in the United States.

> Corporate executives, leading attorneys and government officials all say that criminal indictments are being used increasingly for white collar transgressions that previously might have gone undetected or treated as civil or administrative issues. It is a legal approach that grew steadily during the 1980s and was used with increasing frequency in recent years against alleged uses and areas as

White-Collar Crime Program

Percentage of Convictions in Priority Cases

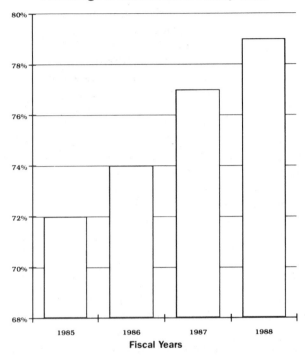

Fiscal Years

Figure 2-4. White-collar crime program: Percentage of convictions in priority cases. (*White-Collar Crime: A Report to the Public, Department of Justice, Federal Bureau of Investigation, p. 31.*)

diverse as government contracting, the environment and high finance.[1]

Why Pursue White Collars?

The decision to focus on white-collar crime is not self-evidently sensible. If you were a prosecutor, where would you devote most of your energies in the 1990s?

[1]"Criminal Indictments: Training Bigger Guns on Corporations," *The Washington Post,* p. A1 (March 2, 1990).

In New York City, there were 292 homicides in 1945. In 1990, that number had risen to 2200. There were 1417 armed robberies in New York City in 1945. In 1990 that number had risen to 100,000—or, as some commentators like to put it, "one every five minutes." Sixty percent of New Yorkers now say they will be living elsewhere in five years, most citing crime as the primary cause of flight. In 1945, 90 percent of New Yorkers considered themselves happy to be there. Washington, D.C., the home of so many white-collar prosecutions, has a homicide rate from two to three times that of New York City. To what degree does it make sense to devote scarce prosecutorial and police resources to offenses against the pocketbook rather than offenses against the person?

The statistics on violent crime are numbing. Murder, robbery, and rape have all marched up every year, reaching what FBI Director Sessions called "an unprecedented high" in 1988. The *New York Post* tabloid had, on *one* day, these subheadlines: "Undercover Cop Shot in Back," "Four Slain in Mob Rubouts," "Bullets Fly on Bleeker Street," "Drug Widower: I'll Fight On," "Dramatic Photos on Pages 4, 5, 7, 8 and 9." Notwithstanding these tabloid truths, then Attorney General Richard Thornburgh shortly thereafter disbanded his long-standing organized crime strike force group, only to create *six* new securities and commodities fraud task forces.

The focus on white collars is not consistent with other statistics, most notably polls reflecting popular opinion. A *National Law Journal*/Lexis Survey asked which crime should receive the highest priority. Forty-seven percent said drug dealing, 32 percent muggings and rapes, 11 percent racketeering, and 3 percent white-collar crimes. The sample surveyed also would give an armed robber more than ten years and an embezzler considerably less, with only 12 percent thinking he or she should serve more than ten years. But increasingly such popular concerns are inverted by prosecutors' offices that invest enormous resources in—and expect proportionate returns from—complex white-collar crime prosecution.

Consider the notorious Princeton–Newport RICO case in which the government brought indictments against various state officials for violation of *RICO*. RICO, or the Racketeering Influenced Corrupt Organization Act, was a statutory reaction to shocking facts unearthed in congressional investigations of organized crime and its extraordinary influence in many ordinary business enterprises. It sought to create a powerful criminal and civil remedy against gangsters who engage in a pattern of racketeering activities that use or influence business enterprises.

The RICO violations in the Princeton–Newport case were premised in turn on allegedly criminal violations of the tax code. One required element of a RICO prosecution is proof of at least two violations within

ten years of some other criminal statute. But the underlying tax violations in the Princeton–Newport case were hazy at best and not separately charged. The interesting thing about the indictment was that it
had no independent counts alleging tax fraud. If the predicate acts
were so clearly wrong as to constitute racketeering, why weren't they
separately charged? After a lengthy trial, the defendants were nonetheless convicted. But what were they guilty of? The trial transcript suggests
that the jury might well have convicted them under RICO without ever
concluding that the defendants violated any specific tax law. That was
part of the government trial strategy. Prosecutors assured the jury, "You
don't need a fancy tax law expert because common sense tells you it's
fraudulent, it's phony."

The Wall Street Journal, commenting on the case, found in this a like-
ness to the classic exchange in the movie *Treasure of the Sierra Madre:*

> MEXICAN BANDIT: We are the Federales. You know, the Mounted Police.
>
> HUMPHREY BOGART: If you're the police, where are your badges?
>
> MEXICAN BANDIT: Badges? We ain't got no badges. We don't need no
> badges. We don't have to show you any stinking badges!

Indeed, jurors interviewed after the trial said they were persuaded
not by any arguments about the tax code, but by the "sleaze" argument.
Discussions between traders included, "You're a sleaze bag." The prejudicial conversations slipped into the record raise issues worthy of discussion. Did such tapes reveal, as one commentator put it, "more about
Wall Street's saucy conversational style and gallows humor" than guilt or
innocence?

The Second Circuit saw the danger in prosecuting like this and
abruptly reversed the convictions. But cases like Princeton–Newport
raise even larger questions. As *The Wall Street Journal* puts it:

> With a rampage of violent crime turning cities into war zones, many
> prosecutors are elsewhere engaged, devoting thousands of investiga-
> tive man-hours to whether Chicago commodity traders are giving
> fair value or Wall Street arbitrageurs are guilty of "insider trading."
> Why this incredible diversion of effort to "crimes" that often are
> not clearly defined by statute and where identifiable victims are sel-
> dom found?[2]

The question deserves more serious discussion than it normally re-
ceives. One of the reasons for the increased interest of prosecutors is, of
course, the fact that white-collar crimes happen. There is an increasing

---

[2] *The Wall Street Journal* (August 21, 1989).

sensitivity to the way people can obtain wrongful gains without pointing any guns. Woody Guthrie used to sing of men "who steal millions with a fountain pen." Clever people find ingenious ways to defraud. Greed is also a mother of invention. Multicount indictments reveal business behavior that few would defend. While the fact of white-collar misbehavior does not speak directly to the priority question raised by raging street crimes in the nation's cities, it does explain why many are not offended with the new prosecutorial emphasis.

Prosecutorial Interests

But another practical factor cannot be ignored. Prosecutors enjoy white-collar crime prosecutions more. Such prosecutions have higher prestige and lead to greater advancement and distinction for those who specialize in them. Prosecuting an assortment of malnourished drug addicts is not as rewarding as getting a prominent professional or business executive within the cross hairs. Drug addicts often have hands that glow in the dark from the dusting chemicals the Drug Enforcement Agency uses to coat packages of cocaine sent from Colombia to the dope peddler. Their defenses are nonexistent. Trials are routine and uneventful and almost always end in convictions. A white-collar crime prosecution, on the other hand, is exciting and high profile, something young prosecutors can get their teeth into.

It is true, the Supreme Court has said, that the prosecutor's interest ought not to be simply to "win a case, but that justice shall be done."[3] But to those for whom pecuniary rewards are not the primary measure of accomplishment, the temptations of a more interesting practice are real.

In the United States Attorney's Office for the Southern District of New York, which includes New York City, for example, young prosecutors have to pay their dues in purgatory before attaining paradise. The first two years are on general assignment for street crimes. There is then a two-year rotation prosecuting drug offenses. Assuming that young prosecutors successfully navigate their way through those four years of conventional criminal prosecutions, they can graduate into the white-collar crime program, which has the highest prestige and the most interest for any budding U.S. Attorney.

One of those inflexible laws of nature is that what you reward, you get more of. If you reward white-collar crime prosecutions, you get more of

---

[3]*Berger v. United States*, 295 U.S. 78, 88 (1935).

them. DeLorean, Milken, Boesky, Deaver: these are names that excite the blood more than the forgettable surnames of faceless defendants from slums and barrios.

Public Encouragements

The press also encourages such prosecutorial interests. Indictments of corporations are often front-page news and the subject of approving editorials.

There are political justifications given for this heavy tilt toward favorable publicity for criminalizing business decisions even at the expense of violent crime prosecution. Prosecutors can avoid the perception that their enforcement of the law favors the rich over the poor. High-profile prosecutions of business are warmly received by consumer and environmental activists. The Reagan defense buildup and the billions spent for defense, combined with stories of hundred-dollar toilet seats, raised public anger, mollified in part by "get tough" procurement prosecutors. A decade of bullish markets, leveraged buy-outs, hostile takeovers, and golden parachutes conveys a perception of greed, and prosecutors win points for confirming its reality. The press generally applauds these trends.

The fact of an increased emphasis on the prosecution of corporate wrongdoing is thus taken as a given. In criticizing attempts to reform RICO and to prune its somewhat unanticipated growth, *The New York Times* on its editorial page said:

> The House today takes up the latest attempt to gut a law that is proving to be especially useful in a period of rampant white-collar crime in the nation's financial institutions.[4]

The New York Times went on to say, "Congress, itself deeply responsible for the national plague of financial lawlessness, needs to remember the victims, including every taxpayer."[5]

There are almost daily reminders of prosecutors' successes in remembering these victims:

- General Electric Company and two employees are convicted of fraud in connection with a battlefield computer system, which the government claimed cost it $10 million.

---

[4]*The New York Times* (September 24, 1990).

[5]Ibid.

- Boeing Company pleads guilty in November 1990 to obtaining two Pentagon secret documents illegally, and, in January, a marketing executive is sentenced to years in prison.
- RCA pleads guilty to obtaining secret Defense budget reports.[6]

The examples are plentiful. One lawyer noted, "There is no question that activities that years ago were subject only to regulatory enforcement through administrative channels have now become common fare for the criminal justice system."[7] As another white-collar defense lawyer, Bob Bennett, pointed out in *The Washington Post,* "For years, procurement fraud was handled by guys in green eyeshades. Now it is being handled by police with a nightstick."[8]

The contrasts are clear-cut and sharply defined. Before 1983, no major defense contractor had been convicted of procurement fraud. In the seven last years of the decade, 20 of the 100 largest defense contractors had been convicted. In fiscal 1985, there were 40 indictments and 37 pleas and convictions for environmental crime; in fiscal year 1989 there were 101 indictments and 107 pleas and convictions, including convictions against Ashland Oil, Inc., Texaco, Inc., and Ocean Spray Cranberries, Inc.

The trend has spread to Great Britain. In February 1990, the prosecution began its trial in the Guinness PLC case, claiming that the defendants, including the former chairman and CEO of Guinness, Ernest W. Saunders, and a group of his associates, including Sir Isador Jack Lyons, millionaire financier and art patron, were "carried away by greed and ambition" during the 1986 takeover of the distiller's company.[9]

More Conquests, More Cases

Greater success leads to even greater emphasis. As *The Washington Post* noted:

> Prosecutors agree that in the past several years more resources have been devoted to attacking white-collar crime. They also note that Congress has been passing stricter laws in recent years, courts are handing out tougher sentences and the U.S. Sentencing Commis-

[6] *The Washington Post* (March 2, 1990).

[7] "Criminal Indictments: Training Bigger Guns on Corporations," *The Washington Post,* p. A1 (March 2, 1990).

[8] Ibid.

[9] *The New York Times,* p. D3 (February 19, 1990).

sion is considering a proposal to further stiffen penalties for convicted corporations.

The prospect of easier prosecutions and stiffer sentences leads to an
increased allocation of agency work forces to white-collar crime efforts.
The Inspector General's Office in the Defense Department (which
investigates allegations of fraud and waste) has grown from two or three
dozen people in 1983 to about 1400 people now.[10] Fifteen years ago,
there were three white-collar crime agents in Orange County, California, looking largely at embezzlement cases under $3000. Now there are
22 white-collar crime agents in that county who investigate fraud cases
of $1 million or more.[11] Before he resigned as Attorney General, Dick
Thornburgh announced that the Justice Department would double the
number of investigators of financial fraud, adding more than 400 additional investigators, FBI agents, and federal accountants to complete
8000 pending cases and open new investigations.[12]

The growing interest of prosecutors in white-collar crime prosecutions has even created several ancillary cottage industries. Former special agents, FBI agents, and financial investigators are hanging up
freshly minted shingles to offer special services. As *The Washington Post*
reported in 1989, "In a period of proliferating investigations of the
white collar crimes . . . two former Internal Revenue Service investigators have opened a Washington office of a national network of private
financial sleuths." The company, it turns out, has various fee schedules,
including fees for "garbage pickup," or going through the trash for
leads.

Whatever the reasons for the "explosion," the craters are obvious. As
Bob Bennett puts it, "They are making criminals out of people and companies who are not criminals."

The Consequences

One of the results of this *overcriminalization,* of course, is that the cost of
doing business has been increased. There are additional layers of management and internal controls necessary to cope with an increased
number of criminal investigations. Such complaints fall on deaf ears
from people like Russell Mokhiber, former member of Ralph Nader's

[10] *The Washington Post,* p. A20 (March 2, 1990).

[11] *The Los Angeles Times,* p. 1 (August 27, 1989).

[12] *The Los Angeles Times* (December 8, 1989).

Corporate Accountability Research Group and now editor of *Corporate Crime Reporter,* "I think what [corporate defense attorneys] mean is that their clients are executives at major American corporations" and therefore should not go to jail.[13]

But there is a consequence more frightening than the prospect of greater costs of doing business. Such costs, as sandbags laid against future disasters, are a reality for the regulated business. That many more companies are being indicted is bad enough. But there is worse news. The penalties these companies face are increasingly harsh.

As the Pharisee looked upon the publican, he could imagine the kind of whipping the publican was headed for. If the Pharisee conceded for a moment the possibility of his coming under judicial scrutiny, he certainly would have supposed that his crimes of spirit or attitude would be subject to significantly less penalty than those of the notorious publican.

Most middle-class people feel the same way. They hear of white-collar criminals being given a ceremonial tap on the wrist, while street criminals bear the brunt of judicial sanction for inappropriate behavior. Such examples are, increasingly, largely hypothetical: if anything, white-collar criminals are given more severe penalties than others. In Minnesota, for example, burglars face no serious risk of going to jail until their third conviction, according to the state sentencing guidelines. This is so, notwithstanding the fact that their activities are furtive, intrusive, culpable, and frightening. White-collar defendants, however, face the very real possibility of at least a year and a day in federal custody for their first offense, for activity that frequently is no more personally remunerative and almost always far less frightening than the behavior of the street criminal.

Sentencing guidelines in the federal courts, and in some states, consider a number of factors that are not favorable for white-collar criminal defendants. Chief among the *aggravating factors* is the absolute magnitude of the allegedly ill-gotten gains, even though these gains are not realized by the defendant personally. Companies that make a small savings by using a questionable formula that does not comply with federal regulations, for example, may find their small savings converted to a multimillion-dollar swindle in the government's eyes when that small savings is multiplied over the number of products sold using the formula. The result is ominous. White-collar criminals frequently go to jail for longer periods than many state-court street criminals.

The best example of this is Michael Milken. While Milken admittedly

[13] *The Washington Post,* p. A20 (March 2, 1990).

made hundreds of millions of dollars each year from investment banking, numbers readily retained in mind by the public and the prosecutors, the charges against him were viewed by many seasoned observers as novel. His guilt was not self-evident. On some of the charges, some commentators believed that Milken appeared likely to be convicted. On many others, creative prosecutors attempted to expand the horizon of his potential liability by charging him with manipulative practices that two decades ago would not have been considered criminal at all. The federal government also used RICO in creative ways not envisioned by its authors, as a ten-pound sledgehammer aimed squarely at Milken's head. Milken had, of course, no prior offenses. He was from all appearances a dedicated family man. He had an admirable record of giving to charity. His crimes had no obvious identifiable victims.

When a combination of pressures, that lethal leverage at the disposal of the federal government, prompted him to plea bargain, he and his lawyers reached an agreement on the number of counts he would plead guilty to, but had no agreement with the government as to any "cap" on the sentence.

Although his lawyers argued for community service (it was clear he would be required to pay millions of dollars in restitution in any case), the judge had other plans. Milken was sentenced to ten years in prison. Milken was given a significantly more onerous penalty than the average first-offense bank robber, child molester, arsonist, or perpetrator of an aggravated assault with a deadly weapon.

Given the reputation for leniency created by "Club Feds," federal prison farms, such as Lompoc near Santa Barbara and Danbury in Connecticut, and the perceived demands of a watchful public, courts seem increasingly determined to demonstrate a "get tough" attitude toward the white-collar offender. But should Milken really get twice the sentence meted out to those who were convicted and sentenced at the same time for the "wilding" episode in Central Park, New York City, that led to a merciless beating and rape of a young professional woman who was left bloodied, brain-damaged, and naked in the mud by teenaged assailants? They got a minimum of five years.

The trend is also seen in huge fines given to business entities. In December 1987, a Denver-based corporation was convicted of 16 counts that charged, among other things, "knowing endangerment" under the Resource Conservation and Recovery Act. Because the corporation was found to have disposed of hazardous wastes in such a way that innocent employees were placed in imminent danger, the corporation was sentenced to a $7.63 million fine, ordered to deposit $950,000 into a trust fund to pay future medical expenses of three employees, and ordered to clean up the facility at an estimated expense of $2.3 million.

The United States Sentencing Commission, organized in 1985 pursuant to a federal statute, further confirmed the trend. Its purpose was to set guidelines making sentencing more uniform. More than 350 companies are sentenced each year by federal courts for criminal violations, and thousands more are sentenced by state courts. These multiplied prosecutions make disparate treatment increasingly likely and justify attempts at standardizing.

But the work of this commission, finally enacted into law in October 1991, shows that unevenness will be solved by ratcheting up to greater severity—its guidelines increase the harshness and hence the negotiating leverage of federal prosecutors in white-collar crime cases. So severe were the recommendations that a federal district judge, J. Lawrence Irving, resigned from the Commission in September 1990 because he felt the sentencing guidelines for individuals were so harsh. "If I remain on the bench, I have no choice but to follow the law," he said while announcing his resignation.[14]

Reading the Signs of the Times

When prosecutors, prosecutions, police, public sentiment, and penalties all tend in the same direction, the most stiff-necked Pharisee should get the message. The pin-striped suit is often traded these days for the plain-striped suit.

The puritan divines said that it was important often to think of one's death. Jonathan Edwards, one of the wisest of American philosophers and theologians, made it his New Year's resolution to think every evening about enfolding himself into a casket so that his retirement every evening would lead him to consider the brevity of life and the certainty of judgment.

The prospect may sound dour, but business executives of today must consider all of the decisions they make through the eyes of a jury, suspicious of members of the business community and ready to find unfair behavior lurking in every transaction.

As criminal prosecutions work their way from the crime blotter on page 8 to the headlines on page 1, all of us need more of the attitude of the publican: "God be merciful to me a sinner."

We ought to feel *The Wall Street Journal* rip apart in our hands and face the lonely walk to a courtroom where our fate and future will be decided.

---

[14]*The New York Times* (October 1, 1990).

3

It's the Law: How Elastic Laws Can Stretch to Make Criminals of Us All

The law is a ass, a idiot
MR. BUMBLE
Oliver Twist

All good citizens, whether Pharisees or not, love laws against criminals. Some of the Pharisees were even given to carrying them about on their foreheads. If they had had automobiles, they would have admired the bumper stickers displayed by their latter-day cousins exhorting the citizenry to "support your local police." The local police go after the "criminal element." It was hard for them to imagine a criminal law so idiotic or asinine as to threaten them. But therein lies the problem.

The reason that the well-dressed professional in the parable got convicted for "white-collar" crimes is the reason many reputable business people run afoul of the criminal laws in ways they would never have imagined. Their strong self-image reflects back to them no trace of wrongdoing.

19

An inability to see yourself as a defendant means first that you cannot imagine the costs you may later be forced to bear for present conduct. It is like the externality question in economics. If a smoky factory is not forced to pay for the soot it blows onto neighboring stucco, graying unrelated buildings and sheets on other people's clotheslines, it would not appreciate the true costs of its activities. There are external "diseconomies" that must be collected and priced to reveal the true costs of a particular method of production. So too, the true costs of staying too close to the line of questionable business behavior are never appreciated by one who does not foresee what it might be like to see the risks to family, fortune, and freedom that a criminal indictment brings with it. One would be far more careful if one could see a six-digit number on his or her own portrait.

The forgiving mirror of personal accomplishment can hide failures of perception as in the following.

1. *The Pharisee cannot imagine himself as a potential criminal.* The Pharisee came to the temple to pray. But his prayer was not a petition for pardon, but a paean of praise that he did not require pardon. "I thank thee," was his celebration of self-worth. He did not see himself as a potential defendant. He was glad that manacles were not made for his manicured hands.

Freud said that no one can imagine oneself being dead. Death is for other people. So the average social achiever cannot imagine himself or herself being indicted, arraigned, or convicted. The achiever, even if the thought suggests itself, is only thankful not to have that problem to worry about.

Once upon a time that insouciance was justified. White-collar crime was an oxymoron. Blackstone, the English commentator whose treatise was law at the time of the Constitutional Convention, laid down that corporations simply could not commit "felony, or other crime in its corporate capacity."[1] In other words, the criminal law was not made for businesses, just individual wrongdoers.

Blackstone's view, once sacrosanct, began to erode in the nineteenth century and ultimately crumbled under the pressures of the Industrial Revolution. As Friedman points out in his *A History of American Law:*

> In every state, every extension of governmental power, every new form of regulation brought in a new batch of criminal law. Every important statute, governing railroads, banks, and corporations,

[1]Blackstone, *Commentaries,* 476 (1765).

or the marketing of milk, cheese, fruit, or coal . . . trailed with it at the end a sentence or two imposing criminal sanctions on violators.[2]

The federal government was not far behind. And by 1890, Congress was providing explicitly for criminal liability for corporate entities which violated provisions of the Sherman Antitrust Act.

How far business insulation from criminal risk has crumbled is increasingly apparent. Businesses are ever more frequently held liable for unanticipated violations. Consider the following case.

The view that use of the criminal law as a method of economic regulation is "for the birds" might find some support in the case of *United States v. FMC Corp.*[3] FMC is known, of course, as an important source of munitions to the federal government. Its ordnance was an important source of supply for the forces in the Gulf War. As a defense contractor, it might well be expected to know the ins and outs of defense contracting and the myriad laws, regulations, and policies affecting government procurement. But its management may have had less expertise in the Migratory Bird Treaty Act.[4] How does the business of a federal defense contractor relate to the strictures of the Migratory Bird Treaty Act?

The story runs like this. FMC had a pond on its property, a fashionable enough statement for many business organizations which seek rustic suburban settings. The pond attracted a variety of migratory birds on their sun-seeking travels. Alas, the pond contained chemicals which were unhealthy for the birds. FMC tried everything from scarecrows to security guards in an effort to dissuade the birds from settling down on the toxic waters. All was to no avail for a number of reasons. The scarecrows were not scary. Some of the guards fell asleep on the job. The source of the pond problem was ultimately discovered. A pesticide had been unwittingly dumped into the pond as a result of equipment malfunction.

Unimpressed by the corporate scarecrows, guards, and other indicia of good faith, the government indicted. The consequences of the poisonous pond were apparent. There was the "corpus delicti": in this case, some dead ducks. What is a prosecutor to do when presented with such "avian mortality"? In Blackstone's day, the answer is nothing. But this is now, not then. The indictment unmasked FMC as murderers of migra-

---

[2]Friedman, *A History of American Law*, 510 (1973).

[3]572 F.2d 902 (2d Cir. 1978).

[4]16 U.S.C. §703.

tory birds, even though no prosecutor could seriously allege that there was any corporate or individual intent to engage in avian genocide. Not one individual had intent to damage ducks. But the various actions and omissions of maintenance employees, sleepy guards, and distracted executives taken together, the court found, constituted a corporate intent. The company was adjudged guilty of a felony and paid a large fine.

The case shows the possibilities of major criminal liability for marginally culpable activity. If FMC can be summoned to court as a serial bird-killer, no business is safe.

The inability to fancy oneself as a criminal defendant blinds one to how one's own conduct appears to others. When we do something inappropriate or even just questionable, we are not our own best prosecutors. It is easy to construct rationalizations which palliate our consciences but are not persuasive to an objective third party. The prosecutor's indictment or, even more painfully, his or her closing argument will have surprising force. There is the law. Its language is clear and unambiguous. Here is the conduct, admitted or undeniable. And there is the motive, money. All the while, squirming in the docks is a defendant who could not imagine such a setting.

2. *The Pharisee cannot imagine the stretch of novel laws that relate to his own conduct.* The Pharisee thought he was in the clear because he was not a street criminal, like the publican. He was not a gangster. He neither oppressed the poor and powerless nor extorted money from hapless taxpayers. He was guilty of neither the simple pigeon drop nor the sophisticated Ponzi scheme.

What he did not understand, however, was that the moral law reached more offenses than he thought. It honed in on his attitude of pride, his hypocrisy, his omissions to do good, his lack of the right spirit toward his neighbor. So, lamentably, business executives may take false comfort in what they are not (to quote a famous president, "a crook") and what they are (reputable, charitable, a pillar of the community).

But the staggering increase in white-collar crime prosecutions over the last two decades shows that every business executive has a growing risk of transgressing an increasingly complex reticulum of federal and state criminal statutes. The reach of such laws and their potential effect on the ordinary business executive or professional are staggering.

Consider the following case.

Two elderly sisters in Texas, frugal and careful seamstresses, run a small tailoring business. After years of use, their sewing machines break down. The machines require a serious overhaul. The repairman comes in, fixes the machines, and later sends his bill.

When the bill is received, the sisters are shocked. It is far higher than they anticipated. They go through the bill like a missionary nurse looking for lice with a fine-tooth comb. Their audit, however, reveals more than lousy invoicing. They believe some of the work was not even done.

They send the invoice to their lawyer. The lawyer confirms their suspicions. It does appear that some of the items were bogus. The lawyer mulls over the options. There is a breach of contract here, but not enough money at stake to justify a lawsuit. The same goes for an action for misrepresentation or deceptive consumer practices—good liability cases, not much damages.

Suddenly, a light goes on. How about RICO? The advantages of making the defendant a "racketeer" are obvious. RICO lawsuits give rise to treble damages. Multiply the recovery by three, and the plaintiffs can recover their attorney's fees. Remove the worry that the attorney's fees would eat up a small recovery. So far, so good. But RICO requires two "predicate acts" of wrongdoing within a ten-year period. The lawyer muses on how to get this dishonest repairman as a defendant in a RICO lawsuit.

Suddenly, another light goes on. He calls up the lawyer for the repairman and asks him to send a copy of the invoice earlier submitted to the seamstresses to him personally. The lawyer makes a photocopy of the invoice, sends it to the seamstresses' lawyer and—bingo—"two" predicate acts, two fraudulent uses of the mails within a ten-year period. Now it is a RICO case.

The case is brought and quickly dismissed by a judge who cannot believe that this is what Congress had in mind by racketeering legislation. Plaintiffs appeal. The case works its way up to the Seventh Circuit Court of Appeals. There, a distinguished federal judge, aptly named Judge Wisdom, says:

> The scope of the civil RICO statute is breathtaking. An allegation of fraud in a contract action can transform an ordinary state law claim into a federal racketeering charge. It may be unfortunate for federal courts to be burdened by this kind of case, but it is not for this court to question policies decided by Congress and upheld by the Supreme Court. The broad language of the statute in the Sedima decision provides us with clear guidance. Material questions of fact exist that cannot be resolved before trial. The judgment of the district court is therefore REVERSED and the case is remanded for further proceedings.[5]

The decision could have as easily supported a criminal indictment under RICO. Soon come the conventional cries of outrage from certain members of the defense bar, commentators, even public officials. The

---

[5] *R.A.G.S. Couture, Inc. v. Hyatt,* 774 F.2d 1350 (CA5, 1985).

periodicals join in. *Business Week* points out, "Increasing use of [RICO] is turning commercial disputes that were once handled in routine suits into federal 'racketeering' cases."[6] A. A. Summer, Jr., a prominent former member of the SEC, said, "It's an absolute outrage. Congress never intended the law to have this reach."[7] But what happened?

The reason for cases like this is not that the laws are silly or that prosecutors are severe. The increasing breadth of white-collar crime penalties is understandable. They reveal a principle and a practical reality. The principle underlying the expansion of white-collar crime prosecutions has proceeded according to the rule referred to by Justice Jackson of the United States Supreme Court over 50 years ago: "the tendency of a principle to expand itself to the limit of its logic."[8] The practical reality that follows from this is also clear: it is increasingly easy to run afoul of federal prosecutors.

Let's see how the principle works. Most entities and individuals charged with crimes are guilty and are ultimately convicted of the crimes with which they are charged if they do not cut short the process by admitting them, by plea bargain, prior to trial. Many of the crimes are at least offensive and sometimes utterly reprehensible. Often prosecutors can easily prove their case.

But the problem comes in the "hard" case. Sometimes technical obstacles arise that threaten the prosecutor's efforts. No statute clearly covers the misconduct; one, perhaps highly technical element, is either weak or missing altogether. There is a natural reluctance by prosecutors to let the guilty go free. The creative prosecutor searches the language of statutes for leeway. The worse the conduct, the more the prosecutor searches. A pull here, and a stretch there, and after many years the elements of the RICO statute are expansive enough to drive a business executive's limousine through without scratching the paint. Hard cases make bad law.

RICO was enacted because too many gangsters were getting away with arson, gambling, vice, extortion, and other familiar gangster activities by using the cloak of normal business entities. As the gangsters were brought to justice under the new RICO law, courts were inclined to interpret RICO liberally, to do justice to the bad actors standing before them. By the time a sequence of racketeers—and whispers of people in cement suits dropped into rivers—had worked its way through the fed-

---

[6] *Business Week* (February 20, 1985).

[7] Ibid.

[8] *Krulewitch v. United States*, 336 U.S. 445, 69 S.Ct. 716, 93 L.Ed. 790 (1949) (concurring opinion).

eral courts, the elements of a RICO violation had often become liberally stretched. Years later, when inventive plaintiff's lawyers wanted treble damage recoveries and attorney's fees from Citibank or Merrill Lynch, or large law firm or accounting firm defendants, they had readily at hand many precedents that had interpreted RICO with understandable elasticity.

The prosecutor presses the limits in the same way. Now the prosecutor, tiring of conventional RICO settings, such as gaming or white slavery, turns an attentive eye to a business executive whose general manager has taken an aggressive position on some government regulation, finds the smoke (or fire) of suspicious circumstances, and indicts, based on interpretation of a law that is far broader than anyone—including Congress—ever anticipated. And soon FMC has highly trained duck watchers at every corporate facility, watching from camouflaged duck blinds for that second predicate act.

3. *The Pharisee cannot imagine the handy, all-purpose tools in the prosecutor's work chest.* You are a judge faced with trying a criminal case. The defendant is an alleged drug courier. Drug crimes are rife. You have sworn to uphold the law. In the case before you, the drug courier claims that a man approached him in Tijuana, held out a leather attaché case, and said, "Take this across the border to San Diego, and I will pay you $25,000." The defendant takes the attaché case across the border. On the other side, he is intercepted by officials of the Drug Enforcement Administration (DEA). The DEA agents open the case and find several pounds of heroin. The man is arrested and the case is set for trial. His defense is that he did not know what he was carrying across the border. You, as the judge, do not believe him. On the other hand, the law requires *scienter*, that is, that the defendant knew the nature of his conduct and intended to violate the law. You decide to instruct the jury on something you call *conscious avoidance* or *willful ignorance.* You tell the jury that a defendant cannot willfully close his eyes or consciously avoid learning what is in this satchel, and that such conscious avoidance may be taken as an evidence of scienter.

A sensible instruction? Of course. Anyone offered $25,000 to cross the Mexican border into the United States must know that one is being asked to do something unlawful. Common sense tells us that even if one does not know the bag's precise contents, one certainly had adequate reason to believe it is contraband and thus has a culpable state of mind.

But now let us jump from the drug courier to the president of a regulated business. He faces not an attaché case, but over 100 volumes of the Code of Federal Regulations (CFR), dozens of which may have some tangential application to his business. Let us suppose that the government has the company dead to rights on a violation of some arcane rule in the CFR. The government has no admission of knowing violation from the executive nor clear and direct testimony from others that the action was knowing and willful.

During the course of the trial, the government shows the jury on an enlarged screen two very simple sentences from the CFR. Anyone on the jury can understand their purport and significance. Anyone can see the offending conduct. The jury is not shown all 100 volumes of the CFR nor instructed on the enormous reticulum of federal regulation of business. It sees only the needle, not the haystack. The judge thus instructs the jury on "conscious avoidance" and "willful ignorance." Did the company and this defendant consciously avoid this regulation? The jury now must evaluate the president's claim that he never read or understood the regulation before authorizing the transaction. They do so in light of evidence that the company made a profit from ignoring the provision. Suddenly, the executive is in a fight for his life.

The risks in such an environment come from the increasing use of white-collar crime as a new form of business regulation. Prosecutors reading Upton Sinclair's *The Jungle* today would begin thinking of innovative criminal indictments to inhibit the development of such unsavory business practices. White-collar crime prosecutions these days are, for the most part, simply another form of economic regulation. When homicide statutes, for example, are used to indict employers providing unsafe work places or designing unsafe products, as in the famous Chicago case of *People v. Film Recovery Systems,*[9] when homicide convictions are obtained for exposing employees to unhealthy vapors, it is clear that another form of business regulation, with sharper teeth, is lurking in the shadows of federal statutes. Curiously enough, the deregulation of many industries during the Reagan revolution saw the simultaneous rise of an inverse pressure to reregulate, by prosecuting criminally offensive business behavior. Nature, after all, abhors a vacuum.

When a prosecutor seeks to regulate criminally, there are several "all-purpose" tools in the tool kit that are the substantive law equivalent of the *conscious avoidance* instruction.

Mail Fraud. One of the most popular crimes in the government armamentarium is *mail fraud.* Designed to snare those who use the mails to entice gullible victims into fraudulent schemes, the statute has come to have a far broader applicability than that core misconduct.

The mail fraud statute reads:

[9]No. 83-11091 (Ill. Cir. Cook County 1983), conviction reported, *The New York Times,* p. 1 (June 15, 1985).

> Whoever, having devised or intending to devise *any scheme or artifice to defraud, or for obtaining money or property by means of false or fraudulent pretenses, representations, or promises,* or to sell, dispose of, loan, exchange, alter, give away, distribute, supply, or furnish or procure for unlawful use any counterfeit or spurious coin, obligation, security, or other article, or anything represented to be or intimated or held out to be such counterfeit or spurious article, for the purpose of executing such scheme or artifice or attempting to do so, places in any post office or authorized depository for mail matter, any matter or thing whatever to be sent or delivered by the Postal Service, or takes or receives therefrom, any such matter or thing, or knowingly causes to be delivered by mail according to the direction thereon, or at the place at which it is directed to be delivered by the person to whom it is addressed, any such matter or thing, shall be fined not more than $1,000 or imprisoned not more than five years, or both.[10]

It has, hidden in the legalese, two principal elements: *a scheme to defraud* and *use of the mails.* But how these terms have been defined shows why prosecutors love to use them.

Fraud has been defined so broadly by the courts that it reaches any "unfair" or "unethical" or "oppressive" business practice. The *use of the mails* has been defined with similar breadth. It encloses any transaction which at some point used the mails, even though the alleged fraud itself was never put in writing, and no misrepresentation was ever put in a mailbox. If someone used the mails at any point and for any purpose in the transaction, there is federal jurisdiction. Putting the two elements together makes a potential federal crime of any transaction that could be sued civilly as common law fraud or misrepresentation. For any arguably "unfair" or "unjust" behavior, therefore, all that stands between the business executive and the criminal docket is the discretion of the prosecutor.

That discretion has been exercised with great creativity. The *scheme or artifice to defraud* requirement has been stretched to include almost every form of unfair practice: influence peddling, political patronage, seduction of women by promising them roles as models, violations of attorneys' ethical rules, stock swindles, writing bad checks, and all the flotsam and jetsam of "bad behavior."[11]

Even authors of books are not, alas, immune. In one case, an author

---

[10]18 U.S.C. §1341 (emphasis added).

[11]See a useful discussion contained in Chap. 9 of *White Collar Crime: Business and Regulatory Offenses,* Obermaier and Morvillo (Law Journal Seminars–Press, 1990), §9.01 and following.

misled his publisher by claiming that he had interviewed the Pope and had obtained extensive biographical information from him. A grand jury subpoenaed the author's notes with respect to the interview. The claimed meeting with the pontiff turned out to be a sham. The material in the book was ultimately exposed as intentionally false.

Counsel for the defendant objected to the subpoena, on the grounds that it is not a crime to write a false book. Once upon a time there was such a thing as criminal libel. Authors had to worry about going to prison for getting their facts wrong, but no more. Inaccurate books are for historians or civil libel lawyers to attack, not for grand juries.

But the federal court in the Third Circuit ordered the subpoena to be enforced. There was according to the court an alleged "scheme to defraud" and there was some use of the mails. It followed that there was, potentially, a federal crime—mail fraud.[12]

As legal observers have pointed out, such expansive judicial interpretations of criminal laws raise important issues:

a. the line between legality and morality, between what is unethical and what is criminal;

b. the line between judicial lawmaking and the doctrine, founded both on due process and the separation of powers, that there should be no common law or "judge-made" crimes; and

c. the line between federal law and the right of the states to have primary jurisdiction over the determination of what behavior is criminal.[13]

For the business executive defendant, these borderlines flex unpredictably from year to year.

For example, has an overly aggressive lobbying effort for your business association crossed a line? Has it become a scheme to defraud? By getting legislation passed through questionable practices, has it deprived the public of the *intangible right* to good government?

Prior to *McNally v. United States*,[14] a 1987 Supreme Court decision, some courts criminalized what they called violations of *intangible rights*, such as the "right to good government," as well as *pecuniary rights*. To such courts, schemes to defraud did not have to violate state or federal

---

[12]See In re Grand Jury, Gronowicz, 764 F.2d 983 (3d Cir. 1985), *cert. denied* 474 U.S. 1055 (1986).

[13]For a discussion of interest to the practitioner, see §9.01 of *White Collar Crime: Business and Regulatory Offenses*, Obermaier and Morvillo (Law Journal Seminars–Press, 1990), p. 9-10.

[14]483 U.S. 350 (1987).

laws or even inflict pecuniary loss on the victim. Reading the laws strictly, these courts found that the mail fraud statute criminalized any infraction against *fair play and right dealing*. If it wasn't "cricket," it was criminal.

The *McNally* case redrew the border. It held that mail fraud meant conventional fraud, involving money. Prosecutors must not proceed with mail fraud prosecutions unless they can show at least that the defendant swindled the victim out of some form of tangible property with pecuniary value (including, potentially, trade secrets). After 1987, your trade association will not be indicted, or will it?

While it was thought that the *McNally* decision was the final word on the *intangible rights* theory, Congress decided to have its own last word on the subject. The modest Supreme Court limitation of a prosecutor's discretion in the *McNally* case proved too restrictive for the Congress. Prior to its adjournment just days before the 1988 presidential election, Congress passed a rider to its comprehensive drug bill that defined scheme to defraud as follows:

> For purposes of this chapter, the term "scheme or artifice" includes a scheme or artifice to deprive another of the *intangible right of honest services.*[15]

This somewhat intangible definition of intangible rights may be greeted with hosannas by prosecutors. But for the business executive attempting to police thousands of employees at different locations, it gives little comfort. Is everybody standing in line at the customer services window, fuming over some misrepresentation by a sales clerk or some defect in a product, a potential prosecutor? What business has never been said—however unfairly—to have deprived a customer of the *intangible right of honest services?* And what, prithee, is the *intangible right of honest services?*

The practical reality is that mail fraud statutes are the prosecutor's safety net. When prosecutors swing into the investigation of some exciting crime, they sometimes connect with something less than clearly defined wrongdoing. But their dogged factual investigation will usually uncover at least some inappropriate behavior to strike out at. Given the embarrassment in admitting that an expensive prosecutorial investigation was all for naught, there is a temptation even for the most honest and sincere prosecutor, to sing the old ballad: "When I'm not near the one I love, I love the one I'm near." As one former prosecutor has pointed out:

---

[15]18 U.S.C. §1346 (emphasis added).

[F]ederal prosecutors frequently will bring a case relatively unrelated to whatever they originally were pursuing, simply because it is an indictable, triable case. The federal agents who work under the prosecutors also are anxious to turn investigations into actual prosecutions. They may press the prosecutor for indictment of whatever offenses appear to be indictable, even if those offenses have little relation to the initial investigation or involve lesser targets or less serious conduct than originally anticipated.

By the time this process reaches the indictment state, agents and prosecutors may find themselves with facts accumulated through the course of their investigation that amount to some sort of improper or dishonest activity but do not fit the traditional criteria for a federal offense ... Quite often mail fraud is the only federal criminal charge to bring against a private individual or a nonfederal public official involved in corrupt activity.[16]

Conspiracy. Another count popular with prosecutors in white-collar crime cases is *conspiracy.* Imagine three employees attempting to parse the Customs rules on constructing a suitable value for products partially assembled abroad. They agree on reading of regulations that, while not self-evident, is arguably correct and saves their company money. A Customs special agent sees it as criminal greed, and refers it to the prosecutor. But as the agent explains the technical violation of the Customs code and the mechanics of *constructing value,* the lawyer's eyes glaze over. A charge of violating the Code of Federal Regulations provokes yawns even among prosecutors. But a *conspiracy* uncovered? That can put a lay jury on the edge of its seats.

The law of conspiracy was designed to bring to justice those who act in concert for unlawful purposes. It arose out of concern that gangsters and racketeers might escape, even though they conspired to do crimes, simply because they did not each perform all the requisite elements of the crime individually. And some of them may have acted in a way that was both objectively innocent and essential to the success of the criminal enterprise.

Trimming away the niceties, modern conspiracy law has, like mail fraud, two elements: knowledge that criminal wrongdoing is occurring and an overt act is performed in furtherance of that conspiracy. When looked at carefully, the potential reach of such a crime is apparent. If a company violates a business regulation, government regulators may believe that the violation was intentional. Having no direct evidence of

---

[16]Hurson, "Limiting the Federal Mail Fraud Statute—A Legislative Approach," *20 Am. Crime L. Rev.* 423, 433–434 (1983), as quoted in *White Collar Crime: Business and Regulatory Offenses,* Obermaier and Morvillo (Law Journal Seminars–Press, 1990), §9.05, p. 9-72.

criminal intent, the government may nonetheless seek to establish it by circumstantial evidence. Investigators may knit together circumstantial bits and pieces—the ambiguous memo, the unusual transaction—into a pattern that suggests a criminal purpose.

Once that is established, one needs to find only one overt act. And overt acts need not be very overt. Take, for example, the standard instruction given to juries in federal court conspiracy cases:

> An overt act under this section need not be unlawful in and of itself. It may be as innocent as crossing a street.

Suddenly, licking an envelope containing a letter written by someone else that the government believes violates its regulatory scheme may become a felony.

Given this breadth, it is no wonder that Judge Learned Hand called conspiracy "the darling of the modern prosecutor's nursery."[17] As Judge Hand said elsewhere in describing the dangers of conspiracy doctrine:

> The distinction is especially important today when so many prosecutors seek to sweep within the dragnet of conspiracy all those who have been associated in any degree whatever with the main offenders. That there are opportunities of great oppression in such a doctrine is very plain, and it is only by circumscribing the scope of such all comprehensive indictments that they can be avoided. We may agree that morally the defendants at bar should have refused to sell to illicit distillers; but, both morally and legally, to do so was *toto coelo* different from joining with them in running the stills.[18]

There are many more examples, to be sure. Given the increasing inclination of government agencies to pursue regulatory infractions as criminal rather than as civil matters, such elastic criminal provisions are disconcerting. If one overt act, done with knowledge of some violation of *fair play* or a consumer's right to *honest service,* can get a business indicted for two felonies—mail fraud and conspiracy—who is safe from an abuse of discretion?

4. *The Pharisee could not imagine the way circumstantial evidence can be used against him, even without direct evidence of guilt.* The publican's offenses were evident and easily proved. Witnesses could give direct testimony of oppression and overreaching. But the Pharisee's sins of

---

[17]*Harrison v. United States,* 7 F.2d 259, 263 (2d Cir. 1925).

[18]*United States v. Falcone,* 109 F.2d 579, 581 (2d Cir.), aff'd. 311 U.S. 205, 61 S.Ct. 204, 85 L.Ed 128 (1940) at 581.

attitude were more subtle. Who was going to prove he committed an offense? Such smug complacency dulled him to the breadth of admissible evidence.

A defendant in a white-collar crime prosecution soon sees the greater liberality of courts in admitting incriminating evidence. Cases against insider trading have traditionally, for example, been proved by direct evidence. Someone with inside information gives a stock tip to a friend or accomplice. That person makes a quick profit in the market. The government has either documents or witnesses (perhaps even the "tipper") that can prove both knowledge and subsequent trading based on the knowledge. In cases like that involving Ivan Boesky, the catching of one tipper or tippee can lead directly to the catching of others, as a result of plea bargains or other negotiated settlements.

But direct evidence is not the only kind of evidence permitted in insider trading litigation. In one recent case, an insider trading case was proved by wholly circumstantial evidence.[19] David Hellberg denied that he had talked to his father about confidential information that David Hellberg had in his possession. His father, Gerald Hellberg, also denied he had talked to his son. No witness came forward to prove such a conversation. The prosecutor was left with suspicious circumstances. He indicted. Gerald Hellberg became the defendant tippee. The SEC produced evidence that Gerald Hellberg's trading was "unusual," "speculative," and lacked any "reasonable basis" other than insider trading. The jury agreed. Hellberg was convicted.

The *Hellberg* case appears to be the first time that anyone has been found guilty of insider trading based on circumstantial evidence. While the SEC was quoted as being uncertain as to what future cases will be brought based merely on circumstantial evidence, such cases will undoubtedly raise the anxiety level of those who occasionally have access to information the SEC might view as insider information.

Let us consider, with gallows sobriety, the following scenario. A lawyer gets a phone call while out of town on a Wednesday evening. The caller is the president of a company. That president advises the lawyer that the company has had meetings just that day with a notorious raider. The raider is pressing the president to sell the company to him. If the company does not agree, the raider says, he will launch a tender offer two days later. The lawyer is asked to represent the company.

In response, the lawyer says that he will be back in his office the next day and will do a conflicts check to see whether such representation

---

[19]See, e.g., *SEC v. Hellberg*, 22 Sec Reg & L Rep (BNA) 1539 (D Utah, October 26, 1990) (nonpublished cite).

would be permissible. The next morning, at 8:45 a.m., the lawyer does the paperwork necessary to check for conflicts. Finding none, he calls the president on his private line and says that he will be able to represent the company. At 9:15, still full of nervous energy from his trip and recent case developments, the lawyer calls his broker. The broker advises him that he has executed three trades on his behalf.

There is no discretionary agreement between the lawyer and the broker, but their close relationship over the years has led to a mutual trust. One of the trades, he says, is a large position in the very company that called the lawyer to represent it in the upcoming takeover battle. While a "public" company, the company is a thousand miles away from the lawyer's office and hardly a household name. The lawyer reacts with a shriek, the broker seeks to break the trade, and their mutual good fortune is that the trade has not yet been processed within the office.

Let us suppose, hypothetically, that the trade was not immediately broken. The lawyer got overwhelmed in representation of various clients and did not check his confirms or monthly statements until 30 to 60 days later, when the stock had doubled in value. Let us suppose that SEC computers, which do not take second place to AWACS radar in picking up "hot" transactions, zeros in on this one. It finds an unusual transaction in size a few days before the announcement of a tender offer. It then discovers that the transaction was executed by a lawyer later revealed to be representing the target. Checking phone records, as the SEC does, it finds a call the night before the subject trade from the president of the company to a hotel room used by the lawyer. It then finds computer documents confirming a conflicts check 20 minutes before the trade. Finally, it finds a call from the lawyer to the personal number of the president of the company 10 minutes before the trade. It talks to the lawyer and finds that he is claiming that his closely related broker traded independently on his own discretion, even though there is no discretionary letter.

What are the chances that a jury would not convict on a criminal insider trading allegation or that the SEC could not win a civil judgment, including the barring of the lawyer from representation of clients before the SEC? Notwithstanding such circumstantial weight, the case would result in gross injustice.

The facts are not as far-fetched as they sound. In fact, the very same set of events befell the author, but, by the grace of God, he found out about the transaction before the order was finally placed, and no trade was ever executed. Given the interrelationships of people in the securities business and the risks of representing people in shareholder litigation, prosecutors and SEC regulators ought to be reluctant to press insider trading cases in the absence of direct evidence.

The breathtaking scope of modern federal business regulation and the circumstantial evidence that can prove it suggest that every company and every individual could probably be indicted for a violation of some federal or state law and not be able to get it summarily dismissed prior to trial.

Dr. Saul Gellerman, Dean of the University of Dallas Graduate School of Management, says, "Some recent studies have shown that almost two-thirds of the largest 500 companies have been involved in illegal activities of some kind which became publicized."[20]

How many more have been involved in questionable activities that could become criminal cases? Fortunately, most prosecutors operate in good faith. Most investigators have a sense of public responsibility. But the bottom line is still the same. The only impediment between you and a criminal charge may be lodged in the common sense discretion of a fallible prosecutor.

[20] *Industry Week*, **232**, 25 (February 23, 1987).

4

"Are You John Fletcher?"

On the Importance of Being Prepared

The busy executive checked his watch as he was about to slip out of the first-class cabin of the U.S. Air 727. This was his third city in four days. He had three meetings in Pittsburgh and a tight schedule.

Grabbing his attaché case and his overnight bag, he strode up the gangway and into the airport, his eyes glazed over from thoughts about the upcoming day. His meditations, however, were suddenly interrupted by an abrupt question.

"Are you John Fletcher?" The question, posed by one of two men standing near the railing at the gate area, caught him off guard.

"Yes, and who are you?"

"Joe Pelagrini of the FBI. Can you come with us to the other corner of the waiting area and talk to us for a second?"

The executive was well known as a hard-driving (to say nothing of up and coming) executive of a Fortune 500 company. His special forte was negotiation. He had a reputation of knowing people and knowing how to get them to his preferred destination. But this was something outside of his normal ken.

"Sure, how can I help you?"

Once in a more private corner, the FBI agents wasted no time. "We believe you have committed as many as six felonies in connection with a negotiation in this area. The grand jury is prepared to indict you next

Monday at 11:00 a.m. But if you cooperate with us, it might go better for you. You don't *have* to talk to us, of course. But if you don't, I'm afraid an indictment is inevitable."

The words left him feeling numb. He had received a promotion three months earlier. He was just now feeling some comfort that his career was established. He was an active, public spirited citizen, well known in his community, active in his church, looked up to by his friends. Now he was 72 hours away from being accused of federal felonies. What should he do? It sounded to him as though he had no choice.

"I've got nothing to hide. If there is anything I can do to answer your questions or explain anything to you, I'd be happy to do so."

The FBI officer smiled. "Why don't you come along with us and we'll go to some place even more private."

He went with the two agents, got into their government car, a gray Dodge car, and drove to a local Marriott hotel. The officers took him to a room with two single beds which looked like all the other rooms the executive had stayed in on the hundreds of trips he had taken for his company. Except for one thing. There was electronic equipment on the desk, including headsets, together with some recording cassettes.

The officers sat down, ordered rolls and coffee, and got about their business.

They explained that he had been identified as a person who had violated federal law. The senior agent, Pelagrini, fingered a file and said, "there are some pretty bad things in here about you." He added, however, that the FBI wanted to be fair and give him a chance to tell his side. "We've only heard one side of the story." He repeated, as though talking for the record, that he had no obligation to talk with them and was not in custody. But again he gave a subtle warning, "Of course, if we don't hear your side, it looks as though things will have to go ahead as scheduled."

Here was another chance for Fletcher to collect his thoughts and make a decision. Again, however, it seemed to him he could not risk calling the bluff.

"Ask me whatever you like."

For the next hour and a half, Fletcher answered questions. He was not told what others had said about him. He had no occasion to review documents, notes, or agreements with respect to the transaction, which had happened many months before. He had no lawyer present to advise him about what constituted a violation of the law in question, or to describe the process he was in the midst of, or to make clear to him what strategy works best with aggressive investigators like Pelagrini and friend.

Confident that he knew how to negotiate in difficult circumstances, he plunged ahead. He would wing it. He talked, and talked, and talked some more. He gave the agent his state of mind, speculated about the knowledge of others, and dropped in every tidbit that he thought might constitute a defense to his actions. The agents took copious notes. Fletcher would have no record of the conversation and would have no right to see the notes, called "302s," unless and until he was indicted.

After the questions were answered, Pelagrini had another suggestion. "You tell an interesting story, but we need some confirmation. I wonder if you'd be willing to help us out on something else?"

Yet another decision was to be forthcoming. "Sure."

"You say that others, including your superiors, didn't think anything was being done contrary to law either. Is that right?"

"Absolutely."

"Well, we'd like you to call your boss, and maybe some other individuals, and have a conversation with them that we can listen in on. Do you see any trouble with that?"

Fletcher was uncomfortable with calling up his boss, the chief executive officer of the company, without warning. But he didn't want to break off cooperation now, when it appeared he was scoring some points. And he really didn't believe the president would incriminate himself. If he interrupted the conversation and asked to talk to a lawyer, it would be a sure sign of guilt. If he was reluctant to go ahead with the call and gave some other excuse, that would seem incriminating, too. He would go ahead.

"Uh, why not? If you guys assure me that there's nothing wrong with it, I'd be happy to do it."

It took only moments for the officers to connect their equipment. Each of them put on a set of headphones. Some questions had already been prepared on a sheet of paper. They were given to Fletcher. Before long, the phone was ringing.

A somewhat confused company president was now on the line answering open-ended questions from a subordinate. Yes, he remembered that transaction. Yes, he remembered there was something problematic about the check. No, he didn't remember anything illegal about the transaction, but does recall there was some concern about it. And so it went. The president had no clue of who his audience was, nor was he guarded in his responses. Since he did not understand why he should be bothered on the matter, his manner was diffident, and he sounded either distracted—or guilty. Pelagrini told Fletcher when the conversation had gone on long enough by giving a gesture, drawing his finger under his chin. It was a gesture, the full meaning of which Fletcher only dimly comprehended.

After one more call to another executive, it was noon. Fletcher had missed his first business meeting. His stomach was churning. He wanted to see what he had bought with his cooperation, and began to wonder whether he should have negotiated his compensation up front.

"Anything else I can help you gentlemen with?" he asked.

The agents looked at each other. "We have some more things we want to get to the bottom of, and we'd like you to be available for another full interview when you get back home after this trip. And we want you to assure us that you'll tell nobody about our conversation."

"That sounds fair enough." He paused for a moment. "If you credit my story, what can I expect for helping you guys?" He smiled nervously.

"As you may know," the FBI agent said somewhat sternly, "I can make no deals on behalf of the United States government. But I would be happy to recommend that all but two felony charges be dropped against you, if you would plead to them. We can, of course, make no agreement as to the sentence."

Two felonies rather than six? Is this the deal for baring his soul? Suddenly, a sense of doom came over him. He had better talk to a lawyer, *fast.* He excused himself, telling the agents to feel free to call him later, and went to a phone to make the phone call he should have made two hours earlier.

To come were indictments and proceedings at which his own words were used against him. Where he had "filled in" his memory in an attempt to exonerate himself, minor inconsistencies with existing documents became an effort to deceive. Good-faith cooperation became an attempt to "pull the wool over the eyes of the FBI" and to "lie himself out of trouble." As far as he could tell, from reading the indictment and from the tenacious, unrelenting, implacable attitude of the prosecutor, he could discern no benefit he had won by his cooperation.

What went wrong? The executive was a skilled businessman, a highly respected negotiator, street-smart, tough, shrewd, and honest. How could he go so wrong, so fast?

The answer is simple. He was playing a game for the first time against seasoned and skillful opponents. He was unsure of the rules. He had no experience against which to test the FBI agent's claim that an indictment was forthcoming. He knew nothing of his opponent's weaknesses or his own strengths in such a setting. He followed his intuition, not knowing that the right course of action in this very specialized setting is counterintuitive. He lost.

This story is replayed again and again in an America that increasingly views "business ethics" as an oxymoron and is increasingly receptive to the idea that businessmen get successful by criminal behavior. The Fletchers often come to their senses too late. How else can one explain the following examples?

- A corporate general counsel, of elite academic credentials, meticulous and detail oriented, an expert in antitrust law, is advised that federal agents are waiting in the reception area of corporate headquarters. When she introduces herself, they produce a search warrant. The company is a much-honored business entity, often written up as an example of corporate ethics and sound business management. She welcomes the agents in. One of them asks if he can interview the president—alone. The general counsel, frightened and unwilling to give the impression that a blue-chip company has anything to hide, arranges a conference room, invites the president and the agent into the room, then excuses herself, leaving the corporate officer and the FBI agent to chat in an interview for which one of the parties is absolutely prepared and knows exactly what he wants, and the other is ignorant, unsuspecting, and still preoccupied with a tough problem in a foreign subsidiary which she had been discussing when she was called away for this meeting. The officer is later indicted.

- A rising young manager with a Harvard MBA working for a sporting goods company is asked by the U.S. Attorney to give a statement in a pending grand jury investigation, with the assurance that "if I have a reasonable doubt that you have done anything wrong, I will acquit you, myself. There will be no indictment. And, of course, you will always get credit for cooperation." The man gives a 180-page statement in which he tries—agonizingly—to give an honest answer to every question the prosecutor asks. Three weeks later, the man is indicted, based in large measure on his statement.

- The owner of one of the nation's most successful small aircraft franchises becomes aware that she is being investigated for theft of an airplane. She is sure that this is some mistake. In an answer to an invitation from an investigator, she walks over to the federal office building in her town and gives a complete statement. She later tells friends who know of the inquiry that her audience seemed "totally convinced." Three months later, she is indicted. The critical fact the government was missing (and that she admitted to without any sense of its importance) was that she had flown a particular airplane over a state border. If she had not admitted it herself, the federal government could not have proved it, and thus would not have indicted her.

- A USDA official begins an audit of a prominent food company. The head of the division the government is investigating is thought to be the most expert manager in the country with respect to a particular type of product. The manager of the company, without telling anyone else, determines that the documents requested by the agent, if turned over, will reveal a regulatory infraction and probably trigger a small fine. Although counsel is available, he does not want either counsel or company to know what he has been doing. He therefore redacts and recopies the critical documents, destroys the originals, and thus converts a potential regulatory infraction into a criminal obstruction of justice.

All of the people involved in these vignettes have many good things in common. They are intelligent, successful, respected, competent achievers. But they all have one critical weakness: they all have decided to play a high-stakes game without the foggiest idea of the rules. Or, some cynics would say, *the rule,* the one that true criminals know by heart: if you don't talk, you walk.

The truth is, as all white-collar crime specialists know, that criminal investigations have very special rules unlike those of business negotiations or civil litigation. One ignores them at great peril. Although these executives would not think of going into a negotiation without knowing the facts, they put their business life and personal liberty at stake, quite readily, based on hunches and suspicions. What are the facts that one ought to know when faced with a potential criminal investigation?

1. *Special agents, whether employed by the FBI, the IRS, or any of the other alphabet soup agencies of the federal government, are hired to find wrongdoing and prosecute it.* It is no slur on the good faith of agents and investigators employed by government agencies to say that they are paid to look for misconduct. Successful prosecutors win convictions. Successful agents come up with prosecutable offenses. Even assuming the highest standards of good faith, it must be remembered that agents are not paid to exculpate. Success for agents is finding criminal defendants and making charges against them stick.

I once visited a wonderful, though somewhat eccentric, Swedish relative in Oakland, California. He spoke with an old country accent but loved his adopted land, where he had attained some success as a sign painter. When I visited him, he asked me if I would like a tour of the bay area. I happily agreed. After a three-hour ride, I had been taken to dozens of points of special interest to my relative. I had seen nearly every sign that he had painted, or supervised the construction of, in Oakland and San Francisco. I had seen the signs of his competitors and learned why they did not measure up to his superior craftsmanship. I had learned the special problems of hanging signs on certain buildings and how difficult regulatory requirements were complied with by creative use of paint and neon. The Golden Gate Bridge, Jack London Square, Nob Hill, and Fisherman's Wharf were not on the itinerary. But I had received the sign-painter's tour from my good, honest, immigrant rela-

tive. To him, the buildings of the bay were all constructed for one purpose: as a convenient place to hang signs.

As the highway patrol officer is paid to spot infractions a normal
driver does not detect, as the auditor is paid to find difficulties in the
presentation of financial numbers not readily seen by a normal reader,
the criminal investigator is paid to find infractions. And by the time the
investigator has opened the file and is actively investigating the matter,
chances are the investigator believes some wrongdoing exists. When an
IRS special agent makes a call, it's most often a sign that this is no ordinary civil audit. When the FBI comes calling—unless they make absolutely clear that they are looking for witnesses to a bank robbery that
happened in your lobby—there is already considerable momentum to
prosecute *somebody*.

The first reality that the interviewee has to deal with, then, is that the
agent knocking on the door, whether smiling or growling, is a potential
adversary, who may well be coming to generate evidence against the
interviewee, and who will view cooperation as a lucky break that will
facilitate a criminal prosecution, not as a persuasive sign of good faith.

2. *A special agent working up a case often needs the cooperation of a business
executive in order to prosecute the executive.* A review of white-collar crime
prosecutions reveals that few major prosecutions happen without
somebody's cooperation. It may be that of a "snitch," a disaffected
employee who bitterly tries to even a score by pointing out questionable
business behavior. It may be an underling who has been secretly
granted immunity and records a conversation with an unsuspecting
superior. But not infrequently, cooperative witnesses turns out to be the
potential defendants themselves.

How do agents get these potential defendants to act so contrary to
their own interests? As Burke said, no one surrenders a precious possession such as liberty save under the power of some great delusion. Special agents have long experience and training in getting information
out of a potential defendant by delusion, whether the defendant-to-be is
a hard-core street criminal or a business executive who may be said to
have violated some regulation. Although these devices are simple, they
are effective, and skilled investigators know them well. They come in
two forms, the carrot and the stick.

The carrot is an implicit or explicit promise that cooperation will lead
to some future consideration—and perhaps exoneration—during the
course of the investigation. Alas, such promises—implicit or explicit—
need not be kept. Those who have not had a brush with the criminal
justice system do not realize it, but much investigatory strategy is based
on the axiom that the end justifies the means.

Sometimes the average citizen sympathizes with reliance on this axiom when it comes to street crime. In a prominent case featuring rape charges against three prominent athletes, the alleged victim had gone back to a motel room to have "a party" with three Division I basketball players. She testified that when she got back to the motel, she went into one of the rooms and found out that the players had a "party" in mind that was somewhat different from what she anticipated. Soon, she said, she was being raped by at least three men and compelled to perform a variety of indecent acts. When she reported the incident the next morning, she could not recall the names of the three men, and knew that there was at least one man who had raped her whom she had not been able to see in the dark. The police intercepted the basketball team before it left on its morning flight back to its home campus and asked one of the players some questions. His answers were evasive and unhelpful.

Then, with practiced interviewing techniques, the police officer held up a piece of paper across the table. "I have here, Jim," he said, "a statement by your friend, Lloyd. He says that you were the person who raped this girl. You were the first one in, and she was really resisting you and not anybody else. Unless you can tell us something to the contrary, it looks like you're going to be the one charged. Me, I think he's probably trying to hang the jacket on you because he was involved. But unless someone tells me to the contrary, that's all I've got to go on."

Jim thought for a moment, and then blurted out, "He's lying. He went in first, and I went in later. And we weren't the only ones. Tom went in, too. And she resisted Lloyd more than any of the rest of us."

Charges were, of course, soon filed against all three. The public was generally pleased about the result, notwithstanding the fact that the police officer had lied. Lloyd had made no such statement. The paper was not what the officer represented it to be, but an unrelated mimeographed sheet having nothing to do with the case. Jim was tricked. But a case was made. Few sympathized with the outrage of Jim and the others who felt that they had been tricked and badly used.

Business executives similarly duped may feel the same outrage the players did, especially when they feel they have done nothing wrong but at most are guilty of reading complicated regulations differently from the government. Internal government manuals make clear that investigators use this strategy frequently. They are prepared to lie about what they know or about what they will do in order to get incriminating information. The special agents' guide for one agency suggests that old maxim, "honey attracts more flies than vinegar," is also true of investigations. A conciliatory and friendly, indeed personal, approach, the agent is told, is often the best way to elicit information. Promise suspects that if they cooperate, things will go well for them. This is often the best way to get incriminating information that will lead to a successful prosecution against them.

The strategies of other criminal investigators are similar. It is not uncommon for agents to promise some vague consideration in exchange for testimony or even explicitly to promise that witnesses will not be criminally prosecuted if they cooperate. When witnesses take the bait and then shortly thereafter feel the jerk of the hook, they can do nothing. Courts have uniformly held that the promises of an agent cannot bind the United States government. Indeed the promises of a United States Attorney have been held not to bind the government. In one case in the District of Minnesota, a prosecutor promised that a party would not be indicted in federal court, then announced that he had reneged on the promise and prosecuted the party. The district court convicted her, notwithstanding the argument by defendant's counsel that the conviction was obtained based in part on bad-faith government behavior. The prosecutor admitted that there had been a promise, admitted that it had been breached, but nonetheless asked the court to sustain the conviction. The district court found no problem with conviction, promise or no promise. While the Eighth Circuit reversed, the case ultimately was not dismissed after further review by the district court.[1]

The other weapon in the government armory is the stick. With Mr. Fletcher, the stick looked like a large 2×4 beam. An indictment was going to come down in three days. He had one last chance to avoid the blow. What he didn't know, of course, was that there was no indictment. There had been no evidence given to the grand jury. The matter was in its early stages of investigation. The government needed information from him before he could even be said to be a "target" of the investigation. But how was he to know? The impact of an indictment, regardless of whether he was later convicted or not, was so enormous that he could not take the chance that the agents were bluffing.

Because the law has special rules that apply when persons are interrogated in custody, including the provision of *Miranda* warnings and the like, agents want to make clear to witnesses that they are not in custody and can go as they please. But investigators desperately want them to stay, so incriminating information can be obtained from them. One of the best ways to do that is to freeze the witness in place with an implicit threat. It may be a bold lie, like the one that entrapped Fletcher. It may, however, be more subtle. "If you don't talk with us, I guess we'll have to go on the information we already have, and that's not flattering to you." Or it may be a question. "Do you really think you have something to

---

[1] *United States v. Amy Frances Johnson* 861 F.2d 510 (8th Cir. ___).

hide? In my experience, people cooperate with the government when they have nothing to hide." Or it may be basically reassuring, with just a hint of a threat, a small cloud no bigger than a person's hand in an otherwise blue sky. "I don't really view you as a target, assuming you tell me what I think you will. Of course, you know what they say about dogs. Run from them and they might bite you."

Such approaches are an attempt at delusion. The truth is quite the contrary. One of the most dangerous positions in the criminal justice system is sitting in a government interview room giving an off-the-cuff interview to an agent who suspects the interviewee may have done something wrong.

The agent is telling the truth with the statement that a number of people have cooperated. But that is rather like the old fable in which the fox invites the chicken into his dark lair. When the chicken protests that it looks risky, the fox points to all the chicken prints on the ground that indicate that other chickens have followed the same path. The wise old hen quite properly responds, "Yes, but what worries me is that all the prints of my fellow chickens are going in, and none are coming out."

3. *If you've got some information to sell, don't give it away.* Adam Smith lived over 200 years ago, but his truths keep marching on. Business, he taught us, is based on the idea of exchange. If you want to get in business and stay in business, you have to know what the marketplace needs, know value when you see it, and assign a price to a product that will maximize profit.

If the government comes knocking, asking for information, you know there is consumer demand. The government wants you to open your safe and empty its contents into its agent's bag. The jewels that they would like to make off with are facts. The fact that they have come to you means they have a demand for something of which you have a supply. That suggests, in turn, that there may be some price they are willing to pay. That price must be negotiated in advance, preferably by someone who knows value.

The government may, for example, be willing to give a witness immunity. But it will give immunity only if a witness insists on it. The testimony of the witness may be suspect in the eyes of the jury if the witness has been immunized, and going through the Department of Justice to get a judge to sign an order of immunity is both cumbersome and politically dangerous, since it is subject to second guessing if the immunized witness in retrospect appears to be more culpable than the one being accused. Often, the government will say immunity is impossible, all the while knowing that it will ultimately give immunity if it is demanded.

If the safe is opened and all the jewels are poured out without anything of value being exchanged, the government will walk off with them and happily put them in its treasury. And no price will be paid later. For that reason, it makes no sense to give information free of charge.

4. *Politely refusing to give information without immunity makes it less likely that one will be prosecuted, not more.* Average business executives do not think of themselves as criminals. I remember the poignant comment of a young chief executive officer, a Stanford Business School Ph.D., prominent in the Young Presidents Organization. He had just made his first appearance in a criminal matter. He had been wrongfully accused by a general manager he had fired for embezzlement and other defalcations. He would later be acquitted of all counts by a federal jury. But now, after his first contact with the magistrate, after being fingerprinted and photographed for his mug shot, he was looking stunned. "You've got to understand," he said, "it will take some time for me to think of myself as a criminal."

Most hard-working, overachieving business people think of the Fifth Amendment as a refuge for scoundrels. They recall old television footage of Kefauver and McClellan Committee hearings where prominent mobsters, their double-breasted lapels flapping, stormed out of hearing rooms with their sharkskin-suited mouthpiece after "taking the fifth."

If they refuse to talk with the government, how can the government think anything else but that they are hiding something? And if they are hiding something, will not the government vindictively seek to prosecute them merely for their lack of cooperation? That intuitive feeling drives an individual toward cooperation.

But the intuition is wrong. Business executives who, in kind and polite voices, advise investigators that they would "love to be helpful," but "of course" must run it by corporate counsel first, are not thought to be criminals, but smart and well advised. Shrewd business executives who do something as silly as the examples given at the beginning of the chapter are not respected. Agents see it as a serendipity, making their job far easier than anticipated. Raising the cost and difficulty of a potential prosecution to busy federal agents means, in a business sense, that they will undertake fewer prosecutions. Witnesses who talk freely and without adequate preparation or binding order of immunity will almost surely prove the Biblical proverb: "In a multitude of words there wanteth not sin."

5. *Many business crimes that are prosecuted happen after the commencement of the investigation.* The Wall Street Journal is increasingly full of prominent names of businesses and executives indicted by grand juries. A

surprising number of these prosecutions happened for conduct that occurred after, not before, the government's initial interviews.

The reasons for this are not hard to understand. Complicated regulatory crimes are not easy to prosecute. It is difficult to get a jury to walk attentively through the cluttered landscape of a complicated regulatory scheme. It is difficult for a jury to have the same outrage when confronted with a *malum prohibitum* (a crime that is only a crime because a government regulator says so) as with a *malum in se* (a crime that is obviously wrong and immoral, like a rape or assault). It is far easier to prosecute under U.S. §1001, prohibiting false statements to federal officers, than it is to demonstrate that a customs declaration did not adequately take into account nonpecuniary "assists" or properly allocate overhead on imports from the People's Republic of China. A false statement to an investigator is a lie, pure and simple. The motive is obvious: to avoid criminal liability for some other behavior far more difficult to prove. The intention (or scienter) underlying acknowledged wrongdoing can be readily inferred from the false statement itself. And a three-month trial might be reduced to a one-week government prosecution.

A seasoned white-collar crime lawyer knows from personal experience that many clients would have not been prosecuted for the underlying wrong but are nonetheless prosecuted for mistakes they made after the investigation began. Former Secretary of Labor Ray Donovan was prosecuted not for some underlying wrongdoing allegedly committed by his construction company, but for allegedly lying to a grand jury about his business later. His later acquittal confirmed his vigorous assertions of innocence. But would he have been indicted in the first place if he had chosen to go before a hostile prosecutor and grand jury? Many grand jury witnesses are prosecuted not for what they testified about, but for the fact of an inconsistency in their testimony. Persons can be prosecuted for their testimony before a grand jury merely for contradicting themselves, and the government need not establish which of the contradictory comments is true, as long as it can show to the jury that the witnesses made contradictory statements as to a material fact out of their own mouths. And so witnesses, testifying in the isolation of a grand jury chamber, nervous, without the benefit of counsel in the room, may say something they can reconcile, but which appears to be a contradiction to the prosecutor, and find themselves prosecuted only for the sin of testifying in answer to a grand jury subpoena.

6. *Beware of impulses, most notably the impulse to prove you are innocent.* The first thing some defendants want to do is to take a lie detector test. They want to prove their innocence. But, unfortunately, lie detector tests are peculiarly unsuited to determine guilt or innocence in a com-

plicated regulatory crime. They are generally inadmissible in evidence. The prosecutor will not believe them unless they tend to show guilt. And a mass of experts will, for a fee, come into court and testify that they are as unreliable as a divining rod.

They are, however, sometimes useful in determining the *bona fides* of a client. While walking down the corridors of the courthouse one day, I was corralled by a friendly judge who wanted to appoint me immediately to represent a difficult defendant. Charles Smith, we shall call him, was on trial for a variety of offenses. He was thought by the police to be a procurer of women. He was now insisting on going to trial without representation, creating difficulties for the judge and court system. The judge asked me if I would represent him, at least for the day, as a personal favor. I took the "appointment."

Charles was initially unhappy with my counsel. "I don't need no public defender. I need a real lawyer, but I can't afford one," he said.

"But what do you have against public defenders?" I asked.

"They always plead me when I'm innocent. Four public defenders, four pleas. I've had it up to here. This time I can prove I'm innocent. No deals."

I explained to him that I would be happy to take his case to trial if a plea were unacceptable. This appeared to comfort him.

When I got into the facts, I found he was claiming an alibi. He was not in the city at the time of the crime. "And, man, I've got six witnesses." Charles gestured to a long bench outside the courtroom. There sat six young women, all dressed for the evening at 9 a.m. in the morning. Leather miniskirts, spike heels, and cigarettes between thumb and forefinger were the style of the day. "Just talk to the girls," Charles said.

I interviewed them, not in company as Charles suggested, but one by one. I came back to give Charles the results. "The good news is that all agree that you were not in town, Charles," I said.

"That's what I told you, man," Charles said.

"The bad news, Charles, is that they have you in six different locations at the time of the offense. I think we had better not use them."

Charles was not intimidated. "Man, we've got two hours to trial, we'll get it together."

By this time the judge was getting impatient. He and the prosecutor presented a deal that would allow Charles to escape without time for pleas to two of the charges. It was a good deal. I advised Charles of the possibility. "There you go again, another public defender deal. Didn't you listen to me, man? No deals!"

I brought the bad news to the judge and prosecutor. The judge was now pleading, "Could you try one more time?"

I went back to the defendant. "I think I've got a deal for you. If you take a lie detector test and pass, the judge will dismiss the charges. On the other hand, Charles, if you fail, you will agree to plead, and the judge can impose an appropriate sentence. If you really weren't there, I think it's a great deal."

Charles' brow screwed together in a look of earnest thoughtfulness. The solemnity of the moment was broken by an ejaculation from one of "the girls." "Yo! Did he say Charles would take a lie detector test? Charles? A lie detector test?" The girl put hand to mouth, wiggled her shoulders, stamped her feet, and rolled her eyes in one convulsive laugh. It was contagious. Soon the entire bench of witnesses was chortling uncontrollably.

Even Charles could no longer maintain the seriousness. He smiled broadly. "Lie detector test? No lie detector test, man. Tell the judge Charles Smith is ready to plead."

7. *One who shoots from the hip may find a bullet in one's foot.* The witness who confronts an investigator for the first time is usually not prepared for it. The essence of the investigative interview is to catch a person off guard. With Fletcher, it took the form of two agents at an airport. For many others, it is an agent dropping by the house at 9:00 in the evening. Or there is an agent lurking in the parking lot at the close of a busy workday.

Targets do not appreciate how much investigators may already know. Witnesses themselves are utterly unprepared. It is unlikely that they know the elements of the crimes they may be charged with, because they probably have never talked to a lawyer about the incident in question. They have no idea what documents investigators have reviewed and may indeed have forgotten memorandums they have written on the subject themselves. They do not know whom investigators have talked to, or what has been told to the investigators. Critical details of the transaction may be unclear in their minds. But, as responsible employees, proud of their reputation, they do not want to appear wavering or uncertain. And so, like Fletcher, they wing it.

An old politician used to say, "Never engage in a war of words with an adversary who buys ink by the barrel." His target was the media. But it would be wise to have a similar caution when talking with a highly trained agent. Never give an unrehearsed story to a person who knows more about the details than you do. The agent is not coming to the interview without having distinct impressions of the case and without being armed with more facts than you think. Speculating to the agent, filling in facts that are foggy in your memory, and resolutely denying doing or saying things because you do not currently recall doing so are all fraught with risk.

I was looking over a list of old files recently, and among the hundreds of clients I recognized that there were one or two files I did not have the foggiest recollection of. When I summoned them up from the vault, I was shocked to see my signature on the file opening sheet, and eventually some brief notes refreshed my recollection. But for seeing the files and the notes, I might well have sworn under oath that I had never represented the client. If I were more cagey, I might have said, "I have no recollection of representing that client." Either statement could lead to a prosecution for perjury. It was, after all, Mr. Deaver who was indicted for saying, "I don't recall" about something the government believed he recalled. While he was later exonerated, it was only after a grueling court process. There may be few "nevers" in life, but this is one of them. *Never give a statement without being meticulously prepared.*

All of these rules lead to an inevitable conclusion. The conclusion is simple and, on reflection, self-evident: *Use your head.*

If investigators come knocking, be kind, courteous, and undefensive. Tell them how much you appreciate their efforts to get to the bottom of the matter. But advise them that, since there may be some legal dimensions that you do not understand, you will have to talk to counsel as a matter of corporate and personal policy. Take their cards and tell them you will get back to them. Have your counsel make all further contacts.

Second, be resolute and tenacious. The investigator will probably say, "You're quite right. You have a right to counsel. I think it's a good idea for you to talk with your attorney. But if you wouldn't mind, perhaps you can clarify some details unrelated to the substance of the investigation. What's your title again?" One cannot accept this invitation without jeopardizing one's position. The proper response is, "I'm sorry. This may sound picky or petty, but I really don't feel free to talk with you even on such mundane details until I have talked with my counsel." Witnesses must be as tenacious as their interlocutors, however friendly or unfriendly their countenance.

Third, get counsel experienced in criminal investigations. Getting counsel and getting the right counsel are both important. Many otherwise talented lawyers, indeed some civil litigators, have thrown an unsuspecting client into the lion's den, assuming that civil and criminal tactics are probably much the same. It is important to get a counsel who knows what he or she is doing.

Don't try to fight this battle yourself. Always get help. The decisions that one makes may have a significant impact on oneself, on one's family, on other officers of the company, and on the corporation itself. This is no time for free-lancing.

The *Song of Roland* tells the story of a heroic young knight named Roland. He was a protégé of Charlemagne, the great emperor whose throne was in Paris. Roland had two weapons: his sword, Durendal, and his trumpet, Olivant. With both weapons at the ready, he went about his business in Spain with his friend Oliver. Suddenly, he came under attack by fierce Moors. He quickly unsheathed his sword and began to leave his assailants in heaps on the battlefield. But he was horribly outnumbered. His equally courageous comrade, Oliver, began to implore him to rely not on his sword, but on his trumpet.

Meanwhile, in Paris, Charlemagne was increasingly anxious about his young protégé. He waited with his vast army ready to march at a moment's notice upon any sign that Roland was in difficulty. But Roland kept fighting until, finally, a thrust of the sword got through his defense. He was now bleeding. Belatedly, he put Olivant to his lips and blew the trumpet with such a fearful blast that birds fell dead some distance from the battlefield.

Charlemagne picked up the signal and came with his soldiers to rescue young Roland. But when they arrived, they found Roland just about ready to expire. He had waited too long. The Emperor cradled Roland in his arms and said, "your reckless hardihood was fraught with woe for us."

So too, the business executives who by reason of intimidation or arrogance try to bull their way through a potential government assault will too often learn that their "hardihood" is both reckless, and "fraught with woe," for themselves and for others.

5
Entrepreneur Beware: The Strange Case of Dakota Cheese

You are, like most entrepreneurs, eager to find a way to build a better mousetrap. Your chosen business is well suited to the task. It is the cheese business. Your specialty is mozzarella, that increasingly popular staple of a cholesterol-conscious American diet, famed for its creamy pliability and seductive "stretch."

You find that thousands of years of cheese making still leaves room for innovation. After countless lost batches and experiments that go awry, you discover a new recipe for mozzarella that is both wholly natural and cheaper to produce. When challenged by government regulators, you are able to produce two expert witnesses. One is a professor of cheese science who has been described in international publications as the world's foremost authority on cheese. He swears under oath that your cheese is a genuine innovation and that in every nutritional category it is both totally natural and superior to all the requirements contained in the U.S. Department of Agriculture Standards of Identity for mozzarella cheese.

You also produce a lawyer who is known as the foremost legal authority on government food laws. He is counsel for the nation's most prestigious institute of food law. He swears under oath that the process you used to produce the cheese is wholly consistent with government law

51

and comports with a common sense reading of an ambiguous scheme of federal regulations relating to the product.

So what is the result? An endorsement from the Food and Drug Administrative and a lucrative product line? Alas, no. Your innovation gets you a criminal prosecution which, through the combination of a law and order judge and a hostile federal prosecutor, forces you out of business.

The strange case of Dakota Cheese shows the truth of the old prosecutor's axiom, "If you have smoke, you don't need fire."

The Making of an Entrepreneur

James Dee grew up in a working-class home, where he learned to work hard and independently and fend for himself. By the time he reached the university, he had decided that he wanted to be in the food business, preferably his own food business. He continued to work hard, did well, and turned down offers to work in some of the giants of the industry, enormous companies that offered him much security and little independence. Instead, he tutored under a mentor at a smaller cheese company until the time was right to start his own business.

A risk-taker by disposition and an entrepreneur by personal motivation, Dee moved to South Dakota and tried to do the impossible: start up a mozzarella cheese company from scratch, without substantial financial backing, and without connection to the network that is alleged to dominate the industry. By long days and the force of will, Dee was able to start his business.

In the midst of his other efforts, he continued to try to find a better way to make cheese. From the late 1970s through 1982 and 1983, he began a series of attempted innovations in the cheese-making process, experimenting with various fortification methods for making low-moisture mozzarella cheese. Fortification refers to a process by which the solids content of the milk used to make cheese is increased. In order to make low-moisture part-skim mozzarella, a cheese maker must obtain a proper ratio between the nonfat solids and the fat of the milk. This may be done by either skimming off some of the fat (cream) or by adding nonfat solids to the milk. The latter alternative is referred to as fortification.

Initially, Dee attempted fortification with nonfat dry milk, but this method did not produce a satisfactory cheese. After a substantial amount of time and expense and scrapping many production runs, he began to experiment with a powder called calcium caseinate. Calcium caseinate is a powdered form of milk protein. Although present in mammals, in commercial form it comes from a cow, and only from a cow. It cannot be synthesized. It is the chief chemical constituent of cheese. More than any other constituent, casein furnishes mozzarella with its softness and pliability. It creates what dairy scientists call "the magic of the stretch."

The use of calcium caseinate in the production of mozzarella cheese was not unheard of in the industry nor was it peculiar to Dakota Cheese. Indeed the government had knowledge of widespread use. But Dee had discovered a new technique in using it that attained greater amounts of high-quality protein and yielded a cheese of unmatched quality. That resulted, eventually, in an exclusive formula using precise proportions of whole milk, nonfat dry milk, and calcium caseinate.

Dee's trial-and-error discovery of a formula for the addition of dry calcium caseinate along with nonfat dry milk to the milk used to make the mozzarella had a remarkable effect on Dakota Cheese's cheese-making process. The use of the calcium caseinate formula resulted in greater yields, and hence the more efficient use of whole milk. Second, the addition of calcium caseinate allowed Dakota Cheese to add greater quantities of nonfat dry milk to the whole milk than would otherwise be possible, which improved the nutritional characteristics of the cheese. Finally, the cheese made using the calcium caseinate formula had superior physical qualities (better meltability, better stretchiness, and the like). By entrepreneurial innovation, the formula allowed Dakota Cheese to build the better mousetrap, to produce a superior cheese at lower cost.

Tables 5-1 and 5-2 show an analysis of how the Dakota Cheese mozzarella compared to U.S. Department of Agriculture Standards for mozzarella cheese.

In sum, the cheese contained 10 percent more protein than the USDA standard and contained higher-quality protein (in other words, protein that meets more of the body's nutritional requirements), while meeting or exceeding all other characteristics.

Table 5-1. Calculated Composition (%) of Low-Fat Part-Skim Mozzarella Cheese
(based on HB 8-1 total solids of 51.43%)

Cheese	Total protein	Casein	Whey protein	WP/ TP%*	Fat-dry base
HB 8-1	27.47	27.17	0.30	1.09	33.30
Dakota	30.20	29.70	0.52	1.72	33.25

*WP/TP% is the percentage of whey proteins of the total protein content.

Table 5-2. Comparison of Dakota Cheese Composition Reported by USDA (151 Lots) with Like Data from USDA AG Handbook 8-1 for Low-Moisture Part-Skim Mozzarella

Cheese	Total solids	Water	Fat-dry base, %	Salt	Protein
Dakota	51.10	48.90	32.50	1.36	30.20
AH 8-1	51.40	48.60	33.30	1.34	27.50

The Wrong Customer for a Better Mousetrap

Dakota Cheese used this formula to produce low-moisture part-skim mozzarella cheese for the federal Commodity Credit Corporation (CCC) for use in the school lunch program. The government itself reviewed the cheese for compliance with physical and chemical specifications. All the cheese was inspected by the dairy grading section of the USDA. Before any lot of cheese could be shipped, it had to be inspected by the USDA graders assigned to Dakota Cheese's plant, who conducted random sampling of the cheese to test the cheese's conformance to the contract requirements. These highly trained graders found the cheese to meet government standards and found all such requirements had been satisfied.

But the decision to contract with the government proved to be critical for Dakota Cheese. By contracting with the government, Dee and the company opened itself to criminal charges of "false claims" or "false statements" if the procedure used for the production of mozzarella cheese deviated in any way from the contract terms. Those terms stipulated that "the cheese shipped to CCC shall be low-moisture part-skim mozzarella cheese as defined by Food and Drug Administration, U.S. Department of Health, Education and Welfare in its Definitions and Standards under the Federal Food, Drug and Cosmetic Act, as amended in effect at time of shipping." In other words, the regulators had the right to second guess compliance with these standards or to accuse the company of criminal fraud if in any respect their understanding of the regulations differed from that of the company.

The Entrepreneurial Personality and Its Dangers

Those risks were aggravated by Dee's personal characteristics. The innovative product that Mr. Dee came up with was matched by an innovative, entrepreneurial personality. Dee, like many entrepreneurs, is hard-working, a perfectionist, impatient with bureaucracy, inclined to believe that government agencies are peopled with bureaucrats who only say "no" and refuse to stretch their minds or their rules to acknowledge innovative products. While loyal to his employees and legendary for his support of the weak and erring, Dee had little patience with regulators. He told them as little as possible. He viewed them as gossips, likely to disclose confidential information to other companies. His lawyers—and later he himself—got into letter-writing disputes with the U.S. Department of Agriculture when he believed their conduct was overreaching or unreasonable.

When these personality traits were combined with another—a near obsession with the secrecy of his production methods—the stage was set for the government to frame a weak substantive case around a fetching set of suspicious circumstances, to offer up a meal that was all sizzle and no steak.

Dee's approach to regulators made a critical decision seem in retrospect inevitable. When contracting with the government for the CCC school lunch program, he neither disclosed his formula nor sought government approval for it. That decision was not unusual.

Few industries in America are more secretive than the cheese business. Kraft cheese, the giant in the industry, refuses to permit public tours of its plants. It does not even permit school children to take field trips to its facilities. It carefully restricts what anyone wanting to inspect the plant may see and never reveals its secret processes to anyone.

Kraft feels the same way about prior government approval that Dee did. When Kraft decided to come out with a "lite" cheese, following in the footsteps of the successes of "lite" beer and "lite" ice cream, Kraft read the government regulations for itself and then brought out its new product with an intense marketing campaign, but without prior approval, daring the government to do something about it. It told the government it had come out with a product; it did not ask for prior permission to do so.

As the seasoned veteran of FDA battles was later to put it, "No one in the industry asks the FDA first before bringing an innovative product. Faced with an innovation, the FDA will always resist: 'It's never been done that way before.'"

But the problem with Dakota Cheese was that it was smaller and more vulnerable than Kraft. Asking for government prior approval is asking for the government to refuse permission. Dee read the law. It was clear to him. He knew when he began to sell his special mozzarella pursuant to the four government contracts that he was required to sell "low-moisture part-skim mozzarella cheese" as defined in the Standards of Identity of the Food and Drug Administration, published in the Code of Federal Regulations, for use in the school lunch program.

I Can Read

Having come up with the new process by himself, Dee had determined by himself that it fit the government Standards of Identity for the product. As the once and future entrepreneur, Dee did not rely on the bureaucracy to tell him what he could do. He looked at the regulations himself. What he found were vague regulations that, while they neither explicitly permitted nor expressly prohibited the use of calcium caseinate, implicitly seemed to allow for it.

Dee went over the big picture. The definition of low-moisture part-skim mozzarella cheese stated that skim milk and nonfat dry milk may be added to the milk used in making the cheese.[1] Dee then looked to see how the regulations defined *skim milk*. The skim milk definition stated that skim milk may include *other milk-derived ingredients* as optional ingredients provided that they meet specified characteristics, including a "protein efficiency ratio" of regular skim milk.[2] Calcium caseinate was a milk-derived ingredient. It could thus be added to his formula.[3]

[1]21 Code of Federal Regulations §133.156-58.

[2]21 Code of Federal Regulations §131.143.

[3]Dee also went over the regulations carefully and in detail, with a businessman's logic:

> Low-moisture mozzarella cheese is the food that is prepared from milk and other ingredients specified in this section by the procedure set forth in paragraph (b) of this section *or by another procedure which produces a finished cheese having the same physical and chemical properties as the cheese produced when the procedure set forth in paragraph (b) of this section is used.* [21 Code of Federal Regulations §133.156 (emphasis added).]

The Dakota Cheese mozzarella certainly met this test. It was a food prepared from "milk and other ingredients" by "another procedure" which Dee believed he could demonstrate produced a finished cheese having "the same, or better, physical and chemical properties" as the cheese produced by the normal procedure.

Dee looked at the milk regulation:

> The word "milk" means cow's milk, which may be adjusted by separating part of the fat therefrom or by adding thereto one or more of the following: cream, skim milk, nonfat dry milk, and water in a quantity sufficient to reconstitute any concentrated skim milk or nonfat dry milk used. [21 Code of Federal Regulations §133.156(c)(1).]

The skim milk section was similarly broad, defining skim milk as "milk from which sufficient milk fat has been removed to reduce its milk fat content to less than 0.5%" [21 Code of Federal Regulations §133.143(a)]. But the regulations also provided that optional ingredients could be used in skim milk. These included:

> Concentrated skim milk, nonfat dry milk or other *milk-derived ingredients* to increase the nonfat solids content of the food: *provided*, that the ratio of protein to

his common sense and with customary
heese typically meant processed rather
cooked, and used nondairy ingredients
ls. The mozzarella standards seemed
natural dairy ingredients like calcium
hysical or chemical properties of the
er without consulting lawyers or the
and went straight ahead.

it would not have made a significant
were made, he asked a prominent lawyer in
Dakota, E. Steeves Smith, to research the issue of whether the
Standards of Identity prohibited calcium caseinate. Both Smith and his
partner, James Taylor, independently researched the issue. Indeed, Taylor placed a "no-names" call to the USDA on the issue. The person he
talked to, with typical government conservatism, said he "could not say
that the use of calcium caseinate was not permitted." After performing
legal research, both lawyers concluded that the regulations did not prohibit the use of calcium caseinate. Both confirmed to Dee that they
agreed with his reading of the regulations.

Indeed, if Dakota Cheese had gone to a specialist, he would likely
have received the same advice. George Burdett is a lawyer who has spent
his life specializing in food and drug law. His career spans 40 years. A
past president of the Chicago Bar Association, Chairman of the American Bar Association Subcommittee on Food, Drug, and Cosmetic Law,
the author of dozens of articles on food law, a man who taught the subject at Northwestern University Law School for 25 years, Burdett was in
the 1980s general counsel to the Food and Drug Law Institute, a prestigious nonprofit organization composed of most of the major food and
drug companies in the United States, which includes on its board the
commissioners of both the United States Department of Agriculture
and the Food and Drug Administration. Burdett had also served as president of the Harvard Law Association.

Burdett independently had looked into the question of whether cal-

---

total nonfat solids of the food, and the protein efficiency ratio of all protein present, shall not be decreased as a result of adding such ingredients. [21 Code of
Federal Regulations §131.143(c)(3) (emphasis added).]

To Dee, the regulation, albeit vague, nowhere prohibited his innovation. He saw he
could use skim milk. He knew that skim milk and nonfat dry milk are interchangeable
and treated identically under the cheese standards. He saw that the regulations allowed
the use of "milk-derived ingredients." And he knew that calcium caseinate was a milk-derived ingredient. *A fortiori,* calcium caseinate could be used as an optional ingredient in
mozzarella cheese.

cium caseinate could be used as an ingredient in the ？
mozzarella cheese in 1985. The regulations were familiar
had attended the hearings on them in the early 1950s. Burde
the same analysis Dee had done. Since calcium caseinate wa
proved ingredient in skim milk, and skim milk was an approved in
ent in low-moisture part-skim mozzarella, he himself concluded that
cium caseinate was a permitted ingredient in the cheese.

The Smoke Gets in Your Eyes

But there is, of course, another side to this story. Notwithstanding Dee's
confidence in his innovation and in his reading of government regulations, he continued to have the same lingering uncertainty. How would
the government view his innovation? And could he keep it to himself?

The cheese industry is notoriously "gabby," and cheese producers are
always looking for a better formula. Faced with these uncertainties, Dee
resorted to his customary entrepreneurial instincts. Inherently secretive, he would take practical steps to make sure that no one—not the
government, not the competition, not even all of his employees—knew
precisely what he was doing. These two decisions—absolute secrecy, no
prior approval—were, to be sure, not peculiar to Mr. Dee. But they were
suspicious.

In Dee's mind, there was a doubt. It was doubt not about his reading
of the regulations, but of the reading the government might give to
them. He knew that his views might not be accepted by the government.
His efforts to keep his process a secret therefore took on a higher priority. He believed he was right, but was not sure the government would
agree. He did not want either his competitors (for competitive reasons)
or the government (for legal reasons) to know what he was doing.

His approach was understandable. There was no legal obligation to
tell the FDA. And he had talked to an old acquaintance, an official of
the USDA. His advice had acknowledged the ambiguity of the regulations: "I can't tell you it's wrong, Jim . . . " When Dee had heard this, he
immediately told others of the conversation. But the USDA official,
when called to the stand by the prosecutor, could not recall the conversation. This consideration to one side, Dee never sought approval
and quite clearly did not want the government to know. In the harsh
light of retrospect, the decision was unwise. The average juror in a criminal case tends to believe that someone would not keep anything a secret unless he was guilty of something. And the extraordinary efforts at
secrecy Dee employed are responsible for the sad saga of Dakota
Cheese.

Dee's secrecy was almost a fetish about this as well as other matters relating to his business. His decisions made clear he did not want any-one to know what he was doing. When bags of casein were emptied of their contents, Dee directed the bags to be burned rather than disposed of in the dumpster. When casein was added, it was always late in the evening after regular business hours. Casein was referred to in internal company documents by code as *white powder.* When government inspec-tors came by to do routine checks, Dee made sure there was no casein evident on the premises. Indeed, his truck driver loaded up bags of ca-sein and took them out to a highway truck stop, so no one could ob-serve them. Dee made clear to his key employees that no one was to reveal anything about company processes.

There were other explanations for much of this behavior, of course. The powder was white and came in white bags and needed to be distin-guished from the nonfat dry milk that came in brown bags. There were so many bags of calcium casein that burning was a reasonable method of destruction for the bags. They filled two dumpsters to overflowing. An incinerator made sense. And the company burned the other paper refuse as well. The milk didn't come into the company until late after-noon, and therefore addition of the casein to fortify the milk could only be done after regular business hours. Secrecy about innovative pro-cesses also makes sense. But the fact of concealment was clear, and to anyone outside the industry, highly suspicious.

A Critical Visit

Then came word that milk auditors were going to do an audit of Dakota Cheese. Dee had had milk auditors visit his plant for years. The milk auditors were employees of the USDA. They monitored milk purchases in connection with a government milk subsidy program, one of a crazy quilt of government interventions in the agricultural marketplace. Though always suspicious of the bureaucracy, Dee had gotten along well with such auditors.

But the auditor who came to Dakota Cheese in 1985 was different. He annoyed the short-fused Dee by sitting around the office, doing little but looking out the window the first day, making demands for coffee and soft drinks of Dee's busy employees. Then he began asking for doc-umentation no milk auditor had ever asked for before. He wanted the financial records of Dee's gas station and certain tax information that, as far as Dee was concerned, had nothing to do with the limited scope of his inquiry: to determine that Dee actually was using the milk he said he was using and that his records on that subject were accurate.

The auditor made a request for invoices from a company that Dee knew well. It was the company that sold Dee calcium caseinate. To turn the documents over would clearly reveal to the government that Dakota Cheese had been using casein, since *casein* was shown on the invoices. Dee could turn the documents over, assuming that the milk auditor might not know the significance of the casein. And even if he did know the significance of it, Dee had good grounds for believing that the process was perfectly legal. Indeed, internal FDA documents, signed by high-level government policy experts at this very time, made clear that the government viewed Dee's reading of the regulations of the skim milk as "technically correct." If Dee had disclosed the casein, it would have led to a straightforward battle with the government on an issue that Dee and Dakota Cheese could, and should, win.

But Dee went to his lawyers and told them the problem. They agreed with his reading of the regulations. But one of them got into his own tiff with the milk auditor. He found the auditor stubborn, obnoxious, and implacable. Later, he gave Dee what turned out to be a critical piece of questionable advice. He told Dee that the invoices could be redacted, so that no casein was showing on the invoices. The milk auditor had defined the scope of his audit at an administrative hearing, and it was clear from his testimony that he was not looking for anything relating to casein. Because the request was outside the scope of the milk audit, Dee's lawyer explained that the only information required was related to the scope of the audit. Other information, including the presence of casein, could be redacted out. The lawyer himself covered up the *calcium caseinate* and stamped over the white paint *starter media*.

The lawyer did not give his advice without some reflection on the issue. He was not trying to subvert the process, only to represent his client zealously. He honestly believed the government was not entitled to more than it asked for at the hearing. He left on the document the trade name of the product, Alenate 2, which would put anyone on notice that the substance was calcium caseinate.

The decision was, however, subject to question. The government had invoices, or certainly could get invoices, from the casein manufacturer. The two sets of invoices would agree in every particular, except one set would say *casein,* and the redacted invoices would say *starter media.* Should the government have them or get them, it would be all downhill for Dakota Cheese thereafter. The amount of smoke seeping from the furtive behavior and billowing from the redaction would get in everybody's eyes—and lead to the company's destruction.

Prosecution Forthwith

When the United States Attorney's office got involved, it executed a *forthwith subpoena* on the company for all of its records. Forthwith subpoenas are disfavored in the law. To drive a truck up to the front of a company and to ask its employees to bring out all of its day-to-day business records and deposit them in the truck without taking copies is an enormous intrusion into normal business life. Judges seldom countenance this action, viewing it to be an unreasonable search and seizure under the Fourth Amendment.

When the company complained here, the judge, a prosecution-oriented federal judge in South Dakota, initially seemed unwilling to order the company to turn over the documents *forthwith*. Then, however, the prosecutor asked if the judge would hear her side secretly in chambers, outside the hearing of the defense.

When the judge came out after that secret conference, there was a new man on the bench. He ordered the company to turn over all of its documents within 24 hours. The judge had heard about the smoke. For all intents and purposes, he had come to a conclusion as to who was right and who was wrong.

The U.S. Attorney's office proceeded with the investigation. It called numerous witnesses before the grand jury. It refused to entertain any civil disposition of the case, insisting on payments of over a million dollars and time in jail. No settlement was possible.

In due course the indictments came down. In the indictment were 38 felony counts, consisting of (1) conspiracy to defraud the United States government, (2) mail fraud, (3) false statements, and (4) false claims.

Every pretrial order by the judge went against the defendants. In one pretrial skirmish, for example, the prosecutor argued that, although Dakota Cheese had produced 21 boxes of documents, totalling over 100,000 pages, to the grand jury, the government had not been able to locate certain documents. It had asked for originals, and Dakota Cheese had only produced copies. Dakota Cheese pointed out that it had produced the documents at short notice, had produced all the documents, and literally had no documents left, either at the company or at its lawyers' offices. Under such circumstances, a court, knowing the government has the documents anyway, will generally accept the company's protestations. Not so here.

The court, without any evidence that Dakota Cheese had destroyed or concealed the documents, found the company in contempt, fined the company $500 a day for every day it did not produce documents it did not have. Because the company did not have the documents, it could not cure the contempt. The fine ran until the time of indictment. Dakota Cheese's tab on the contempt rose to over $100,000 when the indictment finally came down. And when the documents were found in the file drawer of a former partner of the company's local lawyer and immediately turned over, the judge still refused to give the company relief.

The company brought a motion on selected prosecutions, pointing out that this was the first and only prosecution under these regulations—despite underground use of casein in the industry the government knew about—and that there was bad blood between the government and Mr. Dee—caused in part by letters from Dee and counsel to the USDA questioning the competence of their investigators—that should lead the court to hold a hearing to see whether there had been a "selective enforcement" that might cause the court to dismiss the indictment. Such motions for hearings on that issue are routinely granted. This one was denied.

The defendants pointed out that the vagueness of the statute and the fact that the government itself, after an internal study, had admitted the regulations were vague and could well lead to the conclusion Mr. Dee had arrived at. Indeed, an internal memo conceded the Dee interpretation was technically correct. That motion was denied.

The government had hid from the defendant certain exculpatory evidence. The defendants moved for dismissal on that basis as well. That also was denied.

The defendants asked to see full grand jury transcripts of the testimony of its employees before the grand jury, another motion that is routinely granted. Again, the judge denied it.

Trial Strategy

Trial commenced in November of 1988. Defense counsel had two possible issues to raise at the trial. One defense was that the contract terms could be read to permit the use of additional milk protein. The second defense was that the defendants did not know it was wrong to use the ingredient, even if the ingredient was not permitted. Determining how to deploy either (or both) of these defenses was, of course, the central strategic issue faced by the defendants at trial.

The decision was made easier by two developments. Because the cheese industry is notorious for its secrecy (elaborate security; no public tours) and the company was admittedly furtive in its production processes, the government had much more evidence suggesting concealment than evidence proving a substantive wrong. That is to say, the government case had smoke but no fire. Moreover, the court and the prosecution made clear repeatedly throughout the trial that the company's use of milk protein—as with other issues of contract interpretation—raised an issue of fact for resolution by the jury.

Based on these developments, the defendants committed themselves to an irrevocable course. By opening statement, by cross-examination of government experts, by introduction of expert testimony, they hammered on a principal theme: the addition of calcium caseinate was perfectly proper. Mr. Burdett came in to testify as to his belief that Dakota Cheese's process was perfectly legal.

In addition, the defendants introduced testimony from experts Dr. Howard Morris and Dr. Paul Saviano, each of whom confirmed that all technical requirements necessary to the conclusion that the standard permitted the addition of calcium caseinate had been met. Dr. Morris, certainly one of the leading authorities in the world on cheese-making and cheese, testified that these alternative procedures for the manufacture of mozzarella cheese was an innovation that he had not seen before in his several decades of teaching and consulting, and that he wished he had thought of it himself. By performing a detailed analysis of the constituents of the mozzarella cheese produced by Dakota Cheese for sale to the government, Dr. Morris concluded that the Dakota Cheese low-moisture part-skim mozzarella cheese was superior or at least equal to every one of the United States Department of Agriculture's standards for the cheese.

The trial, as it went forward, proved to be two cases in one. The government hammered away at the suspicious behavior, the falsified document, the smoke that reflected a culpable mind. The defense hammered away at the regulations themselves, the technical superiority of the cheese, the widespread agreement that what Dakota Cheese had done was legal. The judge was unmoved. He refused nearly 90 percent of the documents the defense introduced. He admitted all but three of the hundreds of documents the prosecution sought to have admitted.

The question for the jury, therefore, was to be smoke or fire, steak or sizzle. Both the prosecutor and the court stated affirmatively at several points in the trial that the question of whether or not the mozzarella cheese complied with government contract and standards of identity was the central issue for the jury.

Did I Say That?

But on the morning of the jury instructions, after the evidence was in, the judge came up with an instruction neither side had requested. He had reversed himself. He was now going to instruct the jury that the use of calcium caseinate was illegal, as a matter of law. By his earlier ruling that this would be the central issue for the jury, he had influenced the course of the trial. The defendants had placed all their eggs in one basket, attempting to show the jury that the use of calcium caseinate was proper. Now that the case was concluded, the judge changed his mind inexplicably. Pulling the rug from under the defense, he was about to instruct the jury that the only defense the defendants had put forward the jury could not consider.

Defendants argued vehemently that this was tantamount to directing a verdict in a criminal case and violated the constitutional right to a jury trial. The judge had taken an unusual step of putting in a pro-prosecution instruction that not even the prosecutor had the nerve to ask for. But the judge would not be moved. Not only would he give the instruction, he would also insist that the jury take the instruction with them back to the jury room.

The prosecutor seized on this serendipity during her closing argument. She read or referred to the judge's finding of illegal behavior 11 times. The defense case had been exposed by the court as a fraud.

The jury went out after closing arguments and deliberated for many hours. Ultimately, they convicted the company on all counts and Mr. Dee on some counts. The only wonder was why they took so long, given the court's instructions.

A juror, in a later interview, clarified why. He pointed out that the jury believed the defendant's overwhelming case that the Dee process was perfectly legal. On an initial vote, the jury had been inclined to acquit of all charges. But they read the instructions again. They saw that the judge was directing them to find that what Dakota Cheese had done was unlawful. They had another vote, splitting 8 to 4 for conviction. Finally, the holdouts were convinced that the judge was telling them to come back with a verdict of guilty. And they complied.

Weak Case, Light Sentence

The judge, perhaps recognizing he had pulled the rug out from under the defendants, gave a light sentence, far lighter than the prosecution had insisted on before trial or had asked for at sentencing. There would be no prison time. The fine was substantial—$400,000—but less than half of what the government had demanded pretrial. The fine was enough to shut the company down when the government immediately sent out marshals to seize all of the company's trucks and equipment, essentially putting the company out of business before it could even appeal the decision.

And when the appeal came (three separate issues were brought before the Court of Appeals at three separate arguments), one judge— himself from western South Dakota—gave no relief.

Within a space of four years, Dakota Cheese had gone from a profitable business—growing, employing several hundred residents of South Dakota—to utter destruction.

The reason? Smoke. A judge's first impression is often his last impression as well. The judge certainly did not intend to do injustice. He was reflexively pro-prosecution, to be sure. But here he was inclined to go beyond a prosecutor's requests because he believed that he had a bad actor on his hands and that one would not be so secretive unless he *had* done something wrong.

The implacable prosecutor was also not intending to do injustice. She was, to be sure, reflexively antibusiness and ready to believe that companies get ahead by cheating. But the cover-up to her was the critical thing.

The jury was more than willing to acquit on the underlying issue. But when that was taken away from them and they had to determine the defendant's state of mind, the smoke settled in. How could one believe that one with an innocent state of mind would behave with such extraordinary secrecy?

And a friendly appellate court was not going to intervene even when faced with a serious constitutional problem—a directed verdict in a criminal case—when the smoke was so pungent.

The Dakota Cheese scenario can be replayed many times, although in less dramatic form. Whether in Watergate or in Wedtech, the underlying offense may be easy to deal with, but the cover-up is what really gets the prosecutorial juices flowing.

Some Rules of the Game

The strange case of Dakota Cheese suggests some clear rules:

1. *Play the ball where it lies.* Never, *never* try to divert a government investigation by using any tactic that arguably looks like a cover-up or an obstruction of justice.

2. *Get expert help immediately when there is a potential administrative or regulatory problem with the government.* Any regulatory offense can also be a criminal offense. The only thing necessary to make it one is *scienter*, evidence that the violation was knowing. That, in turn, can be supplied circumstantially by suspicious behavior. Remember that what you do after the investigator arrives will generally be more important than what you have done before.

3. *If you must fight with the government, fight in such a way that the focus is on the impenetrable maze of government regulations and the difficulty that an average business executive has in understanding them.* Do not let the focus be on your furtive, guilty-appearing behavior. Come clean and have a fair fight on the law.

4. *Remember that all employees, asked to keep something secret for reasons they may not understand, will probably assume that you are doing something illegal and someday will testify to that effect before a grand jury, or jury of twelve.* If secrecy is necessary in the business, make clear that employees understand why.

Every company has certain smoky cul-de-sacs somewhere in the corporate entity. There is a memo that describes "the risks we took" to get a deal done. There is an underling who believes that he did a great job "in a gray area." Putting out the smoke in such circumstances is as important as putting out the fire.

6

Caveat Employer: Spotting Criminal Risks in Your Organization

Bernie Laker came home that day in uncommonly good spirits.

"What are you so happy about, Bernie?" his wife asked.

"It's been a very good day," Laker replied.

Laker took a piece of paper out of his briefcase, walked over to his wife, and ran it by her face. "Do you see this?"

Then he took the document, which looked like a memo of about 20 or 30 pages, and walked over to the safe, opened it, and inserted the memorandum, there to lie quietly with his other valuables. With a gesture that signaled self-satisfaction, grinning from ear to ear, Bernie summed it all up: "Honey, now I've got them by the [expletive deleted]." As they used to say in *Esquire*'s "Dubious Achievements" issue, why was this man smiling?

When his employer was about to start a subsidiary in the Far East, it placed a blind ad in *The Wall Street Journal.* The Philippines looked like an excellent opportunity. The government was encouraging U.S. companies to set up shop there with various incentives, not the least being a tax holiday in certain defined manufacturing zones. It also offered an intelligent and skilled labor force working for far less than the able, but more highly paid, employees at the company's midwestern headquarters. The opportunity was there, but nobody at the company had significant foreign experience, hence the solicitation for résumés. Laker's résumé, on its face, looked ideal. He had a good education, foreign experience, some technical expertise in plastics, all of which cumulatively represented the ideal applicant. When he came to Ohio for an interview, most of the company's employees were even more impressed. A feisty and slight Englishman, he was witty and quick on his feet. Glib with language, he also seemed to know what he was talking about.

The interviews did not go uniformly well. The vice president of research and development, a well-known leader in the industry, suspected this pleasant applicant might not know as much as he claimed. He began asking him some more substantive questions about plastic manufacture and found Laker embarrassingly ignorant. "I think this guy's a phony," he reported on his evaluation.

But one blackball could not knock the pins from under an otherwise pleasing impression. The president was impressed, as was the chairman of the board of this family-owned enterprise. Laker would go to Manila and set up the company's foreign subsidiary from scratch.

During the first few years of Laker's tenure, company executives were congratulating themselves about the wisdom of their choice. He had been able to attract a retired Filipino general to be his right-hand man. He attracted an apparently knowledgeable Chinese accountant to be his financial officer. He had put together plans for a manufacturing facility and all the other accoutrements that suggested that the plant could be very successful indeed. Although occasionally stubborn, and just a little secretive, Laker was turning out to be even better than anticipated. And he was promising soon to turn the corner on profitability.

But one day, Laker reported a crisis. He said that the continued viability of the company required the chairman of the board, a prominent public figure, to meet with him in Manila to discuss some urgent business.

The somberness of tone and the urgency of the request made the trip seem necessary. The chairman and his lawyer were soon on a plane headed for the Orient. When they finally reached Manila, they met a somber-faced Laker. A day or two of meetings later, they fully understood why.

Over the last year, Laker had been demanding more and more money to get his operation in the black. The company had transferred a substantial amount of cash to the subsidiary. As far as the company was concerned, this was merely an infusion of working capital. The costs of manufacturing the products were fully and fairly represented in the company's work papers. If the company had not gotten behind in the start-up phase and accumulated a deficit, the price the company was currently charging its parent company in Ohio would have been more than adequate to cover the manufacture of the products.

This was an important fact, because the company paid duty in the United States based on the price of the product coming into the United States. If in fact the Ohio company had been holding down the price that it was paying to buy its goods from its subsidiary, it would have been saving significant Customs duty. But if it had been "holding down" the price paid, while at the same time secretly transferring money to the Philippines to keep the company afloat, it was arguably defrauding the United States Customs. A company could hypothetically pay virtually nothing in duty for purchases from a Filipino subsidiary by the simple expedient of claiming that the products it purchased were produced for a penny apiece, even though the actual value was $10.00 apiece, and then secretly give back the $9.99 to the subsidiary under the table to cover the true costs of production.

Before making the transfers, the American company had cleared them with its Big Eight accounting firm. The accounting firm concluded that it made sense to apportion the profit made by the U.S. parent between the parent and its subsidiary, since the subsidiary was also in part responsible for the company's profitable bottom line. Such an apportionment was permissible under the U.S. rules if it had some rational basis. This one did.

The transfer of some profits to the Philippines also made practical sense because of the "tax holiday" offered by the foreign government. The more profits the company could justifiably transfer abroad, the more could be sheltered from U.S. taxes. In determining how to apportion the profit, the company took into account what percentage of its sales overall were attributable to Manila and how much to Ohio.

Laker's management had not been seriously questioned by headquarters. But it did appear that he used occasionally provocative or peculiar language in some of his telexes to his boss, the president of the company. He would, for example, occasionally talk about "subsidies" necessary to reflect the full price of the products he was manufacturing. At first, such references were ignored. But finally the president had had enough. He ordered Laker to stop referring to these transfers in a way that might raise undue suspicion as to what they really were—simply apportioned profits to take advantage of the tax holiday and provide more working capital.

But nothing had prepared the company for this meeting at the Manila hotel. Their general manager had a bombshell. Laker confessed that it had been necessary for him to pay a bribe to "get the right treatment" for the transfers of capital. He said such payments were typical in Manila, that in this case the payment was absolutely necessary, and that a second payment would be necessary soon. He wanted the green light to go forward.

The American guests were outraged. How could he have paid a bribe that would imperil the company's continued operations? It was both wrong and stupid. He must pay it back immediately.

Laker's response was agonized special pleading. He could not pay the money back without exposing the official he had paid the money to. That official he could not risk offending since the company depended on his good will. Paying back the money would lead perhaps to Laker's imprisonment and the cessation of company activities in the Philippines. He really needed to make the second payment as well.

After two days of tense conversation, Laker was instructed to pay no more money, under any circumstances, and told that the company would get back to him. The lawyer went back to the United States with the chairman and was instructed to prepare a full report of the trip with recommendations as to what to do. There was some serious discussion as to whether the general manager should be fired. But given the customs of the country, as he described them, the fact that he was apparently acting, however mistakenly, according to his perception of the company's interests, and his personal pleading for himself and his family, it was decided that he would be reprimanded but not terminated. But under no circumstances could any bribe go forward. That would have to be very clear.

The result of the lawyer's efforts was a 30-page "trip report." It was detailed, well-written, and factually accurate. To the lawyer's eyes, it was a first-rate product. It served his client well. It highlighted every issue, recounted key facts and meetings, gave an overview of the applicable law, and made some good-faith recommendations. But, from the point of view of a litigator, it was also flawed. First, while condemning any further payment, the trip report spoke mysteriously of an "understanding" among the three that "some small gifts or concessions" could later be paid so long as they were not connected, or seen to be connected, to the first payment. Second, the memo ventured forth into a discussion of Customs laws in which the lawyer did not have adequate background or training. Without understanding the full rationale behind the transfers, the author assumed that the profit transfer was a violation of the Customs laws and should not be repeated. Third, the memo was not sent merely to the chairman who had requested it. It was copied to others, including Bernie Laker.

The document that Laker tucked so merrily into his safe that December evening was something that would later fuel lengthy litigation and a million dollars in attorneys' fees. The apparent confession of past misconduct with respect to Customs and the remark about the "small gifts or concessions," which Laker would later claim was code for further bribery, were all he needed. In fact, "small gifts or concessions" was simply an accommodation to Laker, who claimed he still needed to give the traditional New Year's presents of a bottle of wine or candy to the local officer. But in Laker's hands, this memo would prove to be a very sharp sword.

Why Laker was so happy became apparent a year later. One day an invoice was anonymously sent by a conscience-stricken secretary in Manila to headquarters. The invoice suggested a transaction with K-Mart that the company knew nothing about. K-Mart was the largest single purchaser of the company's products. But this product rang no bells. The company did not make one. The invoice made no sense.

Further investigation, the gentlest of tugs on this thread, began to unravel an amazingly complicated fabric of wrongdoing by Mr. Laker. He and the general had developed a product on company time, using company facilities, had told the company it was not worth pursuing and then had begun secretly to manufacture it, using company employees and company manufacturing facilities. Laker entered into a huge contract with K-Mart to buy the product. The business opportunity was, of course, excellent for Mr. Laker. The cost of goods sold was essentially zero. All the profits went to him. Not only was he interfering with the company's best customer, he was also filling his pocket with company money.

The investigation went further. Suddenly, hundred-footed creatures were scurrying out from under every rock: prostitutes on the company payroll, numerous visits to a notorious red-light district outside of the city where the hotel room key entitles one to nearly limitless immorality of every kind and description, billed to the company, where Laker would later say he could "fulfill all my fantasies," and a series of defalcations both great and small.

The evidence was conclusive. Prestigious local counsel was retained to confront Laker with his wrongdoing and terminate him. A series of meetings were held in the fall of the year. A surprisingly calm Laker demanded substantial separation payments and then lobbed the big one. "You know you can't fire me." Taking some documents out of his briefcase—the trip report, a few of his suspicious sounding telexes back to the home office—and waving them menacingly across the table at his adversaries, he said, "I've got the goods on the company." He advised that he had copies of the documents in various locations with instructions on how to deliver them to relevant U.S. and Philippine agencies.

The company was unfazed and resolute. It turned Mr. Laker into the local authorities and commenced litigation against him in the United States.

But, his threat unavailing, Laker began meeting with officials at United States Customs. He had a simple story. The company had been

losing money on its products. It had seen an opportunity to save substantial customs duty by systematically underpricing the goods coming
from Manila to the United States. It would then give the "under the
table" payments back to Manila. The purpose was to defraud Customs.
In order to carry out that scheme, it was necessary to bribe certain government officials.

Always a smooth talker, whether interviewing for a job and claiming
knowledge of plastics when he had none, or attracting a prestigious
general to be his manager, Laker could make a sale. The initially wary
Customs agents were quickly eager buyers. When they asked for documentation, he had it. Like a guide leading bewildered tourists through
the sights in an exotic location, he took the Customs agents by the hand
and explained the true meaning of "small gifts or concessions," why the
report had concluded that there were violations of Customs laws, and
how he had been silenced by the president of the company for being
too clear in his telexes about what was going on.

First impressions are lasting impressions. The Customs agency made
up its mind and never changed it, not as other evidence accumulated,
not even after the company had won acquittals on all counts of a federal
criminal indictment. Not even Laker's criminal conviction abroad or
his other obvious defalcations moved the government. The choice,
from one point of view, was believing a criminal or believing a company
that had a reputation for being straight-laced, even puritanical, an old-
fashioned upholder of midwestern verities. The government believed
the criminal.

The Laker personality is only one of a number of dangerous employee types who frequently gets companies into unanticipated criminal
difficulty. The decision in the Manila hotel, motivated by compassion
and not cover-up, was only one of a number of decisions that had far-
reaching ramifications. The trip report, which would have earned an A
on a law school examination that requires good writing and "issue spot-
ting," is only one type of documentation that gets an ethical company in
serious straits. The ultimate vindication of the company made the mistakes less painful, but the pressures and stress of a criminal investigation
can never be fully compensated.

Some Critical Caveats

Some lessons emerge.

1. *Beware of wolves in sheep's clothing.* There are roving wolves in every
organization. They do not, unfortunately, look the part. The manager
must be more perceptive than Little Red Riding Hood because the

wolf-like characteristics are not always apparent. But there are several common species.

a. *Managerius Lupus corruptus.* We may call Laker—the personally corrupt manager—*Managerius Lupus corruptus,* the person who tries to entrap others in ethical compromises. Few wolves look as innocent in sheep's clothing as the cunningly corrupt con man, like Laker. Few so carefully premeditate their long-range strategic plan. Investigators eventually concluded that Laker never paid a bribe in the first place. He saw a potential violation of law, worded ambiguous messages on telexes to create such an impression, was delighted when he was silenced, and set up the bribery discussion with a prestigious public figure, all to one end: to have leverage if his own misconduct should ever be revealed.

In retrospect, there were several opportunities to detect Laker's lupine nature. His phony claimed expertise was a serious problem not taken seriously enough. A person who passes himself off as something he is not is all the more dangerous when he is also glib and persuasive. His authoring of memos that sounded suspicious and did not correspond with the reality of the transactions they described was a further sign that he might be up to something. But his confession of paying an alleged bribe should have been conclusive evidence. He should have been terminated at once, with full disclosures to local authorities. But the very sort of Christian virtues that characterized the company led them to show mercy to the "sheep" that had apparently gone astray, rather than to take decisive action.

b. *Managerius Lupus ego maximus.* A second type of wolf is recognized by how its ego drives it to mysterious, premature, almost inexplicable successes. This is the entrepreneurial employee whose numbers seem too good to be true. They usually are.

Take, for example, the star of one of my first securities cases. When a national brokerage house hired George Reynolds, they found quickly they had a remarkably successful broker on their hands. While a difficult employee to manage, since he was so full of himself, no one could deny that his numbers tended to confirm his self-appraisal. He was so successful that he led the entire national sales force of the firm in gross commissions—in his first year in the business. Two, and then, three years went by with spectacular success. Earning $400,000 a year in net commissions in the relatively slow mid-1970s, Reynolds was rapidly becoming a megastar in the business. Soon he was assistant manager of the office. How could a young broker be that good that soon?

However concerned the Compliance Department might have been about Mr. Reynolds, they did little to penetrate into Mr. Reynolds' peculiar modus operandi. After acquiring a reasonable customer base early—no one ever claimed Reynolds was not a talented talker—he would occasionally simply take down a large number of securities early in the day and allocate them to his customers' accounts. They had neither ordered them nor even discussed them with Reynolds. When concerned customers called him, he was uniformly apologetic and reassuring. "I blew it. Listen, we can break the trade. But the stock is already up two points, and I'm selling it to a lot of my other customers. Do you want to keep the profit and run up with the stock, or do you want to break the trade?" Customers normally wanted to keep the stock.

If the stock went down in value, Reynolds would reportedly tell his customers, "I blew it. Not only did I put the stock in the wrong account, but it's down a point and a half. But I've got some information on the stock that is almost too hot to pass on. I can tell you this thing is going through the roof. I guarantee it. And I'd strongly recommend that you hold onto it. If I have to break the trade, I will, but it will hurt me with Compliance. Look, hold onto the stock. I think you'll like where it's going. And I'll do something else. If you hold onto the stock, I'll pack you into the next hot new issue that comes along. I get the best allocation in the office, and I save the best new issues for my best customers. So trust me on it. Okay?"

This strategy worked for years. But then came a series of racketeering lawsuits, a move to another brokerage house, then a move to a questionable gold and silver house, a silver coin house, and ultimately a criminal prosecution, where it was revealed that Reynolds had lied, cheated, and stolen, comforted by heavy doses of cocaine and copious supplies of women. Reynolds is merely the apotheosis of a usually less colorful tribe. Managers who do too well too early are frequently sources of trouble within the organization.

Such success is often driven by the vainglorious personality that wants the perquisites and badges of accomplishment even more than the reality of accomplishment itself. Such employees are not only threats to loot the company but also to expose the company to risks from the government. Ego-driven managers may find ways to cut corners that make their bottom line look good and the company ultimately look bad. One manager of a major food company turned his division around. Alas, he did so by pumping too much water into his meat products and selling some of the meat out of the back door. The company lost two ways: missing meat *and* a criminal investigation. An executive told me later, "The guy always said he was the best in the business. He just didn't tell us which business."

  c. *Managerius Lupus controllus.* The third type of *Managerius Lupus* is the entrepreneurial, control-oriented *Managerius Lupus controllus.*

They either subtly or actively resist managerial supervision. They crash through obstacles, disdain bureaucracy, trample underlings, and think the lawyers in the General Counsel's office are nervous nellies who have never seen a way to make a profit that they like.

The entrepreneurial spirit is, of course, commendable and indispensable. Its willingness to take risks is what makes for great business success stories. But in the corporate organization, its excesses are also fraught with peril. To the naked savage entrepreneur, regulations are silly. Cautions about legal risks are impediments to progress. Looming problems can be ignored. If they present themselves, they can be bowled over or stormed through.

A manager for a Fortune 500 company came on board to manage a failing subsidiary and wanted to turn things around quickly. The subsidiary had been losing money for years. There was a real question of survival. But then came the opportunity. An American company representing a foreign country wanted a substantial amount of product. If consummated, the order would be the largest in the company's history.

The "can do" manager leapt at the opportunity. Soon a letter of credit had been put together and the wheels were turning to get the product out within two to three months. But in the interim, the government slapped export restrictions on goods exported to that country with few, if any, exceptions. The embargo effectively made the order impossible to complete. In-house counsel so advised.

Through adept negotiation, the company was able to keep a significant portion of the letter of credit, because of ambiguous state laws in Texas about *force majeure*. The manager should have been satisfied. Instead, he read the regulations, got counsel from outside the company, and determined the goods could be sold directly to one of the company's foreign subsidiaries. The subsidiary could then sell the product to the ultimate customer. What the regulations appeared to contemplate, to this unlearned but eager executive, was that you could do indirectly what you could not do directly. He claimed he had not heard the law department tell him anything directly to the contrary. And magazine articles in *The Economist* and certain trade publications convinced him that it could be done. To him his plan was not a scheme to evade the law, but to comply with the law by observing corporate formalities.

He knew, as an MBA, that one can often avoid certain liabilities merely by paperwork. If a sole proprietor incorporates, for example, the proprietor is doing the same business in the same way, but now without personal liability for business debts—and all because of a fiction, a piece of paper. If one ships goods into a bonded warehouse, one can avoid Customs duties simply by paperwork designating a quite ordinary-looking warehouse as a "bonded warehouse." Why should it not be so here? The deal went forward.

Ignoring the lawyers' advice and continuing counsel was a major mistake. Lawyers are not, to be sure, always right. They sometimes may be too cautious. Frequently, the lawyers set out the business risks, and it is up to management to evaluate them. A lawyer might tell a client that if she seeks a five-year noncompete agreement for one of its key employees, that agreement might be voided by a court, because its duration is too long. If the employee leaves, he may be free to compete immediately because of the unreasonable length of the noncompete agreement he had signed. A corporation may go ahead anyway, for business reasons, knowing that there is a risk of invalidity. But when a lawyer gives advice with criminal ramifications, the situation is different. That advice should not be subject to a management override absent some clear and convincing evidence that the lawyer is wrong. Some companies, however, create a climate that leads employees to consider all legal advice within the company as merely suggestions, to be rejected by business executives whenever the circumstances require. The result for this company was a four-year, $12 million ordeal: an indictment, fines, a succession of agency proceedings, and a cloud of bad public relations not easily dissipated, all visited on a company that had been an entity highly praised by presidents, a supporter of worthy causes, obsessed with ethics.

d. *Managerius Lupus europus.* Another risk is the employee with European experience, or at least a continental attitude toward government regulations. Many companies like to circulate their employees through their foreign operations to give them a broader perspective than they can survey from a sometimes parochial home office. The rationale is sound. But sometimes the learning acquired is different from what management anticipated.

Many European companies play games with government taxing authorities and other bureaus. White-collar crime is not prosecuted there with the same vigilance that it is here. Some European executives view their relationship with the government as a cat and mouse game, or better, a shell game to see if the government can find its revenues in the company books. Certificates of origin are frequently viewed as pieces of paper necessary to get a transaction accomplished. Government forms are often blanks to be filled in as necessary where one makes the expected declarations. Taxes are costs of doing business that ought to be avoided or evaded whenever the tax man can be appropriately bamboozled. As one Dutchman told me, "The Swiss and the Dutch have the same three loves: good cheese, good chocolate, and playing hide-and-seek with the bureaucrats."

e. *Managerius Lupus prevaricatus.* The classifications lead inevitably to a discussion of a particularly lupine species, the casual liar, *Managerius Lupus prevaricatus.* No one is as dangerous as the practiced liar. Traditional philosophers detected three types of liars: the jocose liar, who lies for the fun of it; the exculpatory liar, who lies to get him or herself off the hook; and the pernicious liar, who lies to defraud others. Whether a practical joker or a devious plotter, the employee who does not tell the truth is a criminal prosecution waiting to happen. Dostoevsky describes the personality type through the lips of Father Zossima in *The Brothers Karamazov:*

> The man who lies to himself and listens to his own lie comes to such a pass that he cannot distinguish the truth within him, or around him, and so loses all respect for himself and for others. And having no respect he ceases to love, and in order to occupy and distract himself without love he gives way to passions and coarse pleasures. . . . The man who lies to himself can be more easily offended than anyone. You know that it is sometimes very pleasant to take offense, isn't it? A man may know that nobody has insulted him, but that he has invented the insult for himself, has lied and exaggerated to make it picturesque, has caught at a word and made a mountain out of a molehill—he knows that himself, yet he will be the first to take offense, and will revel in his resentment till he feels great pleasure in it, and so pass to genuine vindictiveness.[1]

The liar, full of offenses and eager for vengeance, may choose to employ his skill before a U.S. Attorney, and what was an in-house molehill may erupt into a highly visible mountain.

In one circumstance, an American agricultural company was acquired by a multibillion-dollar foreign giant. Some of those foreign employees came to the United States and began making laid-back, European decisions. They executed "close enough" certifications (inaccurate, but reasonably close to accurate) and misleading representations regularly, all the while assuming the appearance of fastidious rectitude. When the special agents arrived with their search warrants, the officers were incredulous. How a government could take such necessary white lies as something serious was beyond their comprehension. The results were again ominous: a dragnet investigation alleging millions of dollars of alleged fraud and a blemished reputation for a previously unsullied company.

f. *Managerius Ostrichus incompetus.* The final category of employee is not so much wolf as ostrich. The author of the biblical proverb ex-

---

[1]Dostoevsky, *The Brothers Karamazov*, Pt. I, II, 2.

pressed amazement to God for his creating a beast as dumb as the ostrich, which puts its head in the sand and leaves its eggs in plain view for pillaging by any desert creature. These employee ostriches are promoted to their position at the government desk, even though only marginally competent. The loyal secretary is promoted to customs manager, or the cost accountant to the regulatory compliance desk.

The choice of such employees for such work is understandable. The company wants its ablest employees engaged in activities that make money for the enterprise. Making sure that the company has complied with all the formalities of government regulation and that it has filled out all the right forms is both monotonous and uninspiring. It would be a shame to take the most capable people and make them shufflers of forms.

Employees who take such jobs acquire skill at checking the normal boxes, but often they do not understand the purpose of the document nor can they recognize or sniff out danger. If something comes up that is unusual or troubling, the employee responds with ostrich-like caution by burrowing its head deeply into the sand and letting the transaction proceed. To go to the boss may be a signal of personal incompetence, about which this insecure employee may be very sensitive. Better to plunge ahead and fill out the form as usual.

Hazel was such an employee. Loyal, and meticulous, she had served a company I represented in various clerical capacities for over 20 years. In her last ten years she was rewarded by being placed in charge of compliance with government regulations. One agency regulated the company. She acquainted herself with its rules. She liked the job; she was at last a *manager*. All but 0.1 percent of her work was pure tedium. And she was exceptionally good at it. Every blank was filled in. No signatures were missing. The proper number of forms were sent to the appropriate people.

But on one occasion, there was a transaction that did not have a normal pattern. A question needed to be answered that could conceivably be answered either "yes" or "no" depending on one's interpretation. Worse, the question concerned a decision the company had just made that all would say was "sensitive," most would add "aggressive," and some would call "reckless." It should have set alarm bells clanging for someone who had more training. She was concerned, but not so concerned that she would seek help. She signed off on all the forms even though she must have known, in the back of her mind, that the representations could be read as not totally accurate. Little did she know what lay in store because of one confused judgment.

Hazel, a mother of four and 57 years old, making the equivalent of

$15,000 a year, was indicted by a federal grand jury, with her superiors, for conspiracy. Her eventual acquittal did not compensate her fully for the terrors of two years as a target and defendant, all stemming from one plunge into the desert sand.

2. *Decisions must be made decisively.* Modern management styles often favor those who are *people persons.* They criticize constructively, mixing praise with blame. The quality of mercy they will not strain; they pour it on to the employee who has fallen.

But mercy to the mistaken is one thing. Mercy to the crook is something quite different. One does not empathize with crooks. One fires them.

Laker deserved the quick trigger. He had confessed to a bribe. He had subjected the company and its officers to significant risks. He should have been out—immediately.

When an internal investigation reveals regulatory offenses, discipline should be sharp and severe. Severe discipline can be an absolute deterrent to future violations. The fired employee will never expose your company to risk again. But it is also a good education for other employees who might be tempted to cut a corner. If a company has a code of conduct, it should be resolutely enforced. As the old adage correctly points out, "Never do business with a snake." However teary-eyed the pleading, decisions must be made. One who is unfaithful in little, we are told, will also be unfaithful in much. Cut off unfaithful employees early, before they fully prove that axiom.

The principal criminal charges triggered by Laker's malefaction would have been avoided by resolute action at the beginning. So it is in many settings. Let us consider another case. An employee is caught with his hand in the till. He confesses, weeping, when presented with incontrovertible evidence of his wrongdoing. Then he pleads for mercy. He will disclose his entire wrong and make an agreement to pay the company back, if only it will not turn him in to the federal or state authorities.

The deal seems sensible. His apparent penitence is a good sign. It is difficult to know exactly what he has stolen unless he comes forward and talks about it. There is no business reason to be vindictive. To turn him in criminally would harm him, his family, and the company, as bad publicity emerged about its internal controls. The agreement is given.

But, unfortunately, there is more to it than that. It is an ethical violation for the company lawyer who negotiates the agreement to use criminal prosecution as a threat to coerce a civil settlement. Now, of course, that is not what happened here. The idea for a settlement came from the crook. No one ever threatened anything. But the deal that was arrived at was a clear quid pro quo: no criminal prosecution if some consideration is given. The lawyer has, however innocently, violated an ethical canon. Moreover, there is an ancient doctrine of *misprision of felony.* A company is not obligated to turn in someone who has defrauded it. But if it enters into some agreement with the wrongdoer that somehow benefits the company for not turning the wrongdoer in, the company could be prosecuted for misprision. If the employee's wrong had some regulatory impact—on the company's tax returns, on certain required public disclosures, or potentially defrauded customers or contractors with the company—an argument could be constructed that the company entered into an arrangement to cover up the felony to its benefit. That would also be under federal law an *obstruction of justice.* A prosecutor could allege that the company frustrated a government interest in prosecuting a crime in order to avoid unsavory revelations about its own business. Again, an unwillingness to make a tough decision out of misplaced compassion led an innocent company to the brink of disaster.

3. *Do not reconsider decisions you know are right.* Many times, a company officer will say, "I should have fired her the first time this came up." Take, for example, the case of JFQ Manufacturing, Inc., a prospering minority business. Jack Queen was the owner, a bright and engaging black man. Queen had gone from a successful career with a major defense contractor to starting a company of his own. He quickly built it into a successful supplier of government munitions, supplying ordnance and high-quality parts at prices that were the best in the industry.

Queen did not forget where he had been nor those who had helped him. He made sure, for example, that he hired his old boss, Tommy McCrae, at high wages, to run his production facility. McCrae, a craggy-faced Scotsman, had treated him with real dignity when he was one of the few minority employees at the old company. He hadn't forgotten that treatment. Now he wanted to reward it.

But his old boss was not as grateful a man as Queen was. Soon, McCrae began taking off early on Friday afternoons. Then he was caught taking too many days vacation. One day, he was caught working on a part that had nothing to do with company business. The signs were becoming clear. He was moonlighting for his own account on company time with company parts. When confronted, McCrae resolutely denied it. He was kept on board.

When he was caught again, six months later, he was fired. But Jack Queen couldn't sleep at night. He remembered his old friendship. McCrae pleaded for another chance. Queen hired the manager back, over the objections of the in-house government inspector, the company accountant, and two other managers. More problems came, more near terminations. But McCrae was always received back in good graces.

What Queen did not know, however, was that the employee was be-coming increasingly systematic in seeking to build his own clientele in the same industry, manufacturing essentially the same products. His plans were deliberate and well conceived. He needed customers. He began making plans to talk to key contacts on JFQ's customer list. He needed skilled employees and began talking to other employees of the company about joining him.

Finally, he needed a weakened JFQ. Proposals he formulated to major suppliers began to be mysteriously underbid. (Fortunately, the custom-ers admired the minority company so much that they made adjustments to the contract price that allowed the company to survive.)

But McCrae was not through. He had discovered that other employees had modified some invoices during negotiations with the government to supply spare parts to the Army. The effect of the modification was to overstate the number of hours required to perform the work. This he saw as an opportunity. When his own business was about ready to take off, he went to the government and triggered a far-reaching federal in-vestigation of the JFQ, Inc. As a result, the company suddenly was facing criminal prosecution of itself and its officers, and the real risk that the government would bar the company from entering into any more con-tracts or subcontracts for government work. Meanwhile, McCrae had jumped ship with three friends, and they formed their own company.

Thus went the JFQ roller coaster: from a company started with $20,000 of borrowed money to a company approaching $10 million in sales and then back again. All because a failure to decide firmly and finally is a decision itself.

Fiat justitia, ruat coelum reads the Latin inscription on many a court-house: *Do right, though the stars fall.* The homely paraphrase of the Latin maxim is a good piece of advice. The company that learns of arguably criminal activity by any of its employees is wise to do right, right away, regardless of the short-term consequences and regardless of embarrass-ment or pity.

4. *Getting counsel about possible white-collar crimes is wise; documenting them is not.* Many people, and most lawyers, are natural scribes. They love to put words on paper.

The trip report from Manila was a useful document in the abstract. In practical terms, it was a big mistake. First, no one should document pos-sible crimes without being sure that they are in fact crimes and being willing immediately to confess to them. Lawyers are not obligated to dis-close past criminal actions about which they are consulted (future or pending crimes are another matter). Lawyers can hear, consult, and give advice about past behavior without any necessity of turning the cli-ent in to the authorities. In the Laker case, there really was no crime, as

a jury and judge later found. Putting the lawyer's tentative conclusion
on paper made it all the worse. Indeed, a subsequent letter aggravated
it. The lawyer laid out the likely fines and pointed out that "no reasonable jury would believe the defense that we acted in good faith"—not an
easy letter to explain to a jury that fancies itself reasonable.

While it may appear that no lawyer would write such a statement unless it were true, that view is far too simplistic. It is not at all uncommon
for lawyers, much less employees, to believe that a crime has been committed when none has been. Most people can recognize an assault or a
robbery. These are crimes historically called *mala in se.* They are crimes
that are wrong in themselves. They are immoral on their face. The murder and mayhem street criminals specialize in are usually recognized as
crimes by everyone. But there is another form of crime called *malum
prohibitum.* That form of crime is wrong only because the government
says it is. There is nothing immoral or particularly wicked about pumping 35 percent water and other fluids into corned beef to make it tender, rather than say 20 percent. It may make the product taste better.
But the government can make it a crime simply by saying so. Such regulatory crimes are often vague and difficult to interpret. Regulations do
not cover each and every occurrence. One can sometimes navigate between or around regulatory strictures without offending anyone and
without having a guilty frame of mind.

Sometimes an overzealous employee will become convinced, however
mistakenly, that the company is doing something illegal and will write
an appropriate memo documenting the fact. One employee of a billion-
dollar company wrote the following memo to four managers:

> As we all know, we have been violating federal law for years on the
> sale of propeller blades abroad. These shipments require licenses.
> We have not obtained them. I enclose a copy of the relevant regu-
> lations. If this is ever discovered, someone will go to jail. I suggest
> we change this policy at once!

As often happens, his understanding of the law was faulty. As the American folk humorist once said, "It's not what we don't know what hurts
us; it's what we know what ain't so." Such compunctions of conscience
are harmless when regulations clearly permit the activity. But when the
conduct may indeed be "in the gray," such documents can be the ruin
of a company.

It is even worse, of course, when the documents come from lawyers
who seek to cover their own anatomies by lecturing their clients. Discuss
theories of wrong, yes; just don't document them.

5. *In taking precautions about sensitive documents, some paranoia is appropriate.* The trip report we read was circulated to someone who had

admitted to dishonesty. Copying sensitive information to many people
is a sure recipe for disaster. For every ten honorable employees, there
may be one with his or her own agenda—and with a safe every bit as
secure as Mr. Laker's. If such matters need be written down, they ought
to be marked clearly "privileged and confidential" and given only to the
person or persons with a real need to know.

Some sequences of events cannot be anticipated, to be sure. But
many occurrences can be anticipated and should be. All employees
ought to be sensitive about what they write and for whom, as well
as what they receive. Some document plucked out of context,
emitting some foul odor, might lead to an unjust—and devastating—
prosecution.

"Evil companions corrupt good manners," the proverb says. Ancient
proverbs advise what good companions really are, and who ought not to
be trusted as an agent or employee: an immoral or corrupt person, a
liar, a slothful person, a person who wants to "get rich quick," a tattle-
tale, an indecisive person, a rash person. Mastery of these character
types may avoid great trouble—and a day in court.

7
Beware of the Convergence of "Hot Spots" and Blind Spots: You May Get Burned

Theologians tell us that we remember only the hundredth part of the sins that cling to our soul. Psychologists agree, although in somewhat more clinical language. They confirm that we forget—or suppress—over 90 percent of the bad things we do.

This convenient amnesia creates blind spots. As our field of vision has a blind spot, in which the brain fills in surrounding background so that we think we see all but do not, so portions of our character and past actions become hidden from us. Sometimes these blind spots create real jeopardy from unseen dangers.

Shaklee Corporation was a major success story. Founded by an old student of P. T. Barnum and circus strongman, named Forrest Shaklee, the company grew from humble origins as a source of "natural" remedies dispensed in a chiropractic clinic to a $500 million a year business with professional management and a listing on the New York Stock Exchange. The company was part hocus pocus (the alleged superiority of the "natural" vitamin discovered, so it was said, by Dr. Shaklee himself, for which he still gets no credit from the scientific community), part ingenious marketing (the multilevel distribution scheme created an army of well-scrubbed bourgeoisie enlisting friends and relatives into their "group" to win overrides of $10,000 or more a month, Acapulco vacations at the Princess Hotel, and fancy cars), and part good timing (the new emphasis on health, wellness, and the grudging admission of the medical community that put increasing emphasis on diet and nutrition).

The combination led to great wealth for the Shaklee family and many shareholders, and cultlike status for the "Doctor" himself. While it was widely believed that Dr. Shaklee had multiple doctorates in medicine, biochemistry, and other daunting disciplines, later company literature cautioned distributors to be "humble" about their beloved doctor. While the reasons for such humility were never made clear to the masses, humility was justified. Dr. Shaklee had a chiropractic degree (through correspondence) and a degree in divinity from a mail-order seminary purchased at the market price. His products were not, as many thought, given to him by "nature" while he slept. They were bought "off the peg" from conventional sources.

As the company sought legitimacy and turned increasingly to professional managers, the myths so current in the field were at once convenient and somewhat embarrassing. When the Doctor emerged in all-white apparel under a flattering spotlight at conventions, the screams and tears and efforts to touch the hem of his pants were not directed to P. T. Barnum's pal, but to a "genius," the inventor of vitamins, a man totally in harmony with nature.

Such a disjunction between myth and reality should have made the company cautious about throwing its weight around in courts of law. The company lived in a shiny glass house. The facts—those secret and untidy realities—were the stones. But the company became increasingly aggressive in asserting its rights.

In 1978, the company heard that a prominent Utah distributor, Franklin Gunnell, who had enjoyed a meteoric rise in company ranks, was questioning the company's alfalfa product. Gunnell, a rugged American individualist, rancher, and a former Speaker in the state legislature, was a man of strong convictions who was unafraid to give voice to them. He was troubled by rumors of immorality in Shaklee management that contradicted both the wholesome, family image the company had carefully cultivated and his own Mormon beliefs. Tipped off by a former Shaklee executive, he had also had some of the company alfalfa tested by a local laboratory. He had found the results not to his liking. Given his growing uncertainties about Shaklee, he was considering adding another line of health products for his sales force, something he was legally entitled to do but which Shaklee had strongly discouraged in a way Gunnell, at times, found threatening.

When the company heard of Gunnells's concerns, they took aggressive action. They terminated him, held a meeting in Salt Lake City before his coworkers to describe his bad actions, and sued him for defaming both the company's management for sexual immorality and the company's alfalfa—a popular product with no known value for human nutrition. The idea apparently was to make an example of this individual, steamroller him with the prospect of costly litigation, and get him to back off.

Alas, the company did not know the man. Gunnell and his wife, El Marie, were not about to accept injustice. Like Yeltsin climbing on top of the tank, the rugged rancher decided he would stand up for the right. He hired counsel and fought back. In that emerging battle, it became apparent that Shaklee had misjudged something else in addition to the man—a misjudgment even more costly than its underestimation of the Gunnells's wills. It had forgotten a serious corporate blind spot.

Discovery in the civil suit began. Soon, prominent Shaklee executives were called to give embarrassing details about their private lives, an inquiry made necessary by their pleading the morality of their executives. One had to admit staying at an "adult" motor hotel near company headquarters known for its whirlpools, pornography, and "masseuses." But such embarrassments were not as important as a more serious problem—a hidden company scandal relating to alfalfa, the very product the Gunnells were accused of defaming.

After stonewalling, dodging, and evading, the company was finally required by the judge to turn over documents about the alfalfa that were, in the words of Shaklee's counsel, "bad, real bad." They revealed the following:

1. Shaklee had had an infestation of salmonella in some of its alfalfa.

2. The company had treated the salmonella with ethylene oxide (ETO), a treatment not appropriate for organic material.

3. That treatment had left a heavy residue of ethylene chlorohydra (ECH), a suspected carcinogen.

4. Tests revealed high levels of ECH and ETO on the alfalfa.

5. Countermanding recommendations of some employees, the company authorized distribution of carcinogen-laden alfalfa, apparently for financial reasons.

6. In-house lawyers had written internal memos describing the potential criminal ramifications of this behavior.

7. The company knew that some customers were taking 20 or more tablets a day to ward off arthritis or other conditions that, of course, could not be cured or prevented by alfalfa.

These facts ultimately came out. *The Wall Street Journal* jumped on them. It ran a lead story on the titillating peek into the true nature of this "natural health" company and the exploded credentials of its founder. The Securities and Exchanges Commission had briefly suspended trading in company stock. After trial and appeal, and the prospect of a costly and even more embarrassing retrial, the company settled with the Gunnells—but only on the condition the Gunnells agreed to keep the financial and other terms confidential. Frank and El Marie continue to ranch and enjoy life in Utah.

But how could a sophisticated company like Shaklee put in issue the sex life of its management, the *bona fides* of their deified founder, and the quality of a key product—when the inquiries with regard to each was at least, embarrassing, and at the most, could lead to criminal indictments?

The answer is the blind spot. As the child who kicked the porcupine said, "It just seemed like the thing to do at the time."

The case is one of many examples of companies and individuals rushing to court, not knowing how fragile their glass house really is.

"Hot Spots"

These blind spots become especially combustible when mixed with government "hot spots."

President Reagan was a conviction (rather than consensus) politician with a mandate for new ideas. Among his strong themes was the view that extreme environmentalism is unreasonable and should be balanced by a common sense approach that permits more development. The press snickered at the talk of trees exhaling pollutant poisons and crowded around James Watt to catch a malaprop, but the President had his way. James Watt, Mrs. Burford, and others took control of environmental policy.

But when Watt finally got in public disrepute due to his off-the-cuff comments, and when Burford was criticized for a lack of candor with Congress, a new team came in. The new head of the EPA decided it was time to put some teeth into environmental regulations. Within three months of assuming these duties, the EPA had initiated over 40 criminal cases. In the vanguard of this new determination to treat breaches of environmental regulations as crimes were Operation Desert Junkyard assaults on every kind of alleged environmental wrongdoing. It would typically have the makings of the typical government investigation: a snitch, suspicious circumstances, and a "hot" area. It proved an incendiary mixture.

In our case, a property manager was charged criminally for disposal of hazardous wastes. One of its shopping center tenants had done woodworking. When the tenant moved out, it left behind some shellac, paint thinner, and a few cans with a ring of dried paint at the bottom. A foreman not used to cleaning up for woodworkers put the cans in a garbage can. The garbage collector reported it to authorities. Suddenly, the company and its employees were in the local paper as alleged "environmental criminals."

The author of Ecclesiastes talked about the seasons to rend and to sow, to embrace and to refrain from embracing, to laugh and to weep. There are also seasons for prosecution.

In the mid-1980s the government decided to "tilt" toward Iraq. Iraq was up to its neck in desert sand in the "Jihad" with Iran. Iran was still viewed as the prime threat to American interests in the region. The United States did not want Iraq to lose the war and wanted to strengthen its ties with Saddam Hussein.

As a part of this program, the government agreed to provide guarantees for letters of credit in connection with exports to Iraq. The problems of dealing with countries like Iraq are self-evident. Companies will not export to Iraq unless they have some assurance they will be paid. They demand letters of credit. But banks will not issue letters of credit without some assurance that they will be paid. Given these hurdles, few transactions were done. The United States Department of Agriculture decided to facilitate agricultural shipments to Iraq by providing guarantees on letters of credit. Both the company and the banks issuing the letters of credit would therefore know that they would be paid. It would be good for U.S. commerce and exports, good for our Iraqi friends, and good for U.S. policy throughout the world.

The regulations adopted to implement this policy were characteristically ambiguous. They referred to this shipment of U.S. goods abroad but they did not clearly prohibit the use of any foreign constituents in those products. The concept of "origin" has always been one of scholastic interest to trade lawyers. In an increasingly interconnected world economy, fewer and fewer products are exclusively from one country. They all have parts from exotic locations.

So ambiguous is the concept of origin that in many countries, one can certify that the product is of local origin if there has been any value added in that country. Given the opportunity to sell to oil-rich Iraq, however, many agricultural exporters saw an opportunity to expand international sales. They took advantage of the program. Some of these companies were themselves foreign-owned or at least had related foreign subsidiaries or sister companies. When products were sent out from a U.S. location to Iraq, they were certified as being of U.S. origin.

In 1988, sensing the ambiguity of the regulations, the USDA issued a press release which said, essentially, that although the regulations were clear, it would clarify them. Guarantees would be available if 75 percent of the product was of American origin, but only the American origin material could be subject to the guarantee program. The message was typically bureaucratic. These regulations have always been crystal clear. And so let us clarify what they always meant. U.S. origin now meant that 75 percent of the goods shipped were of U.S. origin.

Given the complexities of determining origin, the government might not have cared much about different standards of measurement. But then came Saddam goose-stepping into the pubic stage as the conqueror of Kuwait. Congressional leaders began to investigate the United States Department of Agriculture program. Political opponents of the administration seized on the apparent hypocrisy of building up Saddam, both militarily and economically, and then lamenting how strong he had become, militarily and economically. Some of the opponents began to delve deeper into how Saddam had grown to his current monster status. They found examples in this program, and others, of us feeding him.

The USDA, in turn, wanted to avoid any allegations of misconduct on its part. The answer was obvious: a crackdown on abuses under the guarantee program. Investigators began to prosecute agricultural companies and other entities. One company was fined $5 million. Others were subpoenaed before the grand jury. Why? In part, because their practices in international shipments, however conventional or typical, were subject to real question. In part, because their business was a "hot area" for criminal prosecution.

Bank Robber and
Banker-Robbers?

Banks used to be thought of as the victims of crime. When Willie Sutton was asked why he robbed banks, he replied, "because that's where the money is." Their contact with criminal law came either as victim, when nylon face masks presented themselves before tellers with scribbled notes, or as witness, when authorities wanted to use bank records to impale a criminal customer.

But then came the indictment of the Bank of Boston in early 1985. The Bank of Boston was accused of violating the Bank Secrecy Act, which requires banks to report certain kinds of currency transactions. The purpose of the act was to frustrate efforts of money launderers to use American banks to wash the proceeds of drug transactions. The Bank of Boston's failure to comply with that act in a host of apparently routine financial transactions served as a "wake-up call" for many other banks throughout the country. More than 100 came forward to admit that their systems of compliance were also inadequate. Another bank in the area, the Bank of New England, was later indicted and convicted of a violation of the act.

These hot spots are like fashions. They change from season to season. In the early 1980s there were task forces created to sniff out defense contractor fraud. Suddenly, indictments were coming down all over the country against long-time government contractors such as McDonnell Douglas, Sperry Corporation, North American Rockwell, General Dynamics, and Boeing. Then came a renewed emphasis on foreign payments. Suddenly, there were massive investigations of questionable payments abroad.

The pattern is true not only of hot areas by subject matter but also is true of emphasis on white-collar crime generally. When FBI agents are told to look for white-collar crime, they will inevitably find it. When the savings and loan collapse threatens to cost the government billions, there is an investigation to find fraud. Fraud is found. When the government searches for contractors who are taking advantage of the *minority set aside* money, by having some nominee minority in charge of a business not at all controlled by minorities, cases will be generated.

Let's look at some examples. In April 1983 an investigation, code named *Thimble*, began. A defense contractor had been solicited for a bribe and told the government. The FBI decided to have an extensive undercover operation, with court-ordered electronic surveillance. The FBI went after five different corporations and 19 individual subjects, in an effort to prove that close to $100 million in contracts had been fraudulently awarded. A total of 120 corporations and individuals have been either suspended, debarred, or proposed for debarment from doing any further business with the government. Several million dollars in restitution was recovered in fines. Additional indictments are expected.

Recently, the FBI started its well-known *Ill Wind* investigation. The FBI and other law enforcement agencies sought to address the issue of bribery and fraud in the procurement process of the Department of Defense. There the FBI used the typical investigative tools at its disposal: covert electronic surveillance, 44 search warrants in 14 states, and conventional investigative techniques. Figure 7-1 shows the fines, recoveries, and restitutions from years of emphasis on the Department of Defense fraud.

Department of Defense Fraud

Fines, Recoveries, and Restitutions

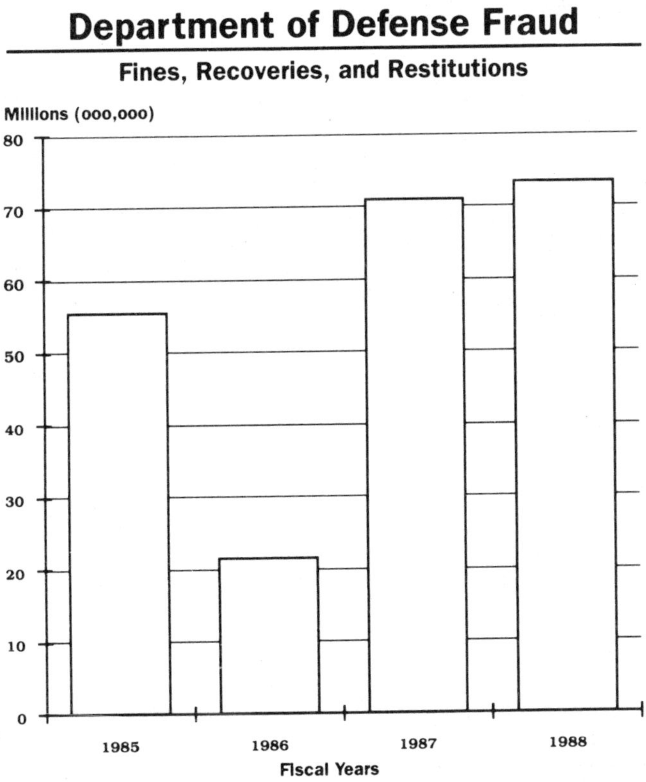

Figure 7-1. Department of Defense fraud: Fines, recoveries, and restitutions. (*White-Collar Crime: A Report to the Public, Department of Justice, Federal Bureau of Investigation, p. 6.*)

The environmental crime area shows what can happen. The FBI has ranked environmental crimes as "priority" investigations. Every environmental crime allegation is given such priority. As a result, from 1984 through 1988, the FBI caseload on environmental crimes increased by 397 percent. Figure 7-2 tells the story.

The priority is reflected by the extraordinary lengths law enforcement will go to when it sniffs a hot area.

Many recall the famous FBI sting operation called *Abscam*. Notwithstanding indignation in Washington, the FBI was unrepentant about having a bogus sheik offer bribes to a variety of Congressional leaders. The sheik's efforts were so successful that Senator Larry Pressler became something of a folk hero by being the only public official to turn

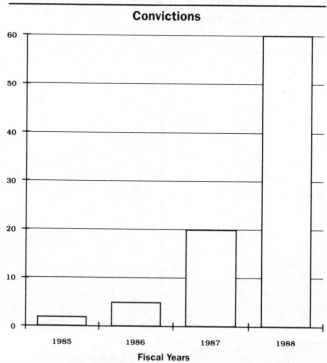

Figure 7-2. Environmental crimes: Convictions. (*White-Collar Crime: A Report to the Public, Department of Justice, Federal Bureau of Investigation, p. 13.*)

the bribe down. Such efforts continue to be used in white-collar crime matters.

More recently, a number of FBI agents posed as commodities traders in the pit of the Chicago Mercantile Exchange and tape-recorded conversations between commodity traders in the pits of the world's largest futures exchanges. The kind of tactics usually reserved for mobsters was now clearly being applied to successful business executives. Like armies in war operations, the FBI has the pleasure of naming their operations: *Abscam* (a combination of Arab and Scam); *Brilab* (a combination of bribery and labor); *Brispec* (a combination of bribery and special interests venued in Sacramento); *Sourmash* (Chicago Board of Trade investigation named after distilled grains used in whiskey); *Greylord* (an investigation of the Chicago court system, named after a horse depicted on a racing form being read by an agent when asked about the investigation); *Hedgeclipper* (Mercantile Exchange undercover investigation of hedging futures contracts); and Operation *Safe Bet* (organized crime and gambling investigation). And the government is willing to lay out the money to carry the operation off. The commodities investigation required over $1 million to get off the ground. As one U.S. Attorney put it, "I don't think that just because people have a position of wealth or power in the community that they ought to be immune from prosecution."[1]

The Los Angeles Times reported:

> Just another day in the life of the FBI's white collar crime division, which increasingly using electronic surveillance and undercover operations in an effort to apprehend the thousands of con-artists who steal billions of dollars every year from corporations and individuals throughout Los Angeles and Orange counties.[2]

Such methods show that "White collar crime is the FBI's number one priority in Southern California . . . "[3]

Dan Webb, United States Attorney for the Northern District of Illinois in the 1980s, spelled it out: "[I]n recent times we have more and more attempted to find at least in some cases a better method of trying to develop evidence of whatever criminal activity is going on inside the particular structure or enterprise. That method is also controversial,

---

[1] *The Los Angeles Times*, p. 6 (February 12, 1989).

[2] *The Los Angeles Times*, p. 1 (August 27, 1989).

[3] Ibid.

that is using undercover operations to infiltrate ongoing criminal activity and develop evidence that is not just retrospective in nature, but develop evidence that actually is being developed as the crime itself is being committed." He goes on to say, "They essentially come in the simplest form, consisting of law enforcement agents, pretending to be somebody they are not, infiltrating an ongoing course of criminal activity and gradually develop evidence, layer by layer against people who are culpable in the scheme, hopefully eventually tracing the misconduct up to the top of the scheme. We do that through another controversial means, and that is electronic eavesdropping. We use a lot of electronic eavesdropping in the course of undercover investigations . . . "[4]

It's the Pits

Business Week wrote of the commodities investigators as "wired FBI agents prowling the trading pits." The prosecutor in the commodities markets investigation, Anton R. Valukas, the magazine reported, "appears ready to bludgeon traders already suspected of wrongdoing into cooperating with investigators in order to implicate other, more prominent figures at the exchanges."[5] *Business Week* concluded:

> But don't expect Valukas to show his compassionate side in the ongoing federal probe into trading practices at the exchanges. He has invested hundreds of thousands of taxpayer's dollars—and great personal prestige—in the investigation. He can ill afford to come up empty handed.[6]

As the best-selling author, Scott Turow pointed out, "It's hard for me to applaud the government's tactics, but there is nothing unusual in them."[7]

The rationale underlying such sting operations often smacks of the aphorism about "all is fair in love and war." As the Supreme Court itself has said:

> Society is at war with the criminal classes, and courts have uniformly held that in waging this warfare the forces of prevention and detec-

---

[4]Minutes of Chicago Bar Association, Volume 51, 175–8, January 1, 1985.

[5]*Business Week* 30–36 (February 6, 1989).

[6]Ibid.

[7]Ibid.

tion may use traps, decoys and deception to obtain evidence of the commission of a crime. Resort to such means does not render an indictment thereafter found a nullity nor call for the exclusion of evidence so procured.[8]

There is, to be sure, a hazy line between those who would resist what Justice Frankfurter called "ordinary temptations" but fall into sin as the result of entrapment, and those who are looking for a way to commit crimes and are merely provided with an "opportunity" by law enforcement officials.

But courts have traditionally believed that defendants are responsible moral agents who should be able to struggle successfully against temptation. If they cannot do so, that reflects a criminal mind that ought to be punished. One court, for example, put it this way:

> [Entrapment] would be but the repetition of the plea as ancient as the world, and first interposed in Paradise: "the serpent beguiled me and I did eat." That defense was overruled by the great law giver, and whatever estimate we may form, or whatever judgment pass upon the character or conduct of the tempter, this plea has never since availed to shield crime or give indemnity to the culprit, and it is safe to say that under any code of civilized, not to say Christian ethics, it never will.[9]

But others read the constraints of ethics differently, believing with the famous southern preacher of the last century that "it is never right to do wrong to do right," or as Justice Brandeis put it, in a stinging dissent seeking to establish the law of entrapment:

> I am aware that courts—mistaking relative social values and forgetting that a desirable end cannot justify foul means—have, in their zeal to punish, sanctioned the use of evidence obtained through criminal violation of property and personal rights or by other practices of detectives even more revolting. But the objection here is of a different nature. It does not rest merely upon the character of the evidence or upon the fact that the evidence was illegally obtained. The obstacle to the prosecution lies in the fact that the alleged crime was instigated by officers of the government; that the act for which the government seeks to punish the defendant is the fruit of

---

[8] *Sorrells v. United States*, 287 U.S. 435, 453 S.Ct 210, 77 L.Ed. 413 (1932).

[9] *Board of Commissioners v. Backus*, 29 How. Pr. 33, 42 (N.Y. Sup. 1864) as cited in *White Collar Crime: Business and Regulatory Offenses*, Obermaier and Morvillo (Law Journal Seminars–Press, 1990).

their criminal conspiracy to induce its commission. The government may set decoys to entrap criminals. But it may not provoke or create a crime and then punish the criminal, its creature. If Casey is guilty of the crime of purchasing 3.4 grains of morphine, on December 31st, as charged, it is because he yielded to the temptation presented by the officers. Their conduct is not a defense to him. For no officer of the government has power to authorize the violation of an act of Congress, and no conduct of an officer can excuse the violation. But it does not follow that the court must suffer a detective-made criminal to be punished. To permit that would be tantamount to a ratification by the government of the officers' unauthorized and unjustifiable conduct.

This prosecution should be stopped, not because some right of Casey's has been denied, but in order to protect the government. To protect it from illegal conduct of its officers to preserve the purity of its courts.[10]

The Brandeis view, however, was in the minority then and is in the minority now.

Of Means and Ends

As a result, even reprehensible conduct by the prosecutor often will not lead to the dismissal of an indictment. In one case, a lawyer felt the pressure of an imminent criminal investigation. He decided to make haste to the courthouse. In exchange for his cooperation, he was able to win for himself favorable treatment from the prosecutor.

To do so, he willingly wore a "wire" in conversations with his own client. He cheerfully recorded attorney–client privilege discussions about past and present and future criminal concerns, as well as tactical and strategic discussions which reflected his client's state of mind. The prosecutor was able to get inside the attorney–client "war room" and monitor all such discussions. During the course of these secretly recorded sessions, the lawyer continued to serve as the client's counsel in pending matters until he was found out.

When indicted, upon learning of this subversion of the attorney–client relationship, the defendant moved to dismiss the indictment for prosecutorial misconduct. The indictment was not dismissed because, as the court was later to write, the actions were "not so outrageous as to shock the universal sense of justice."[11]

---

[10] *Casey v. United States*, 276 U.S. 413, 419, 48 S.Ct. 373, 72 L.Ed. 632 (1928) at 423-425.

[11] *United States v. Heller*, 830 F.2d 150 (11th Cir., 1987).

Indeed, so broad is the government's powers when in hot pursuit, that it can sometimes be authorized in deceiving the court. In one case, for example, the government issued a bogus subpoena to a grand jury. Grand jury subpoenas should only issue, of course, based on good-faith need for a witness before the grand jury. The lawyer who obtains them for the prosecution is an officer of the court. But in the case of the bogus subpoena, the prosecutor felt he needed to protect his "mole" from detection, and so he was issued a grand jury subpoena along with some other targets of the investigation. Because he was a part of the "party," the other defendants to be had confidence in him and gave incriminatory statements. To the district court that reviewed this prosecutorial behavior, after a motion to dismiss, its duty seemed clear. The indictment had to be dismissed because the prosecutor's manipulation of court processes "obviously exceeds the bounds of propriety."[12] But the Third Circuit in *United States v. Martino*[13] disagreed and reinstated the indictment.

Such tactics can be even more colorful. The FBI, for example, has used a prostitute as an informer, even while knowing that she was regularly having sex with the principal suspect. An indictment based on her testimony was not dismissed.[14]

Sometimes the Mata Hari technique is as innovative as it is alarming. In a recent investigation in Los Angeles, federal agents again hired two prostitutes. Their mission was to "get close," quite literally, to the targets of the investigation and to win from them some pillow talk admissions while performing their services.

In an investigation of lawyers charged with fictitious or unnecessary legal billing to insurance companies, one lawyer member of "the alliance" wore a wire for almost two years. The lawyer even recruited clients to help him in the undercover investigation.

Some courts, to be sure, have disagreed with such methods, sex in particular. As one said, "sex is much too strong and effective an inducement to be used as bait."[15] But the above examples show what the government may do when it smells a rat in your industry. And it shows how little judges are inclined to stop it.

Decisions by the FBI and other prosecutorial authorities are hardly arbitrary. Most people charged with crime plead guilty. Most who do

---

[12] *United States v. Caputo,* 633 F.Supp. 1479 (ED Pa. 1986).

[13] 6825 F.2d 754 (3d Cir., 1987).

[14] See *United States v. Simpson,* 813 F.2d 1462 (9th Cir., 1987).

[15] *State v. Banks,* 499 So.2d 894 (Fla. App., 1986).

not plead guilty are convicted. Problems like fraud in the savings and loan industry, insider trading, or improper disposal of hazardous wastes are prosecuted because serious misconduct does exist. Many of the investigations are, to be sure, influenced by political pressures, unanticipated changes in policy, or newly elected officials with different emphases. Sometimes they reflect an agency's efforts to look "tough" when it itself has been under the gun. They all, however, represent genuine social problems that need fixing.

Heads Up

 But the real import of all this for the business executive is the need for vigilance. The fact that your business or your job is not now typically threatened by criminal prosecution does not mean it will not be in a few months. Those gray areas in your line of work that have never been the subject of criminal scrutiny may become so. Builder, baker, or candlestick maker can all quite easily come under the searchlights of prosecutors eager to make new cases. Prosecutors, like everyone else, want promotions. Promotions come from making cases the boss wants to be made. The greater the pressure to find cases, the greater the likelihood that marginal cases will be selected for prosecution. And marginal cases usually have less evidence of a clearly culpable stay of mind.

In short, nearly every corporation has some blind spot in which a marginal criminal case could be made. If that blind spot becomes congruent with the government hot spot, there is trouble. And soon extraterrestrial yellow jackets are floating down out of the sky to search your facility and files.

To make the illustration personal, let's suppose that the fairness issue again comes to center stage in tax policy. A beleaguered administration is trying to justify its attempts to reduce the tax rate for capital gains. Its opponents dig up a treasure trove of tax breaks for the rich in the current tax code. They find evidence that a billion dollars are being lost at the treasury by improper deductions. They prove that the cowardly IRS has generally only prosecuted people for fraud on the revenue side, for not reporting substantial income, legal or illegal. The IRS has handled inflated deductions for club dues, car expenses, travel, entertainment, and the like too civilly. The President decides to "get tough" with the business deductions in order to facilitate getting his capital gains relief.

The IRS decides to make some criminal cases against ordinary business executives and professional people in the community. The computer spits out your return. No matter how fastidious you have been, there will be some borderline decisions, perhaps some mistakes in your deductions. Those mistakes, whether in deducting a high percentage of the costs for your business vehicle or questionable club dues or other mixed recreational and business ventures, get you halfway to a criminal prosecution. The other question is whether you acted intentionally. But *intentional* means only that you intended the consequences of your acts. And you, a successful professional with a good education and elite credentials, obviously intended to do what you did.

Soon you are sitting at counsel table before a jury of twelve. In one corner of the courtroom is a screen that is 10 feet by 20 feet. On the screen is a copy of the deduction you claimed, together with your personal signature, swearing under penalty of perjury that the return is accurate. Next comes a regulation, verbatim from the IRS code. You were hoping the regulation was more ambiguous. But when you see it, you realize that the jury will clearly understand it. It makes clear that your deduction is wrong. You look up and down the jury box and see people who will believe that $18,000 in deductions over three years is a lot of money. You see them going into the jury room to deliberate your fate.

A far-fetched nightmare? Perhaps. But one ought to act as though it is an imminent reality. A categorical imperative for business executives in the new climate is to treat every decision as one they would be happy to live with a fire-breathing special agent looking over their shoulder. The decision otherwise may prove "too hot" to handle.

8
The Internal Investigation

When the Best Defense Is a Good Prosecution

Sometimes the criminal investigation of a business begins with a bang on the door. Federal agents pull up to the headquarters, produce a search warrant, and cart off hundreds of boxes of corporate records. The federal investigation is well under way, a grand jury is hearing, or is about to hear, the evidence. It is time to start laying in the sandbags.

But other investigations start with a whimper: a comment or request by a government regulator, a phone call from a troubled employee, an invoice that appears tampered with, books that won't balance. The federal government may as yet not have evidence of wrongdoing. But the facts are ominous. The company may have the luxury of time, but how ample or cramped the breathing room is by no means clear. A bit of smoke seeps out of one division of the company. No one wants to be rash, but things do not look good. What does a company do, act or wait?

The strategic need is clear. One must do an internal investigation before the government does one of its own. One must dredge up and organize the facts. Only then can a decision maker evaluate the problem and commit the corporate entity to a course of action. But how does one dredge up the facts?

Who Should Do the Investigation?

One should begin by listing those who should not. Corporate executives should never take it upon themselves to investigate the facts. If they begin interviewing witnesses, reviewing documents, and writing memos to subordinates, they can rest assured that everything they do will be ultimately discoverable by the government. Corporations have no Fifth Amendment privilege against self-incrimination. And there is no other protection or privilege that can shield the candid, extemporaneous observations of the chief executive officer from later scrutiny, since anything the officer sees, observes, says, or chooses to write down may later be used against the executive and the company.

There is a further risk when management does the internal investigation. It may implicate the executive in the criminal investigation itself. If the manager discovers information that suggests a conspiracy within the organization, almost anything the manager does—short of dropping a cruise missile on the offending division—may be seen as an overt act covering up or furthering the conspiracy. Inaction may be seen as an obstruction of justice; ignoring or disbelieving employees may be seen as evidence of evil intent and prior knowledge of the underlying wrong.

Finally, the executive may not be the best person to extract information. No one likes to admit wrongdoing to anyone. But it is especially difficult to do so to a boss who hires and fires. When called on the carpet in such a case, the employee may face a *Hobson's choice*. Is the explanation criminality or stupidity? If the act is wrong, the employee must either have not comprehended its significance or the employee must be a malefactor. Either admission threatens the employee's job security.

Even an in-house general counsel is usually not the best person to do the investigation. Some courts have the tendency to discount the general counsel as a "real lawyer" because the general counsel often has some management or supervisory responsibility, and thus the shield of attorney–client privilege may leak. In addition, the in-house lawyer may find it more difficult to "get tough" with reluctant witnesses, since, as counselor, the lawyer needs to meet with corporate employees regularly on a friendly basis in order to facilitate his or her management functions. The lawyer seeks to be the servant of the other employees, a role that does not comport easily with being a snitch to upper management.

When an internal investigation is done, therefore, it is outside counsel that should do it. Inside counsel can well serve the role of coordination and comfort, scheduling interviews and setting employees at ease by supplying the appropriate introductions. But it is outside counsel, sometimes with the help of an investigator, or other experts such as accountants, who must get to the bottom of what occurred.

Can One Preserve the Secrecy of the Investigation?

The purpose of the inquiry is to discover wrongdoing, not to document it. One dangerous practice, therefore, is to take statements of witnesses. Those conducting the investigation must be careful to preserve the attorney–client privilege. However helpful to memory, it is unwise to take verbatim written statements of one's own employees. Such statements, even when prepared by lawyers, are usually discoverable by prosecutors. It is a much better practice to write memos to file without direct quotations, entitled *work product, thoughts, impressions, and opinions based on interviews*. Courts frequently open to prosecutor scrutiny verbatim statements, or paraphrases that appear to be an attempt to preserve the witness' own words. On the other hand, a lawyer's impressions, opinions, and meditations are protected by the work product doctrine, even if they also have the tendency to preserve the gist of what a particular witness said.

A second dangerous practice is to publish the results of the investigation, or of any part of it, beyond the circle of those within the organization with a need to know. Many complex criminal cases require expert accounting systems. But showing an accountant not employed by the company information gleaned from privileged interviews will usually be a disclosure sufficient to destroy the privilege. There is no such thing as accountant–client privilege.

There is a parallel problem within the organization. If reports on what the investigation reveals are too broadly circulated beyond those with a clear need to know, the court may hold that the privilege has been waived. Once an inadvertent disclosure is made, large chunks of privilege may unravel quickly. The attorney–client privilege cannot be waived selectively or piecemeal. If one thread of privilege is removed, a prosecutor may be allowed to pull persistently at the rest, until the whole body of attorney–client communications is uncovered for government inspection.

Inadvertent disclosure is one common problem in internal investigations; infection is another. There is, indeed, a time when ignorance is bliss. As the old radio quiz show had it, "it pays to be ignorant, to be dumb, to be stupid, to be ignorant." Lawyers who begin interviewing people within any organization can create, spontaneously, a rumor mill, which manufactures bits of information and disseminates them instantaneously to the far-flung reaches of the company.

This rumor mill environment grows nothing but thorns and thistles. A rebellious employee finds an opportunity to turn the company in or seeks to gain some leverage with the company. A nervous employee can trigger panic among other employees; résumés are tuned up overnight. A company loyalist may see it as an opportunity to engage in some self-help redacting or destroying of corporate files. Employees not yet interviewed may prepare their stories, self-justifying responses reducing the chances of any spontaneous (and truthful) response. The chances of hitting upon the truth go down; the chances of aggravating the company's dilemma go up.

There is a special risk of infection for upper management. The president of the company, if a hands-on manager, may want to micromanage the investigation. The boss will say that, as the chief executive, one *has* to know everything. The boss *does not have* to know everything.

Since so many crimes in the white-collar area are *scienter* crimes that turn on the knowledge of the actor, the less knowledge, the better. In a three- or four-year investigation, it will be very difficult for that president to determine what was known contemporaneously with the acts, what was learned early on as a result of the investigation, and what was learned only in preparation for trial. The executives will be much more believable, and much less at jeopardy, if they are insulated from the specifics of the investigation. The company president will not be able to make a final decision on the course of action, of course, until there are enough facts to do so. But even then, there is no need to know the details or conclusions with any specificity.

How Can One Control the Rumor Mill?

Anyone who has done an investigation knows the *in terrorem* effect of the investigation. An employee who is not intimidated by an internal investigator is a rare bird. Regulatory problems can get blown out of proportion. Intense questioning may cause the employee to wonder whose briefcase the lawyer is really carrying. Is this attorney preparing something for the prosecution?

Unless employees understand the problem and the company efforts to fix it, they may take action themselves. An employee group at Northrup, for example, decided to declare war on the company, alleging that the firm overcharged the government on its Stealth Bomber contract. As a result, Northrup was forced to make disclosures in connection with discovery in that litigation that could have an impact on the criminal investigation.

One should not forget that cooperating with the government is not without its inducements. The true whistle-blower who alerts the government to fraudulent activity within the corporation which takes money out of the government's pocket may be entitled to a percentage of the ultimate recovery gained by the government as a result of the tip. Considering that such awards may be as high as 10 percent, and the government recovery may go into the hundreds of thousands or even millions of dollars, the prospect of such a recovery may be a form of *contingent fee* that gives the government witness a significant incentive to see a conviction, with its attendant fines and penalties.

It is important, therefore, to set employees at ease. It is time to talk the language of routine and caution—not fear, dread, and doubt.

In talking this language, however, the employee should not be misled. The employees should be put on notice that the lawyer does not represent them; the lawyer represents the company. While the company will not recklessly expose its employees to unnecessary risks, and while normally the interests of employees and company converge, there may come a time when the company's interests diverge from those of the employees. If that happens, the employees should not have a justifiable claim that their confidences have been betrayed. The ideal is to protect everyone. But the lawyer must make clear who is being represented. Facts may turn up during the investigation that threaten the employee's job. Information may be developed that will lead the company to the conclusion that it is best to cut out a small cancer within the company before it can metastasize. Some of the employees may be demoted or dismissed. To avoid battles over attorney–client privilege, it is important to remind employees that they can retain (usually at company expense) independent counsel to represent their interests.

Doing the Interviews

The interviews should be carried out quickly and face-to-face. Many employees do tell exculpatory lies to those investigating their conduct. When given enough time, cohorts may get together to coordinate their stories. The quicker and the more spontaneous the scheduling and completion of the interviews, the more likely it is that the investigation can get information and rely on it.

Once the interviews are completed, the internal investigation should focus on what occurred, why it occurred (what was the breakdown in corporate control?), and how it can be fixed (both externally with respect to any government investigation and internally so that it does not happen again). Based on the facts and conclusions, one can determine whether to make a preemptive strike and seek immediate peace with the government or stand still, if the offense appears not to be criminal or significant, or hunker down if the government is on its way.

Be Prepared

One part of the internal investigation is to get employees ready for the government investigator. If there is a serious problem that the government is aware of, it will likely not wait to summon people formally before the grand jury. A special agent will be at the employee's doorstep, often quite literally.

At 9:00 p.m. at night an investigator knocks on a door in Shaker Heights. He flashes his badge to an executive. He then asks if he can come in to ask some questions. The law-abiding manager invites the agent in for a cup of coffee. The special agent begins to ask questions. The first questions are innocuous, not accusatory. Further inquiries become more pointed. Before long, the manager is in the middle of an inquisition. His extemporaneous answers then become an FBI "302" that he hears later from a witness stand.

If sophisticated managers make such mistakes, so will employees. Prepared employees will be wary. They will say, quite courteously, that they should talk to one of the company lawyers before the interview. Employees can do this with all cheerfulness and goodwill but must remain insistent. The special agent will otherwise say something like, "I understand you have to talk to counsel, but I have just a few things to clear up. So, maybe I could ask just a few questions now on some uncontroversial things from my records, and then you could talk to counsel about a more substantive interview later." If the employees bite, the early questions ("what is the company's full name again?") will turn ever more substantive and, before the employees know it, they will have given a complete interview. The best response for employees is, "Look, I don't mean to be difficult. And I know that a number of these questions are very routine. But I really think before I have any interview with you that I should talk to someone at our law department."

Some investigators are still not distracted from their duty and go on with something like this. "You are not the target of the investigation. I have no reason to believe, yet, that you are involved in any way in wrongdoing. And so if you really have nothing to hide, I think it would be in your best interests to talk to me now. Frankly, it's easy for me to suspect the worst otherwise. You don't really have anything to hide, do you?"

The Supreme Court has recently determined that any responses to questions after a request to talk with an attorney is made cannot be used against a witness. But the tactic was used many times, and quite successfully, in the past. Even when a court determines that admissions cannot be used against the employee, certainly the information will be known to the government and may give government prosecutors an important advantage in subsequent proceedings.

It is, therefore, clearly in the employees' interests not to say anything until they have talked with a lawyer. And the time of the internal investigation is a good time to make the point. If employees have some exposure, it is imperative that there be no discussion with the government until there is a grant of immunity. If employees are genuinely innocent of any crime, it is all the more important that they not talk and potentially get themselves into unintended difficulty by misspeaking, until they have had a chance to talk with a lawyer. A lawyer will generally be able to get either immunity or equivalent assurances.

The problem for the corporate lawyer conducting the investigation is, of course, how to tell employees what is in their best interests without representing them. It would be easy and honest to tell employees that it is not in the employees' best interests to talk to anyone representing the government about the case without a lawyer present. Any good white-collar criminal defense lawyer would give the same advice.

Unfortunately, the government takes a dim view of this practice. It can easily construe that advice as an obstruction of justice. Here sits an employee with possibly damaging information about the company. Here comes the company's highly paid lawyer with knowledge of the value of this information to the government. Here is the lawyer taping the lips of the employee to prevent him or her from making disclosures adverse to the company.

The company's lawyer has obvious leverage over the individual employees, because employees know that the company lawyer's recommendation can terminate their career or make them a scapegoat in the ongoing federal investigation. When the company lawyer "shuts up" individual employees by giving them counsel not to cooperate with the investigation, many zealous prosecutors would characterize this as an *obstruction of justice*. A lawyer is advising a client not his or her own to do something in his or her own client's interest.

A good lawyer representing a company will, therefore, say something like this:

> As I mentioned to you, I represent the company and not you. It may well be that the government will seek to interview you. Agents may show up at your home, call you at work, or get in touch with you in some other way. They will produce a badge and ask you for the right to have a brief conversation. Now let me make clear that you have an absolute right to talk with the government if you so choose. There is nothing standing in the way of your exercising that right. You also, of course, have an absolute right not to talk to a government agent, without it being held against you in any way. I, of course, cannot advise you what to do in this particular case. I should, however, point out that most lawyers representing clients in this area of the law do recommend that their clients not talk to government agents without

a lawyer present. It is in the government's interest to find out how many people are guilty and prosecute them. And while nothing I have heard here suggests you have any culpability, sometimes we can say things that are misunderstood by others and are difficult to retract. And so if a government agent does come by, you could courteously tell the agent that you'd like to wait and have an opportunity to talk with counsel before having any interview.

To that end, the company will make available to you, free of charge, a lawyer to represent you personally. If someone does contact you, please give me a call and I will recommend someone to you. If you find that lawyer suitable, he or she can represent you throughout the proceeding, at no charge to you.

When there are too many individual witnesses to be talked to individually, it is possible to write a carefully worded release to the employees, giving them the same information. It is not, in fact, in corporate employees' best interest to give free-wheeling interviews with government agencies searching for criminal wrongdoing. And it *is* in their interest to have counsel representing them personally. Reputable counsel will not be influenced by who is paying the bill. It is thus important to get employees in good hands, so if a criminal prosecution develops, there is a cohesive defense team ready to go into the fray immediately. The employee must not be ignorant of the prosecutor's devices.

Prescribing Therapy

Finally, the corporation should be advised what prophylactic measures are necessary to prevent the same problem from occurring again. This report should come to the attention of the board of directors. The board members should normally excuse inside directors who have any relationship, however tangential, to the problems being investigated and should not be sent books or other exhibits for them to keep in some file at home. Any materials should be disclosed to them at a board meeting and then collected to preserve their confidentiality. The board should adopt appropriate recommendations and resolutions to show that it took the problem seriously and acted to prevent its recurrence. Some recommendations boards frequently consider include:

1. An internal audit team, if one does not exist, or specific steps to strengthen internal audit procedures.

2. An instruction of relevant employees in the regulations that were breached in the present case.

3. A code of conduct, making clear that ethical behavior is a company priority, and a whistle-blower provision that commends, rather than

condemns, employees who bring to management's attention genuine examples of potentially illegal or unethical behavior.

4. Disciplinary measures to focus employees' attention on violations, ranging from letters of reprimand through suspensions with or without pay, up to and including termination of parties primarily responsible for the wrongdoing. There is nothing like the sacking of someone who has crossed the line to rivet everyone's attention on good behavior, and to convince other employees that the company is serious about its mission to behave lawfully. Such terminations, however, should not be, or appear to be, scapegoating. Discipline should extend as far up the corporate ladder as the misconduct itself reaches.

None of these measures may be sufficient to forestall criminal prosecution (although, under the recently enacted sentencing guidelines, they will mitigate the punishment imposed on the corporate entity). Some may have countervailing tendencies that require analysis.

Codes of conduct, for example, often promote sound public relations and may indeed have some marginal impact on employee behavior. But they are far from a guarantee against criminal indictment. The explosion of white-collar crime prosecutions has led many companies to enact such codes and often to have seminars, educational programs, and other forms of friendly admonitions. Since a corporation can act only through its employees, and since those employees and agents bind the corporations only when they act within the scope of authority given to them by the company, to what extent are such directions from the corporation's moral codes a defense in a criminal action against the corporate entity?

The leading case in the area is *United States v. Hilton Hotels Corp.*[1] In the *Hilton* case, several hotels in Portland, Oregon, had organized a boycott in an effort to attract more conventions to the city. The boycott sought to force certain suppliers to donate 1 percent of their sales to the "Greater Portland Convention Association." If they did not, the hotels would boycott the suppliers' products.

The government viewed this as a criminal antitrust violation and charged various hotels involved in the boycott with federal crimes. One of the hotels charged had instructed its hotel purchasing agent on two occasions not to go along with the boycott. The agent admitted he had been so instructed. He also admitted that he had violated those direct and unambiguous instructions by deciding on his own to threaten to boycott certain nonconforming suppliers out of what he termed per-

---

[1] 467 F.2d 1000 (9th Cir. 1972).

sonal "pique." While those corporate instructions were certainly admissible as part of the company defense, they did not make the company conviction-proof. The jury was instructed that it could find the corporation guilty even if the purchasing agent's actions were "contrary to their actual instructions or contrary to the corporation's stated policies."[2] The Ninth Circuit Appeal approved these instructions, finding that "generalized directions" to obey the law, when compliance with the law has potentially negative impact on profits, are "the least likely to be taken seriously."[3] While most courts allow evidence to be introduced about such good-faith training programs, they are far from a magic antidote to a lethal criminal infection.

The Lawyer as Prosecutor Pro Tem

To carry out this mission, the defense lawyer has to act the part of a prosecutor. The normal reaction to allegations of wrongful conduct is self-justification. Everyone in the industry is doing it. The government will not find out. The violation is "technical." And even if disclosed, the penalty is not likely to be severe.

It is sometimes essential that a lawyer give the prosecutor's closing argument, putting together the most salient facts as seen through the suspicious eyes of the prosecutor, showing how premeditated and calloused it was, and how much money was made from the misconduct, convincing the jury—whether board or management—that there is a serious chance of conviction.

In the Old Testament it is reported that God revealed the Ten Commandments from Mount Sinai. But the preliminary preparations for the revelation of God's holy law is not often considered. Before the people were ready to receive those moral precepts, God had to prepare them. The ground began to quake under them. Mount Sinai caught on fire. A horrible darkness descended on the mountain top as God's cloud covered his conversations with Moses. A trumpet began to blow. Its piercing call grew louder and louder, until the people could scarcely bear the noise. Once God had the people's attention, they were ready to listen and to commit themselves to do what was right, saying, "We will do all this law."

Sometimes the lawyer's trumpet must blow loud, and management must quake, before sensible judgments can be made.

[2]Ibid., at 1004.

[3]Ibid., at 1006.

9
Repent or Perish

Why Confession May Be Good for You

Two men sat in Room 437 of City Hall, a building that doubled as the county courthouse. Their position and predicament seemed identical.

Both men were in their thirties. Both were in custody. Both had been charged with theft, one of sandwich meat from a local grocery store, one of a car radio. Both were being arraigned before the same judge, Neil Riley. Both were eligible for the services of a public defender.

But the essential difference between the two men could not have been greater.

I had been Chief Public Defender for six weeks that morning. My law firm contributed one lawyer to oversee the Public Defender's office, at no charge to the county, to get trial experience for its litigators.

The first defendant was happy to accept my services, though obviously unhappy to be waiting in the dock. I went through a litany of questions to determine whether he was eligible for my services, and then a number of questions designed to get out the critical facts.

"Any priors?" I asked.

"None," said the man emphatically. "I've got a clean record."

It was always a relief to find a defendant unburdened by prior convictions. Perhaps this was a defensible charge. He denied the accusations vigorously. And with no prior record, he would not be subject to usual cross-examination about his prior offenses. The jury might be more in-

110

clined to apply a strict reasonable doubt standard. And if the defendant did get convicted, he probably would get a relatively light sentence.

After gathering the information I needed, I went over to Al Hyatt, the Assistant City Attorney, to see the police report.

I had a friendly conversation with Al. "I've got a guy with no priors and theft under $100. Could we continue this one for dismissal?"

Al was known for his reasonableness and willingness to negotiate in appropriate circumstances.

"What's the guy's name, Roger?"

"Smith," I answered, "Billy Smith."

Al thumbed through two dozen police reports before finally extracting Smith. After scanning it, his eyes squinting in the dim light, a somewhat cynical prosecutorial smile lifted one corner of his mouth.

"No priors, Roger?" said Al, as he passed over the police report and rap sheet to me. "I hate to tell you this, Roger, but your guy is no virgin."

Stapled to the top of the police report was the rap sheet. Billy was either a little forgetful or this was a clear case of mistaken identity. The rap showed five felony convictions and seven misdemeanor convictions. Billy was not yet 35 years old. I went back to talk to him.

"Billy, you told me you had no priors. But look at this rap sheet. Do they think you're somebody else, or what?"

Billy looked quickly at the sheet and threw it back at me. "That's what I hate about the whole system. It stinks."

I was puzzled at his meaning.

Billy went on. "It's nothing but hypocrisy. Six months ago I was here, and a probation officer told me that if I went straight, good things would happen to me. 'Keep your nose clean, Billy, and you won't have to worry about us anymore,' he said. And I believed him. I went straight. I kept my nose clean."

I gently interjected, "But what about this charge, Billy?"

"That's what makes me puke. I am clean six whole months. Then, one lousy burglary and I'm right back down here again. Hypocrites."

Billy wanted a full-scale defense. He was tired of plea bargains and public defenders. When he saw what he thought was a bit of cynicism in my expression, he said, "Hey, don't worry about me, represent someone else. I'm tired of public defenders. I'm going to get myself a real lawyer."

From that rebuff I rebounded into another one. The second man was also sitting in the holding area, looking grim. I introduced myself. We shook hands. I mentioned to him that I had reviewed his bail report and it looked as though he might qualify for a public defender. I briefly explained the program and my willingness to represent him. "Emil Swanson, three children, unemployed for six months," the precourt screening report began.

Emil would have none of it. "Thanks, but no thanks."

I reminded him that my services were free of charge.

"Yeah, I know, but I don't need you."

I gave him the reasons people need counsel at every stage of a criminal proceeding, even if they thought they knew what they wanted to do about the charges.

He was unmoved. "Look, I don't want to be rude, but I don't need you."

I said, "Okay, fine." But inside, I was saying, "You'll be sorry, Emil."

The clerk began to read the roll of defendants. Each one would come up to the bench and hear the same litany. Name, address, nature of the charge, right to a lawyer, availability of public defender.

Finally, Swanson's name was called. I sat in the courtroom, even though my business was over, to see what would happen. I had a deal with the clerk. I would always give the clerk the list of my clients, and he would, agreeably, call them first.

But I decided I would wait to see what happened to Emil. I was always queasy when I saw a person with some possible defenses go up "naked" before the arraigning judge.

The Court went through the standard questions with Mr. Swanson. "Do you understand what you are charged with?"

"Yes, your Honor."

"Do you have a lawyer?"

"No, sir."

"Would you like a lawyer?"

"No, your Honor. I don't need one."

"If you can't afford a lawyer, one will be provided for you free of charge. I see Mr. Magnuson is in the courtroom, and he would be happy to represent you."

"No, your Honor. Mr. Magnuson has talked with me already. I don't need him or any other lawyer."

"I can give you a week continuance to see if you could retain your own counsel," the judge said.

"No, your Honor. I am ready to plead today."

The judge had more than done his duty. It was time to arraign the defendant. "Emil Swanson, you have been charged with taking three packages of sandwich meat from the Red Owl on 18th and Nicollet on July 17. How do you plead?"

"Guilty as charged."

The judge was a bit stunned with the forthrightness of the defendant. "Mr. Swanson, you can plead guilty with an explanation, if you'd like."

"No, your Honor, just let it show that I pled guilty as charged."

The judge by now was getting curious. He had the clerk bring him the bail evaluation report. It showed that Mr. Swanson had been employed for 15 years before being laid off. His wife did not work. He had three children. He had no prior record. His shoplifting was limited to three packages of sandwich meat. If the defendant did not give an explanation, the judge would try to find one for him.

"Mr. Swanson, it looks as though you've had some hard times lately. Is that right?"

"Yes, your Honor, but I'm not going to make any excuses."

"Well, I appreciate that, Mr. Swanson, but were you stealing this meat to feed your family?"

The defendant's eyes moistened. His eyes fastened to the floor. He took two deep sighs. He cleared his throat.

"Judge, I could give you a lot of excuses for what I did. Some of them might sound pretty good. But the truth is, I did wrong. I knew better. I committed a crime, and I knew what I was doing. It was dead wrong. And you should throw the book at me. I just don't know what to say. I've been in agony over how I could do something this wrong. But I don't deserve any special treatment, Judge. Just give me the maximum."

The judge was uncharacteristically speechless. Now a simple arraignment had turned into high drama in the courtroom. Clerk, court reporter, other defendants, lawyers, and spectators were all watching this man be transformed from just another misdemeanant into something of a guide on a moral odyssey.

After what seemed like a half hour, but was more probably only 30 seconds, the judge said, "And so you have nothing more to say, Mr. Swanson?"

"No, your Honor." Mr. Swanson took out his handkerchief and blew his nose.

Another pause. The judge said, "Mr. Swanson, I can't find it in my heart to sentence you. I'm going to continue this case for 12 months. Your plea is withdrawn and vacated. If there is no repeat of this behavior in the next 12 months, the charge will be dismissed, and you'll have a clean record. If there is any repeat offense, you will be tried for both this offense and the new one. Do you understand?"

"Yes, thank you, your Honor."

The judge thanked Mr. Swanson for his forthrightness and called a recess as the defendant left the courtroom. It was clear to me that Mr. Swanson was right. He had *not* needed my services. He had done much better for himself than I could have done for him.

There were to be many more Billy Smiths in my future as public defender. But no more Emil Swansons.

The contrast stuck with me, as a confirmation of an old maxim. "He who humbleth himself shall be exalted, and he that exalteth himself, shall be abased." There is a time for fighting until the last dog is hung. There is also a time for abject confession, without blame, without excuses.

Many people when accused of anything choose to hunker down. Defend. Dig a trench, entrench oneself in it, and assume a defensive posture. But there are times when confession can be good not only for the soul, but also for the body.

For many years, the IRS had a written policy. If anyone turned him or herself in for tax fraud, regardless of how grievous the fraud may have been, the IRS would not criminally prosecute the person unless, of course, it had already been on the trail. The person would still be subject to civil proceedings and steep civil penalties, but there would be no criminal prosecution if a person came forward and forthrightly confessed.

Since 1972, that formal regulation no longer exists. But there does appear to be an informal policy that still remains the general rule. Many practitioners report success by bringing clients with serious tax fraud to the government. IRS representatives will sometimes give tacit approval in advance to "going civil" with an investigation. The IRS is reluctant to prosecute criminally anyone who has come forward voluntarily.

Once the special agents of the IRS do catch the scent, however, and the books are opened, it will not be long before the book is thrown. A public indictment follows. The IRS loves to defer indictments until February or March and then announce them publicly by press release in early April, to keep taxpayers focused on being honest with their returns. A reputation is destroyed. And one quickly finds the worst of both worlds: enormous restitution with penalties plus jail time. Honesty would have been a better policy.

The policy applies to other agencies as well. In one case, a company distributed parts used in a particular vehicle. The vehicle could be configured for civil or for military applications. The parts were initially sent to Canada. The liberal trade agreement that existed between the two countries made the paperwork for such shipments simple and uncomplicated. The parts could be dispatched from Canada to anywhere in the world.

Alas for the company, one of the many places was Libya. Another was Iran. Between Moammar and the Ayatollah, the company had a corner on the Defense Department's Most Wanted list.

A review of corporate records was not heartening. Some of the shipments were made without a valid export license. Certain Libyan officials had made implicit threats to company representatives not to discontinue parts shipments. How could this have happened?

Some interviews with employees finally revealed the truth. There had been an internal company cover-up. One of the employees had written a memo outlining the problem. He copied three different supervisors. The memo, much of which was typed in capital letters, with boldfaced exclamation points, accused the company of committing federal crimes. It attached copies of the relevant regulations. It was enough, in and of itself, to indict—and probably convict—the company of criminal behavior.

Top management of the company, of course, knew nothing of it— nothing of the memo, nothing of the sales. But when they saw what had been going on, they were both horrified and perplexed. After concluding my investigation, I recommended going to the government and telling all. The company was willing but wanted to understand the risks.

The risks were, of course, staggering. Giving the government these facts could result in criminal liability for the company and several of its midlevel managers, as well as a host of lesser employees. Some of them would likely go to prison. The company could pay an enormous fine. Even more threatening from the company's point of view was the possibility of a debarment. The company's lifeblood was exports. If the company were indicted as a result of the evidence it gave the government, the company would likely be suspended immediately from getting any further government contracts pending final resolution of the criminal charges and might have its export privileges suspended during the same period. If convicted, the company could be debarred from government contracts for up to three years and have its export privileges denied. The decision to turn itself in was, quite literally, a "bet the company" move.

On the one hand, the government might never discover the fraud. However thin the ice was, one might be able to skate over it. On the other hand, if the government did discover the fraud, and the cover-up, and the conscious decision to do nothing about it, the worst consequences would be almost certain to occur.

After lengthy discussions with key directors and top management, the company decided to do what it wanted to do all along: the "right thing."

With fear and trepidation, I and another lawyer walked into the lion's den. There sat a top agency official, well known in government circles for his experience and toughness. The confession began. The documents were laid out. The curative policies the company had put in place were described.

The official seemed to want to downplay the disclosures.

"I can understand how such mistakes occur."

The other lawyer cleared his throat. "We appreciate your inclination toward mercy. But unfortunately it was not, as we mentioned, simply a mistake. These items were knowingly sent out of the country without licenses. The management of the company is horrified, but we don't for one minute want to mislead you that it is less serious than it is. It is very serious, and that's why we came to you with it."

Another official was summoned. The record was reviewed and ultimately a decision rendered. "Put all of this into a letter for our files. Include what you have done to fix the problem. And I think that should be adequate."

"Adequate? Did he say adequate?" There was a great sense of relief.

As we walked to the door, the white-haired official smiled, "Go and sin no more."

The clients were, of course, jubilant. One reason was the remarkable result. At a minimum, it saved the company a million dollars and a million distractions. But another reason was just as important. The company had done the right thing and it had been rewarded.

The letter to the government confessed all, in excruciating detail. The company then worked out with government agencies a general licensing procedure that saved the company thousands of dollars and made worldwide shipments virtually as easy and efficient as local shipments. There was no fine, and no criminal or civil penalty.

There followed several other cases, with several different agencies. In each case, forthright admissions led to astonishing results. One other case is noteworthy.

A major American company was under attack by rapacious takeover artists. The wrestling match between raider and target groaned its expensive way onward as each grappled for leverage. But meanwhile, unknown to the raiders, the company had a serious problem.

One of its key managers, unbeknown to any higher-ups, had been systematically violating a regulation of a government agency. The violation was harmless to the public, and perhaps even made the product better, but it was a competitive violation which saved the company money at the expense of noncompliance with federal regulations. The last thing the company needed during the takeover effort was a criminal indictment. Such evidence of management criminality, or at least management incompetence, could have tipped the balance against the company.

And the government had the scent. The product had been "tagged" by the relevant inspector. The investigation was already ongoing. The howling hounds could be heard in the distance. While they edged closer, an internal investigation was discovering the truth: the violations were systematic and done deliberately to deceive the government. Documents had been mutilated or destroyed altogether. Low-level employees had been intimidated. Agents of the government had been lied to.

An approach to the government under these circumstances was obviously risky. But again management took a brave course. The disclosures were made. In fact, the government was approached as a friend, to see how it could help the company in ferreting out such misconduct in the future.

Two remarkable things happened. There was no prosecution, nothing but a letter of reprimand. The second was even more remarkable. The company was allowed to give the tagged merchandise to charity, getting both a charitable deduction and a public commendation by the government for doing so. And the raider was successfully resisted. The humble were again exalted.

This is not to say, to be sure, that confession always—or even usually—avoids serious penalties for serious wrongs. But it is to say that the government usually reacts well to those who make voluntarily disclosures of misconduct.

Part of the reason for this is in the regulations themselves. Most agencies have a provision for voluntary disclosures. The view of Customs, for example, limits fines and sanctions to those who make a *voluntary disclosure*. Debarment officials consider very carefully how forthright the company has been in admitting its wrongdoing. The Defense Department guidelines also make clear how important it is to government debarment decisions that the contractor had shown the responsibility to confess the wrong, express remorse, and own up to the resulting consequences.

The simple fact is that most wrongdoing goes unprosecuted unless someone reports it to the government. And when there is a genuine case of self-reporting, it is only fair to give the reporter a break. This is why confession has such special significance for debarment.

The purpose of the debarment regulations is to establish whether a corporation is "responsible" in its dealings. The government does not want to deal with, or award benefits to, someone who is not responsible in complying with the laws and regulations of the government. In the case of admitted wrongdoing, how does one establish "present responsibility"? Whether for children or for corporations, the answer is the same. Does the party know that what it did was wrong? Does it admit the wrongdoing? Did it admit the wrongdoing before the conduct was known to the government? Has the party made restitution and put in place measures to ensure the misconduct will not be repeated?

The reason why the preemptive strike is often profitable does not lie simply in the letter of the law. In the dynamics of human interaction, the spirit of the law is sometimes more important. And it is hard to say no to a true penitent.

Whether it is Judge Riley, shocked at the unwillingness of the defendant to agree with the court-provided excuse; the agency head, unable to convince the lawyers in front of him that the offense was not as serious as he wishes it to be; or, for that matter, the mother, confronted with the teary-eyed child who resolutely refuses to make excuses for misconduct or to blame siblings—repentance clears the way for mercy.

Ultimately, it is a further amplification of the parable. The Emil Swansons of the world cast their eyes to the ground and implore mercy. And they often go away from the bar of justice "justified."

10
The Grand Jury

An Invitation from Torquemada

During the Inquisition in Spain, some citizens were invited to Segovia, the home of the lonely compound of a prestigious local leader named Torquemada. There they would be asked some questions about their activities and beliefs.

Torquemada, appointed Grand Inquisitor in 1492, had his own ways of inducing cooperation. Few made the trip to this prefect's house voluntarily. Most had the attitude of a person tarred, feathered, and sent out of town on a rail, "Were it not for the honor, I would rather walk."

Inducements have changed, but invitations persist. Imagine for a moment that you have been accused of wrongdoing. The wrongdoing is serious enough that if proved, you would lose your freedom, your reputation, your job, your civil rights, even your hobby—if you like to hunt.

You feel a bit frustrated about your inability to put your side of the story across. The investigation is going forward without you. You have something to say, but cannot say it.

Suddenly, the invitation (on the next page) arrives.

You will be permitted to give your story to a group of some two dozen citizens. The questions will probably be broad enough for you to make clear what you did and why you did it.

But in looking over the invitation more closely, you see there are some special features to the party. You will not be allowed to have a lawyer in the room with you when you give your story. No trusted advisor will be there at your side to counsel you, to make sure you understand

119

January 18, 1992

Ms./Mr. Jane/John Doe
c/o Lawyer's Name, Esq.
Lawyer's Address
City, State ZIP Code

Dear Ms./Mr. Doe:

This letter is to advise you that you are now one of the subjects of a federal grand jury investigation in this District into contract fraud, and other matters, in possible violation of federal criminal law.

The grand jury has asked me to extend to you an invitation before the grand jury at 2:30 p.m., February 3, 1992, to testify about the matters that are now under investigation. The grand jury has also requested documents described in the attachment to this letter. You or your authorized representative may deliver those documents to the grand jury at 2:30 p.m. on February 3, 1992, or if you wish, you may have those documents delivered to the office of the United States Attorney, as agent for the grand jury.

You must understand that a decision by you to testify and/or to produce the documents requested will be a completely voluntary decision by you and that your testimony and documents could be used against you if any criminal charges should be returned against you.

I would appreciate it if you would ask your attorney to notify me in writing by Friday, January 24, 1992, as to whether or not you will accept the grand jury's invitation to testify and produce the requested documents. If your attorney has not contacted this office by that date, I will assume that you plan to testify.

Very truly yours,

John Smith
United States Attorney

_____

Harry Hanson
Assistant U.S. Attorney

Attachment

the questions and the possible significance of your proposed responses. No lawyer will rise to interpose any objections to the questions you are asked. In the entire party room, there will be no one on your side except you.

The ability to make objections by counsel may seem less important anyway, because there will be no judge in the room. No one will control the prosecutor's questions to make sure they are fair or appropriate. There will be no magistrate to protect you, the witness. In short, there will be no one in the room who can serve as a neutral referee between you and the prosecutor.

Another feature of the proceeding is that you may be asked questions from documents you have not seen or reviewed prior to your testimony, documents the prosecutor has been able to compile through grand jury subpoenas, search warrants, or informants. The prosecutor may ask you if you ever saw a document on some subject of inquiry. You search your memory bank and say no. Meanwhile, the prosecutor has the document at hand. On it, you are shown as a recipient. Satisfied that you have been tripped up, the prosecutor slips it back into his or her folder unseen by you, without giving you a chance to refresh your recollection.

The prosecutor has fully studied the case with government investigators and agents. The other people in the party room also know something about the case, as they heard from other witnesses, looked at documents you have not seen, and know what the prosecutor thinks you did. But you have no access to what those other witnesses said and cannot clarify any apparent contradictions between your story and theirs.

In addition, your fellow citizens are by now well known to the prosecutor. The prosecutor has shared large amounts of coffee and chatter with them over several weeks. They've talked about the weather and baseball or some other sport of the season. The prosecutor has discussed a number of different cases with them and has earned their trust. You, of course, don't know any of them, nor will you or any representative have an opportunity to hear what the prosecutor says about you out of your presence. And, indeed, after your appearance, you will not be able to make any arguments as to why you should be allowed to go on with your life, nor will you be able to rebut what the prosecutor says about you when he or she seeks your indictment.

Finally, anything you do say can be used against you. A court reporter will take down every word you say. Because you are answering questions, you will be speaking extemporaneously, answering unrehearsed questions about events and documents and meetings that might span a decade. If any of your answers are inaccurate as to anything the government believes is a material fact, you may well be prosecuted for perjury. And, if in the course of lengthy testimony you give two answers that appear to conflict to the point of contradiction, the government can prosecute you for false statements before this group—even though it can't prove which of the two conflicting stories is false.

Now, supposing you receive this kind invitation, how do you RSVP?

Such is the question faced by many citizens who receive subpoenas to testify before a grand jury. If the subpoena is directed to you as a custodian of bank records to help document fraud on the part of one of your customers, the decision is easy. If there has been a bank robbery, and you happen to have seen the robber speed away from the scene in a getaway car, your public spiritedness will lead you to comply cheerfully. But when the subpoena relates to questionable conduct in which you were involved, whether or not you feel that you actually may have done anything wrong, the decision is far more complicated.

The Theory of the Grand Jury

Most people, if pressed to recall their civics lessons from tenth grade social studies, could come up with some elements of the myth of the grand jury. They would perhaps identify it as one of the coveted freedoms won at Runnymede from King John, or as another of those English traditions brought over to this country, a legacy of constitutional protections that a free government ought to give its citizens. The theory is decent. When one is charged with serious crimes, one ought not to depend on the happenstance of who is the prosecutor pro tem. An overzealous prosecutor, acting without any significant restraints on his or her discretion, can do horrible wrongs to the reputation and interests of citizens that cannot easily be righted, whatever the ultimate outcome of the criminal case. The prosecutor ought to be accountable to someone other than him or herself.

The grand jury, the perception runs, is this agency of accountability. It is to be the grand buffer between the accused citizen and an overreaching prosecutor. Twenty-four citizens come together in solemn assembly and examine critically the evidence produced by the prosecutor to see whether there is probable cause to believe that the accused did what the prosecutor is prepared to charge him or her with. Arms folded, looking to all the world like Missourians who need to be shown, they probe the evidence, prod the prosecutor, and ask tough questions. If there turns out to be probable cause that the crime has been committed, the grand jury reluctantly comes down with a bill of indictment. If the evidence does not measure up, the grand jury comes down triumphantly with a "no bill."

The grand jury, by conventional wisdom, is meant to be an endorsement of the oft-quoted maxim of Lord Acton, the British political philosopher. Lord Acton warned, "Power corrupts. Absolute power corrupts absolutely." The prosecutor who would like to bring down criminal threatenings on a personal enemy or a political opponent, a scorned minority or an unpopular renegade, is checked and balanced by a grand jury. That jury is to be as important a protector of the defendant's rights as the *petit jury* of twelve peers who will hear the defendant's case if it ever goes to trial for an ultimate finding of guilt or innocence.

Such, at least, is the theory. In fact, grand juries are a convenience to the prosecutor. The misty mythological underpinnings of the system serve merely as a convenient rationale for its continued existence. The reason for this is apparent. The modern grand jury is a vehicle for the prosecutor to discover the facts by subpoena power prior to going to trial.

While the Supreme Court itself has in many decisions helped articulate and reinforce the grand myth of the grand jury as the "protector of citizens against arbitrary and oppressive governmental action," the reality of the grand jury's origins are less sanguine. Created to consolidate royal power in the face of competing baronial and ecclesiastical court systems, the grand jury was from the outset a thoroughly accusatory body. Indeed, in early days service on the grand jury was fraught with risks of its own: failure to accuse a criminal known to have transgressed the law subjected the grand jurors to substantial fines and penalties. If the grand jury carried out its mandate and found probable cause, the defendant went from the frying pan to the fire—sometimes quite literally. Once indicted, the defendant was brought before the King's Court for trail by ordeal.

From these medieval origins in England's Assize of Clarendon, the lore of the grand jury as a staunch defender of individual rights, however belied by its reality, grew ever larger—sometimes bolstered by an occasional grand refusal to carry out the sovereign's wishes (like the grand jury's heroic defiance of King Charles II when he wanted to indict the Earl of Shaftesbury and the Earl's friend, Colledge, for their Protestant convictions), sometimes ballyhooed by judicial pronouncements like this:

> By refusing to indict, the grand jury has the unchallengeable power to defend the innocent from government oppression by unjust prosecution. And it has the equally unchallengeable power to shield the guilty, should the whims of the jurors or their conscious or subconscious response to community pressures induce twelve or more jurors to give sanctuary to the guilty.[1]

---

[1] *United States v. Cox*, 342 F.2d 167, 189-90 (5th Cir.) (Wisdom, J., concurring specially), *cert. denied sub nom. Cox v. Hauberg*, 381 U.S. 935 (1965).

The Reality of the Grand Jury

That lore, while it continues to live on in cases in which courts affirm the importance of the grand jury and its historic protection of the unpopular individual, continues to run head on into reality. That reality was expressed in the Wickersham report, the result of a task force (the Wickersham Commission) appointed by President Hoover. Wickersham, a former Attorney General, wrote in his report:

> As the surveys are efficiency studies of criminal justice, they naturally devote more or less attention to this subject, and where this attention is devoted, the conclusion seems always to be arrived at, that *under modern conditions the grand jury is seldom better than a rubber stamp of the prosecuting attorney* and has ceased to perform or be needed for the function for which it was established and for which it was retained throughout the centuries; that, consequently compulsory grand jury hearing throws an unnecessary work burden upon the administration of justice, which burden should be lightened by eliminating the necessity of indictment and permitting prosecution to be instituted and accusation to be made through the simpler processes of information.[2]

After significant study of the subject, Wickersham noted with classic understatement, "It must be a very weak case which cannot be presented so as to procure an indictment."[3]

The grand jury is no obstacle to the prosecution. Its members routinely do whatever the prosecutor asks them to do. Although there is the occasional "runaway" grand jury that refuses to indict, such grand juries are few and far between. So loyal are they to the prosecutors who spoon-feed them the facts that one experiment showed that a grand jury would indict someone whose name had never been mentioned before them either in documents or by oral testimony—simply because the prosecutor asked them to.

The structural bias of the grand jury is nowhere more clear than in the role of the prosecutor. The prosecutor is an advocate, seeking to persuade the grand jury by showing probable cause that a crime has been committed. The prosecutor is also, however, the principal legal adviser to the grand jury, answering the grand jury's legal questions and providing guidance at every step of their deliberations.

But the reality underlying the Wickersham Report, that grand juries

---

[2]National Commission on Law Observance and Enforcement, *Report on Prosecution*, 124–25 (1931) (emphasis added).

[3]Ibid., at 36.

are virtually never an impediment to a prosecutor, no matter how weak the case, is only half the story. The other side of the story is that the grand jury *is* a significant help to the government.

This has given rise to a political paradox. When there are suggestions that it be abolished, the prosecutors rise up with one voice to speak in behalf of saving this venerable "defender of defendant's rights," while the defense bar calls for its abolition. How so?

In civil cases, both sides may do factual discovery prior to trial through formal processes designed for this purpose. They can require the adversary to disclose documents; they can seek answers to written *interrogatories* that explore the contentions of the other side and the facts supporting them; they can notice *oral depositions* under oath of both neutral witnesses and adverse witnesses. The transcripts of these civil interrogations are an important source of information that can be used later at trial to avoid the "trial by ambush" of yesteryear. At all depositions, of course, both sides are represented by counsel. If a question is inappropriate, the counsel can object. If a dispute over an objection cannot be resolved, a judge will ultimately determine whether the question need be answered or not. Despite complaints about the expense of oral and written discovery in civil litigation, most lawyers and clients recognize the importance of discovery of information to a fair and efficient trial on the merits. Failure to comply with legitimate requests for discovery will often lead to the imposition of sanctions by the court up to and including dismissal.

In criminal proceedings, this discovery is a one-way street. Prosecutors are allowed to conduct all the discovery they like. Using the grand jury subpoena power, the prosecutor can bring anyone before the grand jury at any time. The prosecutor can ask him or her any question without worrying about a lawyer being in the room (one is generally sitting nervously, and ignorantly, outside the grand jury room on a hardwood bench). When the transcripts are prepared, the prosecutor alone has access to them. The prosecutor will supply to the adversary transcripts of the relevant witness testimony (Jencks Act material) intended to be used at trial a day or (if generous) a weekend before the trial starts. Prosecutors are obligated to turn over portions of the transcript which contain *exculpatory* information (*Brady* material)—prosecutors seldom find any—but otherwise they need only hand over relevant portions related to actual testimony to be taken, and that at the last minute. The defense has no right to know which witnesses were called nor the substance of their testimony before the grand jury. At best, the defense can seek to find them and "debrief" them orally immediately after their appearance—if the witnesses consent.

When the indictment is finally returned, the prosecutor has volumes of testimony neatly digested and organized, hundreds or thousands of documents in neat piles, and dozens of exhibits already marked and ready for trial. If the interrogation has been done well, the witnesses are pinned down so tightly there will be no "wiggle room" later. So fortified by the cooperation of the grand jury, the prosecutor is prepared to rise at the defendant's first appearance and insist the defendant be given his or her constitutional right to a "speedy trial"—suggesting there is no need to extend the 70-day period from indictment to trial laid down for criminal cases by federal statute.

Again, it is the defense that argues for the court to abridge a "sacred right" of the defendant and give the defense some time to figure out what the case is all about. As with the debate over the grand jury, the prosecutors fight valiantly to preserve this bulwark of civil liberties.

Torquemada's Inducements

Given these realities, why do so many accept the invitation to appear before a grand jury? There is a short answer: fear. If one claims a Fifth Amendment privilege against self-incrimination and refuses to testify, one may appear to be guilty of the crime charged. Prosecutors will hint darkly that "dogs bite people who run from them." And while hard-bitten, hardscrabble hoodlums could not care less what prosecutors or grand jurors think of them, business executives or middle-class professionals have a hard time believing that a prosecutor will not hold it against them if they refuse to testify.

The fear may be even more aggravated. The person may be in such a sensitive position that an indictment is tantamount to a conviction. If the person is a politician or public official, or perhaps a person in a position of trust in a regulated profession, a preacher, an accountant, or local community leader, the fact of the indictment itself may so destroy a career as to make any subsequent conviction, if it comes, something of an anticlimax. In such cases, with an indictment imminent, why not take the risk? Go before one's fellow citizens and try to make the big sale.

Alas, many do—only later to conclude that they should have listened to their lawyers.

There is an old fable from Aesop that has a fox inviting a chicken into his den. When the chicken expresses skepticism, the fox points out that many other chickens have accepted the invitation. He points to the ground around his den that shows dozens of chicken prints. The chicken wisely considers the argument for a moment but then becomes troubled by one observation. There are many chicken prints going into the den, but none coming out.

Ray Donovan is a good example. The former Secretary of Labor in the Reagan administration was besieged by allegations of pay-offs and other corruption related to activities of his construction company in New Jersey, allegations he vigorously denied. A grand jury began to consider allegations against him. Donovan resigned his post at the Labor Department and went back to New Jersey to confront the charges. He decided to testify before the grand jury investigating him. Notwithstanding his testimony (one might say "because of his testimony"), he was indicted on multiple counts. He was not indicted for any conduct relating to the charge he initially went into the grand jury to defend himself against. He was charged with lying to the grand jury. Although he was ultimately acquitted and exonerated of any wrongdoing, it became apparent that while the government did not feel it had adequate information to indict him on the underlying wrong, it could and did indict him for alleged inconsistencies in his grand jury testimony.

Some Reasons for Caution

A few years ago, I represented a number of executives of a major defense contractor. The company had participated in the development of two sophisticated guidance systems for some of the increasingly "smart" weapons of destruction in the U.S. arsenal. Each project was governed by its own contract agreement. Under one contract a proportion of costs expended by the contractor in the program could be repaid to it if certain conditions were complied with. The company could thus get reimbursed for certain kinds of expenditures that might otherwise be lost to it. The other contract had no such reimbursement feature. The government claimed that engineers who were working on both projects charged their time to the one project that might get the company reimbursement, even though they were working on the other project, for an obvious financial motive: so that the company could collect money it was not otherwise entitled to.

The government said it was a simple as temptation and sin. The company had encouraged the falsification of time cards. It had given an implicit message: write down the time we will get paid for, regardless of what you really did.

The company claimed, on the other hand, that it was much more complicated than that. These engineers were "dedicated" to the incentive-based project by explicit agreement. Their "dedication" meant that they would always work on it first. They were obligated to drop anything else they were doing, when necessary, to dedicate themselves to problems in that program. But sometimes the phone did not ring. There were no inquiries. What should they do during these down hours?

Rather than do nothing and rely on their dedication, it was decided the team should be kept together to work on other programs at the company. Notwithstanding this other work, they remained ready to put it aside at a moment's notice when an inquiry came in about the first project.

That led to the question of how to account for the hours they were so occupied. How should they allocate the hours from their 50–60-hour weeks on 40-hour time sheets? Because there were only eight hours to be accounted for on the time sheets, and many of the employees worked 10 to 16 hours a day, the engineers would generally write down on the time sheets first those hours related to the program to which they were dedicated.

Keeping these employees made good management sense. It had the salutary effect of keeping together a committed core of collegial employees on a new project, rather than having them lose interest and, perhaps bored by lack of any new challenge, disperse to other programs or other companies. But the government saw nothing but a conspiracy to defraud.

After some negotiation, I was able to win immunity for my clients. That protection, conferred by an order signed by a federal judge in Washington, D.C., provided them what is called *use immunity.* In connection with ordering their testimony before the grand jury, use immunity means that the government can make no use of the testimony it hears before the grand jury in any subsequent criminal proceeding against that witness. While technically the government could continue to prosecute, since use immunity is not *transactional immunity* (which immunizes a witness from any prosecution for the entire transaction, regardless of the source of the government's testimony), it is a long-time practice of the Justice Department not to prosecute those who are given use immunity. There are, to be sure, rare exceptions such as the case of Oliver North, who was prosecuted notwithstanding his immunized testimony before the Congress. But such defendants, if later convicted, often—like North—see their conviction reversed. These executives, having been given immunity, were thus safe, or were they?

When they appeared to testify, I asked for a copy of the order signed by the judge. The prosecutor from the Washington task force provided me the whole file. The order was there, signed, appropriately enough, by the federal judge.

But attached to it was an internal Justice Department memorandum, and attached to it was a questionnaire to be filled in by the prosecutor after my witness's testimony. The questionnaire went something like this:

Question No. 1: Was the grant of immunity worthwhile in the light of the witness's testimony?

Question No. 2: What points were established by the witness's testimony that you would not have been able to establish without the immunity order?

Question No. 3: Did the witness testify inaccurately or falsely as to any question?

All of these questions had very few lines of space available for the prosecutor's answers. Then came the next question, that provided a quarter of a page for the prosecutor's response. It went something like this.

Question No. 4: If the answer to question no. 3 is yes and you believe the answer was untrue, state whether or not you have authorized the commencement of a perjury prosecution against the witness, and if not, state why not, in detail.

I eventually returned the file to the prosecutor and the testimony proceeded. The witnesses were then summoned, one by one, into the grand jury room. I was, of course, forced to remain outside. While some 15 states now permit lawyers to accompany their witnesses into the grand jury room, no federal courts do. These witnesses, however, at my direction came out to me after nearly every question. Stepping out of the grand jury after every question to consult with a lawyer has been repeatedly ratified by courts as an appropriate, albeit cumbersome, way to protect the defendant's rights. But the prosecutor exploded like an MX warhead. He accused the witness and me of "obstructing" the grand jury investigation. I pointed out that the proceeding would be somewhat lengthy, but the testimony would also be more accurate and reliable when the answers were given after reflection.

The prosecutor called off further proceedings abruptly, sent the grand jury into recess and on to a coffee break, and went up to see the chief judge in the district. He recounted his tale of woe. "Your Honor, these guys are fully immunized, have nothing to worry about in terms of any prosecution, and yet they're obstructing the grand jury process by coming out after every substantive question. Your Honor, I want you to order this to be stopped."

The judge seemed a bit troubled himself. He asked me what the witnesses had to worry about.

The foreman of the grand jury, a former mayor, university professor, and political friend of the judge, stepped in momentarily to say amen to the prosecutor's arguments.

I replied, "Your Honor, the questions asked concern several years of work and hundreds of time sheets. These witnesses want to make sure their answers are absolutely accurate. And to say that they are safe and secure is not quite accurate, your Honor."

I then gave the Court a copy of the page asking the prosecutor to justify at length why the witness was not to be prosecuted for perjury if any statement was inaccurate.

The judge reviewed it, then scanned a few of the cases I provided him from various circuits which acknowledged the appropriateness of the practice. But he still was not amused. He looked at me wryly. "You know I can find a way to stop you." He cleared his throat. "Mr. Prosecutor," he said, "it looks like Mr. Magnuson has got us on the law, but have you considered seeking to remove him for conflicts for representing more than one witness? The Court would entertain such a motion." The prosecutor said he would think about it, and the process continued.

The case was ultimately settled. No individuals were indicted. Indeed, the judge initially refused to approve the ultimate agreement, thinking it was too sweet for the company. He lectured the government lawyers, made a colorful speech to the press, called for additional justification for the "bargain," asked the prosecutor sarcastically if he knew what side of the table was the "government side," and called for the Justice Department to disclose what part my "tactics" had played in their "caving in."

When he finally did approve the deal, he apparently still believed—notwithstanding government denials—that the case settled without the necessity of pleas from any individuals, due in part to my purportedly obstructive tactics. The legal press was later to report how the government "shot blanks at the company" and speculated why. But my interests were not so grandiose or strategic. I knew from the government's own memo that the grand jury is a dangerous place even for—one might say especially for—the innocent.

The Bamboo Splints, Please

Experienced prosecutors know how to use their leverage. In the late 1970s, a special prosecutor was appointed to look into allegations regarding the Jimmy Carter 1976 presidential primary campaign. Rumors had circulated that the Carter campaign had mysteriously come up with funds at a critical moment. Going into the crucial Pennsylvania primary, the Carter momentum had been arrested. Early polls showing a Carter victory now showed a narrow defeat. The campaign seemed stalled for lack of money.

Suddenly, a large infusion of cash jump-started a Pennsylvania media blitz. Carter narrowly won the primary after these Rafshoon-designed ads detonated on the populace, gained enough momentum to win the nomination, and finally won the presidency itself. Where had this money come from?

Rumor had it that an NSF check from Billy Carter to a peanut warehouse had been honored by Bert Lance's bank, and that Bert had kept the check in his upper left desk drawer until the new president's campaign organization could get enough money to pay off old debts.

I represented a company whose employees were called as witnesses in the investigation. Most of them were "good ol' boys" from the south. Although they had been granted immunity, their testimony was not as helpful before the grand jury as the prosecutor may have anticipated. In the middle of an interrogation, while I sat patiently outside, the prosecutor burst out of the grand jury room with dramatic effect, trailed by my ashen client.

"You tell your client to start telling the truth or I'm going to indict him for perjury! I know he knows things he's not telling. You have a heart-to-heart talk with him and explain the consequences of perjury in the grand jury room. He's about to blow his immunity."

The good ol' boy was physically trembling. He was telling the truth, he insisted. Should he make something up? His heart was racing. He was dizzy. Even his red neck looked gray. He asked me if he could be excused to go to the doctor. Finally, he put his head on the desk and went silent.

The prosecutor's bluff did not work. The witness really did not know anymore. But the terror was real.

The prosecutor ultimately concluded there was insufficient evidence to indict. And no perjury proceedings were initiated. But if the witness could have concocted something incriminating, he would have been tempted to do so.

Who's Who in the Grand Jury Room

A person who comes before a grand jury generally fits in one of three categories. The witness may be simply a *witness*, being called to produce evidence related to somebody else's wrongdoing. While some of the wrongdoing may be known to the witness, there is no indication that the witness may be liable for it.

The second category is *subject*. The subject of an investigation is someone whom the prosecutor suspects may have been involved in the wrongdoing. No decision has been made about ultimate culpability, but questions are being asked about the person's role, and the subject could quite easily become indicted.

A *target* of the investigation is directly within the cross hairs. In prosecutor speech, being a target means that you will be indicted, absent some *deus ex machina* or other miraculous intervention. Targets are not generally subpoenaed before the grand jury but may be provided a *target letter.* In a target letter, targets are told that indictment may be imminent, but that they may choose to appear before the grand jury within a certain time to given an explanation for their behavior. The hope is that the target will come in and try to talk the grand jury out of the action it will otherwise take.

The two key terms of art—subject and target—are given a definition in the *Department of Justice Manual.* A subject is a person "whose conduct is within the scope of the grand jury's investigation." A target is a person "to whom the prosecutor or the grand jury has substantial evidence linking him/her to the commission of the crime and who, in the judgment of the prosecutor is a putative defendant." These definitions from the *Manual* are hardly models of precision. Some prosecutors call putative targets *subjects,* giving prosecutors the right to change their mind. For others, calling someone a *subject* is tantamount to guaranteeing indictment.

Whether one is called a subject or a target, one should expect indictment. The difference is in emphasis. For the target, indictment is only slightly less certain than death or taxes, and the subject has a special "privilege." Like an Oxford undergraduate, a target is "invited" to appear, not commanded to do so. The Department of Justice wants to avoid "the appearance of unfairness" (and lingering memories of the Star Chamber, that horror chamber of interrogation in medieval Britain) that is created when someone certain to be indicted is required to testify at a "command performance."

Although this threefold division gives some modest help to the witnesses and their lawyer in quantifying their risk, it is by no means a guarantee. The categories are ratchets. What Keynes said of wages is true of a prosecutor's categorizations: they are "sticky downwards." Witnesses can move quickly into subject or target status by giving a wrong answer. Subjects may readily become (or already be) targets. But the inverse slide from target or subject to witness is rare.

Some Suggestions

For the above reasons, a cautious approach to the grand jury is indicated, regardless of the nomenclature.

1. *If one is a witness but is related to the transaction the government believes is criminal, it makes sense to refuse to testify without immunity.* No one can be forced to testify before a grand jury without immunity. The govern-

ment can make you appear but it cannot require answers to potentially incriminating questions. If the government believes so strongly that the witness did nothing wrong and is not even the subject of the investigation, why should the government object to providing the witness immunity? It loses nothing. And an immunity forces the witness to testify upon penalty of contempt. An ingenious prosecutor may argue that granting immunity to such a witness does hurt the case because it makes the testimony unnecessarily suspect at trial. But prosecutors, of course, know how to cushion this consequence, and most criminal cases settle without trial anyway. If the concern is real, some more informal immunity may be considered—a letter of understanding or the like—which makes the agreement more plausible to the government and less suspicious to the jury. The witness, with some real assurance of protection, gains additional security and can testify more freely and with greater liberty of expression, knowing there is no personal risk.

2. *If the witness happens to be a subject or target, one should bargain for immunity if there is any reasonable chance to get it.* If there is no chance to get immunity, there is no sense in giving a *proffer* to the prosecutor. A proffer cannot be used against a witness if it is not accepted. It is to be returned in writing and buried in the sea of the prosecution's forgetfulness. But while they may be gone, proffers are not so easily forgotten. They go into the government memory bank and can come back to haunt the defense team later. If there is a realistic chance of settlement, on the other hand, and the witness has information that may be helpful to the government, there is no better time to bring it up than prior to going before the grand jury. Gaining immunity normally ends the risk. The immunized witness wins.

3. *If one is representing a company, one can try for a wholesale immunity.* Frequently, the government is interested in one bad actor. In order to establish that bad actor's crimes, it must call a number of people who perhaps unknowingly facilitated the crime within the organization. But each one of them has some modest exposure. If all are subpoenaed, all will probably retain separate counsel. Those counsel will seek immunity. The prosecutor will have to apply to Washington, and wait a month or two, before the order returns. The approach is cumbersome and costly. Sometimes, counsel for the company, without explicitly representing all of the different individuals, can ask the prosecutor to give some assurances to each of the witnesses by means of *letter immunity*. Letter immunity is functionally equivalent to *judge immunity*. It simply does not bind other United States Attorneys throughout the country. If the U.S. Attorney is willing to give such a letter, the company can save the expense of obtaining lawyers for each witness and the months of time necessary to win immunity orders for employees who are at very slight risk. A sensi-

ble prosecutor loses nothing by finding a way to grant immunity wholesale. Such prosecutors need only be secure enough in their judgments
to know who really did it and who needs to be charged.

4. *Remember the prosecuting risk.* In fairness to prosecutors, the risks of
the immunity are not all one-sided. There is, of course, a risk to the
government in providing immunity as well. If it immunizes the wrong
person, it might find that person coming before the jury at trial and
admitting guilt, while exculpating the defendant in the dock.

For that reason, agencies like the IRS have various criteria for granting immunity. The standards serve as a caution to prosecutors against
granting immunity to a "close family relative" or other friend of the accused, who might be tempted to use the grant of immunity to do a "mea
culpa" while exculpating the friend or relative. The criteria laid out in
the *Department of Justice Manual* include the following:

a. The importance of the investigation or prosecution to effective
enforcement of the criminal law;

b. The value of the person's testimony or information to the investigation or prosecution;

c. The likelihood of prompt and full compliance with a compulsion order, and the effectiveness of available sanctions if there is no
such compliance;

d. The person's relative culpability in connection with the offense
or offenses being investigated or prosecuted, and his/her history
with respect to criminal activity;

e. The possibility of successfully prosecuting the person prior to
compelling him/her to testify or produce information; and

f. The likelihood of adverse collateral consequences to the person
if he/she testifies or provides information under a compulsion
order.[4]

5. *Most of all, remember your risks.* There are also unanticipated haz-
ards for the defense in the grand jury process beyond considerations of
immunity, simply because of the arcane rules that have determined its
function. One lawyer in New York, for example, had a bright idea. He
did not want his client to go before the grand jury. In that respect, he
was a competent defense counsel.

But on the other hand, he was frustrated by his inability to get his
position before the grand jury. He thought his position was so reasonable that a grand jury might decide, in one of those rare acts of defiance, to "no bill" the prosecutor when asked for an indictment. How

---

[4]*Department of Justice Manual* 9-23.210 at 9-484 (1989—2 Supp.).

was he to inform the grand jury of the defense position without submitting a witness to the risks of the process?

He came up with a solution. He would write a carefully crafted account of what occurred for the grand jury. He would put it in a sealed envelope. He would then dictate a letter to the foreman of the grand jury, suggesting the good reasons many people shrink from coming to the grand jury given its structural unfairness to those accused of crime. But in this case, the letter would suggest, it was important for the grand jury to understand the defense position. He had drafted an account of what occurred. If the foreman thought it would be helpful for the grand jury, he could open the sealed envelope, read the report the lawyer had prepared, and share it with other members of the grand jury.

To ensure that no one thought he was doing something unethical or underhanded, the lawyer carefully copied the prosecutor and the chief judge so they could intervene if they thought the procedure was inappropriate. The lawyer was commending himself, no doubt, for the creativity of getting information before a body of citizens otherwise hermetically sealed by law into the grand jury fortress.

But any such self-congratulation was almost immediately dissipated. The prosecutor issued information charging the lawyer with the crime of *tampering* with the grand jury. Federal statues prohibit any communication with the grand jury outside of the normal grand jury process. Notwithstanding the innocence of the lawyer's motives and the openness with which he did it, he was convicted of a federal crime by the federal district court for the Southern District of New York. That conviction was later affirmed by the Second Circuit.

6. *How about the "Big Sale"?* There are, of course, exceptions to the normal rule of avoiding the grand jury. There have been stories, passed down by oral tradition and circulated around the hearth, that tell of members of Congress or other public figures bravely coming before a grand jury. They tell the grand jury that lawyers have advised them against the appearance. The potential defendant discloses why people don't come before a grand jury and concedes that several friends, advisors, and confidants have tried to obstruct the target's way to the grand jury room just that afternoon. But notwithstanding that advice, the target says, "My whole life is at stake in this room. Do not, grand jury, apply the normal rule of probable cause here but the rule of reasonable doubt." The message delivered, humbly but with conviction, is "If you indict me, you destroy me. My life is in your hands. Don't hide behind the anonymity of what you do, or talk about probabilities. I'm talking about certainties. You will destroy me if you find probable cause I have committed this crime. I have come to show you that I didn't. My life, in addition to that of my family, is with you and your discretion."

While such a pitch may work under the right circumstances, it will normally be ineffective. It will disclose secrets of the defense to the grand jury and to the prosecutor that should not have been disclosed until they are testified to at trial, with maximum advantage of surprise, and will lead to admissions on the record that will be grist for a tough cross-examination by the prosecutor later, as Mike Tyson discovered in his rape trial. "Did you not say when you were called before the grand jury, and I quote, . . . ?" Further evidence of crime, further counts in the criminal indictment, giving up the tactical advantage of silence and surprise, and providing, inevitably, a substantial amount of testimony for future impeachment argue against an appearance before the grand jury, even in cases where the indictment is tantamount to a conviction.

The fact is, if prosecutors do not have enough evidence to prosecute without your providing it, you ought not to provide it. An invitation to a hanging is one thing. An invitation to a hanging where you are to supply the neck is another. If prosecutors do not have enough evidence to make them think that they can get their conviction, their suspicions about why you are not appearing are not enough to get them to indict anyway. On the other hand, if prosecutors have enough evidence to indict you, their minds and the minds of the grand jurors are not going to be influenced by the most poignant and persuasive appeal.

No one sounds very good in self-defense, whether a seven-year-old with cookie crumbs on his or her lips, or a senior executive with a mistaken tax return. The rule is true in almost any area of negotiation or persuasion. When you are defending yourself, you are losing. And that's all people do before the grand jury: defend themselves. Everyone expects a defense. No one really expects to be persuaded. That expectation usually proves true.

A Concluding Lament

This lesson is, unfortunately, not always easy to sell to white-collar criminal defendants. They usually got to their places in life by persuading others. Each step up the corporate ladder has been a step of persuasion. The corporate executive, the member of congress, the professional, etc., are usually schooled in making presentations that sell both their product or service and themselves. It is tempting for executives to think that a grand jury is just another board of directors. They pride themselves on control of their board, their clients, or their customers, and they believe they can control a grand jury as well. A little self-deprecation, a touch of humor, a becoming sense of gravity, and a moist-eyed appeal will certainly not be lost on any group of objective spectators. If the nervous Nellies advising executives would just "let Reagan be Reagan," they would twinkle their way through the mine field without ever finding the trip wire and emerge safely on the other side.

It is thinking like this that gets many prominent people indicted. People who resist the invitation for vindication will not be thought guilty. They will be thought well-advised. Torquemada may be a charming Spaniard with fine china and a good kitchen, but you wouldn't want to come to a party organized by him (as Inquisitor pro tem) only to find that the bamboo stalks have purposes other than to provide wood flavor at the barbecue.

The best thing to do in such situations, absent a grant of immunity, is to send the kindliest of "regrets."

11
Parallel Investigations

It was classic Jack Benny—another of an almost infinite variety of variations on a single theme, all of them funny, all of them masterfully timed.

A robber confronts Jack Benny on a sidewalk in Beverly Hills. He shoves a gun in Benny's ribs and demands, "Your money or your life." There follows Benny's sidelong glance at the audience, palm pressed against his cheek, a pregnant pause, "I'm thinking, I'm thinking."

As in all good comedy, one finds a sad truth about the human condition. There is not always a good option. Sometimes there is only a least-bad option. Such is the meaning of a *Hobson's choice*.

The principle has special application to regulated companies facing a federal investigation of unknown scope. The choice may come down to your money or your life.

Once upon a time, it was easier. Everyone knew what a criminal looked like. The big ones dodged out of Kefauver or McClellan hearing rooms covering their scowls behind one of their double-breasted lapels. The little ones loitered in unsavory neighborhoods wearing their distinctive social uniforms. Neither kind regularly crossed the paths of reputable business executives—or their legal counsel. Corporations were, to be sure, occasionally accused of misconduct by fractious minority shareholders, business competitors, or government agencies. But however unpleasant these occasional altercations, they remained civil matters that were resolved, well, civilly.

No more. The reality today is that every major corporation has, lurking somewhere within its far-flung reaches, wearing various disguises, some potential "criminals": employees who cut corners thinking they are benefiting the company; low-level employees promoted to a regulatory desk at the company for which they are not really qualified; "can do," "hands on" managers who think they understand the purpose and spirit of the rules and believe the letter of the criminal laws surely cannot apply directly to them; disaffected memo writers within the company who want to protect themselves by littering the file with their own scruples and questions of conscience and by giving a conspiratorial flavor to questionable management decisions.

Once this behavior is exposed, gimlet-eyed government employees look under the sheepskin to find the wolf. If they decide the actions are worthy of investigation, they may, after the investigation, believe that the misconduct should be pursued civilly or criminally. The problem for those protecting the interests of the corporation and its executives is that the government need not elect which path to pursue—and may indeed choose to go down parallel paths essentially simultaneously and without telling those being investigated which path it has in mind.

For the regulated company, a government agency which believes the company has done something wrong has, therefore, a double-barrelled gun in its hands. It can refer the case to friendly cousins in the prosecuting office as a criminal prosecution. When the regulator sees a potential infraction of the law that may be intentional, the government can, quite literally, "make a federal case out of it." But the agency can also destroy the target with a second barrel. Regardless of whether the agents fire the criminal salvo, they can seek to prosecute the company and its officers administratively.

In some circumstances, this second option is even worse than the first. A criminal charge, with a $10,000 fine, with some modest term of imprisonment, sounds terrible enough. But the complete termination of the business may sound even worse.

Let's suppose, for example, that a small company makes a particular receptacle for the Department of Defense (DOD). Its price is lower than that of any competitor. The part has always worked. Any wrinkles with the DOD had generally been quickly ironed out.

Now it appears that one of this small business's employees had wrongfully estimated the number of hours necessary to perform a task in connection with a negotiation over price before the contract was awarded. The government auditors believe the estimate was intentionally false. Notwithstanding the fact that the government still got the best price available in the market, and perhaps the best product, it now commences the investigation.

It is normal to fear a potential criminal charge most of all. The targets of this company know this fear well. There is a litany of federal charges that can be brought: false claims, mail fraud, conspiracy, and the like. All have substantial penalties. But the second barrel may be even more lethal. Under the DOD regulations, the government can totally debar the company from doing business with the government. If it is primarily a government contractor, the business is dead. One can hardly resolve the criminal case without some knowledge of what the debarment people will do.

It is not only government contractors who have this worry. Any regulated or public company can face the same issue. The Securities and Exchange Commission (SEC), for example, requires regulated companies in the brokerage industry to maintain certain records. Disclosure of these records is mandatory. Very mandatory. Refusal to turn over information to the SEC can trigger a penalty of up to $500,000 plus five years in prison. If the document requested may reveal a separate basis for criminal charges, one cannot stand on one's constitutional rights. The mere withholding of the document will itself trigger criminal charges.

The complexities of these *parallel investigations* make a lawyer's job especially difficult and a client's understanding of what the lawyer is doing equally so. Again, the process seems counterintuitive. Why doesn't the company lawyer simply represent everybody? Why do counsel seem to multiply like vice presidents at brokerage firms? Why do lawyers spend so much time drafting "stand still" agreements when everybody ought to be on the same side? Why can't we just get together in one big meeting, disclose everything we know, and get the matter over with?

In the face of these questions, the lawyers seem almost, well, too legalistic. Their answers are often seemingly too cautious and too expensive. The business executive, used to drawing very straight lines between two points, blames the lawyers, understanding better the line of the poet, Robert Frost, "Why does the hearse horse snicker when he hauls a lawyer away?" But a lawyer seeking to represent a client in a parallel investigation, and do the client justice, faces some increasingly complex issues.

The backdrop for these issues is the murkiness of government intentions. The darkness concealing government intentions can be frightening. Penalties may be severe in any case. On the administrative side, they may include enormous civil monetary penalties, delicensing, debarment from government contracts, suspension of export privileges, any one of them so draconian that it may in some circumstances result in termination—with prejudice—of the company itself. On the criminal side, regulatory infractions, however apparently *malum prohibitum,* may be transformed by application of prosecutorial discretion into felonies, leading prominent executives to prison and personal ruin. But not knowing which barrel the government is going to fire and when complicates the lawyer's decision.

The high stakes are thus inversely related to the small amount of information available to those defending against such a parallel proceeding. What is the government really after, and how should one deal with its requests? The businessperson has questions, too. Why are there so many counsel, so many fronts of combat, so much expense? Why can't the matter be dealt with quickly?

The answers lie in the need to make careful decisions on critical questions that may have a significant impact on the corporation's future.

The first critical decision in such cases, of course, is to determine who the client is. Lawyers who regularly represent corporate clients in shareholder disputes have experienced the sometimes serious, sometimes merely tweaking, judicial probing about the identity of the lawyer's client: Whom are you *really* representing? Is it management? The Board? The controlling shareholders? All shareholders? The fictitious corporate entity's "best interests"? In parallel investigations the question of whom to represent raises especially sensitive issues, both of propriety [under the American Bar Association (ABA) Code of Professional Responsibility[1]] and prudence.

Most experienced litigators like the feeling of strategic and tactical control provided by joint representation of a corporation and members of its top management. As Justice Frankfurter remarked years ago, joint representation is a bastion of strength in the face of an actual *common attack* from without, and a potential *reciprocal recrimination* from within, the company camp.[2] It also prevents a variety of headaches: an ineptly chosen maverick counsel who frustrates an otherwise carefully balanced joint defense, a successful "divide and conquer" strategy of the government, an enormously duplicative and expensive deployment of multiple legions of counsel.

Multiple representation is sometimes possible. It is not typically improper per se. But it is risky. Government lawyers are increasingly aggressive in bringing motions to disqualify lawyers representing multiple clients. If the investigation goes criminal, representation of more than one defendant or target is essentially impossible, and prior representation of multiple parties will disqualify counsel from further representation of *any* client in the criminal proceeding. See *United States v. Agosto.*[3] Even before indictment, during the grand jury proceedings, the repre-

---

[1]§ C-5-11 through 5-20.

[2]See *Glasser v. United States,* 315 U.S. 60,62 (1942).

[3]528 F.Supp. 1300 (D.Minn. 1981) *aff'd* 625 F.2d 965 (8th Cir. 1982).

sentation of more than one target—and occasionally even more than one witness—is the frequent subject of successful motions to disqualify. See, e.g., *In Re Grand Jury Investigation.*[4] Agencies such as the SEC are attuned to the tactical advantages of dealing with multiple counsel and sometimes seek to disqualify counsel from representing both the company and individual witnesses, *In Re Merrill Lynch, Fenner & Smith, Inc.*[5]

The arguments used by the government to justify its insistence on multiple counsel can sound compelling. They have, after all, the defendant's interests at heart. Multiple representation of targets, they say, denies each of the targets effective representation of counsel under the Sixth Amendment. A broadly scaled government investigation almost always creates possibilities for individualized resolutions and thus thorny conflicts of interest. A corporate lawyer may advise individuals to take positions more in the corporate interest than in their personal interest. In negotiations of a global settlement, there are subtle nuances in the strategy of bargaining that affect each client differently. Some remedies affect one party more than another. And multiple representation, the government may suggest darkly, gives rise to possible *collusion* and *orchestration of testimony* that frustrates the government's investigative purposes.[6]

If those arguments are successful, and they usually are, the problems of defense multiply. The need for multiple representation especially (and inevitably) complicates matters for the lawyer representing the corporation. It multiplies the expense to the company, of course, but it also multiplies the difficulty in finding out the facts and in both devising a strategy and implementing it. Although it is common for potential defendants to agree to a *joint defense* strategy and to insulate shared confidential communications from waiver of attorney–client privilege and subsequent disclosure, communications never proceed as freely as when only one counsel is representing everyone.

The problem continues during more formal discovery. The SEC [via Rule 7(b)] permits witnesses to be sequestered at the discretion of the SEC during the giving of investigative testimony. It can use that power to ban lawyers seeking to represent an individual in the lawyer's corporate capacity when the individual is also represented individually by personal counsel. When clients are represented by individual counsel, therefore, corporate counsel is not allowed to participate in their investigative testimony. The lawyer representing the company may get a post mortem debriefing, but they are black and white snapshots without

[4]436 F.Supp. 818, 820 (WD Pa. 1977).

[5](1923) CCH Fed. Sec. & L. Reg. 79, 536 (1973).

[6]See, e.g., *In Re Grand Jury Proceedings*, 428 F. Supp. 273, 278 (S.D. Mich. 1976).

the color, motion, or *Sturm und Drang* of being there. And when it is time to choose some strategic option based on this discovery, even the most smoothly organized defense team still requires decision making by committee—with all its complexities and compromises.

The second critical decision is whether to offer the client, once identified, to the government for testimony. That such a decision need be made at all may seem strange to the civil litigator.

Litigators in civil practice know how to deal with the rules of discovery and the requests of regulators. They are cautious, courteous, and generally forthcoming. They know that discovery is the rule in civil litigation. They realize that an open and cooperative spirit is generally appealing to bureaucrats, whose lack of adequate remuneration is at least partially compensated for by the deference they customarily receive from private practitioners. An important objective of civil practitioners is to facilitate smooth ongoing relationship with the government.

But lawyers who have experience in criminal proceedings have a different perspective. Criminal litigators are used to standing on their constitutional prerogatives, a strategy the government prefers to call obstruction. They give nothing they do not have to, and rehearse to themselves elegant legal maxims like "If you don't talk, you walk." They know the protections of the Fifth Amendment and deploy them. To them, the enforcement regulators are simply prosecutors in embryo, and they know how to deal with them.

When litigators representing a regulated company get a preliminary request for information from the SEC, a visit from an agent of Customs, the USDA, the FDA, or a procurement fraud auditor, they have to know whether or not to go with their genteel leaf-raking civil instincts or with the pit bull approach of the criminal lawyer.

Did You Ever Have to Make Up Your Mind?

The difficulty of choosing a course of action is manifold:

1. *If the first salvo is a grand jury subpoena or a search warrant, the litigator knows this is a criminal problem.* The likely outcome, however long delayed, is an indictment of someone. The strategy is simple: protect the company and its officers. The tactics are also obvious: give no incriminating information other than that required by law. Information simply arms the adversary with your story in advance so it can be destroyed later. Or worse, voluntary testimony may be viewed as perjurious. A parade of government officials (Donovan, Deaver, et al.) have been indicted and convicted in recent years of perjury based on voluntary testi-

mony—and not charged at all for the underlying conduct they were presumably most worried about.

2. *If, on the other hand, the problem is a routine audit called for by the regulations, made by familiar government agents friendly with the company, the tactics are usually equally clear: open the files, sip coffee, be fulsome in cooperation.* If the issue is a possible broker–dealer revocation, for example, stubborn resistance is usually not sensible. Make peace quickly.

But many times the problem resists classification. Is this a secondary audit or a tax fraud that the agent is investigating? Is it an administrative slip-up or a potential conspiracy count in a criminal indictment? Is it a routine SEC inquiry or the precursor of a major prosecution referral? Is it an audit inquiry or the first step toward a major procurement fraud criminal investigation? Will the invocation of the Fifth Amendment be taken as a sign of guilt—turning a routine inquiry into a criminal prosecution—or as a sign of careful lawyering? Can a cooperative spirit so shape the inquiry that the agency will be satisfied without resorting to serious enforcement proceedings?

Moreover, the problem may have no easy solutions. The SEC requirement to maintain certain *mandatory information,* mentioned earlier, is a good example. When the SEC makes the request for *required records,* there is attached to the request a reference to the federal statute which makes it a crime, punishable by five years in jail and up to $500,000 in fines, not to turn over mandatory information. The provision of that information may, however, lend itself to criminal sanctions, hence the Hobson's choice.

The client may be faced with debarment if there is a decision not to provide information necessary to get export licenses or to ship certain regulated products abroad or necessary to sell its products to the government. The client may choose not to disclose the information to regulators and hunker down for a criminal proceeding. The result, however, may be debarment from making sales or shipments necessary to keep in business.

The government can thus use the prospect of civil or administrative proceedings to enforce requests for information that may be incriminating. And if these draconian consequences are not enough, companies and individuals face a risk that taking of the Fifth Amendment may result in a negative inference at any civil or administrative proceeding that may ensue.[7] One can take the Fifth Amendment as an officer of an investigated company, but at a later trial the court will assume that one's

---

[7]See *SEC v. Stewart,* 476 F.2d 756 (2d Cir. 1973).

answers would have been adverse to its cause, and it will then unleash the vast armory of administrative sanctions that the law provides: disgorgement, debarment, delisting, delicensure.

Another consideration is, of course, the impression the strategy causes. If one guesses incorrectly and overreacts, that overreaction may become a self-fulfilling prophecy. There is an old German maxim that Dobermans only bite children with guilty consciences. What the axiom says of Dobermans is sometimes true of government agents. As the biblical proverb has it, "the wicked fleeth when no man pursueth."

If one assumes an aggressive criminal defense posture in response to what might be a routine administrative inquiry, it may signal to the investigators that they are on to something significant and may prompt a referral to the local prosecuting authorities. What might have been perceived as routine now is seen as smoke concealing fire.

Such impressions are important to reputable clients, of course, regardless of their actual impact. Even in cases where a conservative approach might be the best policy, clients frequently have to be tackled before offering voluntary testimony, the legal ramifications of which they may only dimly understand. They may think that only criminals take a hard line on Fifth Amendment issues. They do not want to appear to be uncooperative stonewallers.

Given these difficult considerations, what strategies suggest themselves?

1. *If there is any serious prospect of criminal prosecution, it is usually better to be safe than sorry.* This means that there ought to be no unnecessary cooperation in practice, however fulsome in proffer. It means that separate counsel must be retained for people who could become subjects or targets in the investigation and that special counsel ought to be retained with expertise in handling criminal investigations. It means that potential targets ought to avail themselves of the Fifth Amendment.

The law makes clear that the Fifth Amendment, while it cannot be claimed by the corporate entity, may be asserted by an individual in any proceeding: trial, grand jury, administrative hearing, interrogation by an agent. The problem comes when there are certain civil ramifications to the assertion of the Fifth Amendment privilege. Can the government use the assertion prejudicially in a parallel civil proceeding? Can they seek sanctions for failure to provide information, sanctions such as debarment, which may be life-threatening to the company?

To mitigate these concerns, counsel may seek to enjoin the civil proceeding or at least suspend discovery in it. There is some good language in the cases undergirding this approach:

> [T]he government may not bring a parallel civil proceeding and avail itself of civil discovery devices to obtain evidence for subsequent criminal prosecution.[8]

On the other hand there is bad language as well:

> It would stultify enforcement of Federal law to require a government agency such as FDA invariably to choose either to forego recommendation of criminal prosecution once it seeks civil relief, or to defer civil proceedings pending ultimate outcome of a criminal trial.[9]

Many times the government will cooperate in this effort, seeing pitfalls for its own criminal case (dismissal or loss of evidence). Some agencies (Customs, for example) have explicit policies that the criminal case goes first, the civil case later. Usually, however, efforts to stay the civil proceeding, or even discover depositions, are unsuccessful.[10]

2. *It may well be that the first request for information has been innocent.* The government probably does not know what it has, but it will soon find out. However slender the thread the government is pulling on, it may inexorably lead to an overwhelming problem. The pursuit of a single thread, that is to say, leads to a fire-breathing minotaur in the corporate bosom. The facts are bad. The government will inevitably get them. Once it does, the litigator knows that any cover-up or evasion may be worse than the underlying wrong.

At this point, counsel will consider seriously a preemptive strike. Do a thorough investigation, taking careful steps to maintain attorney–client privilege. Based on these facts, develop a submission that is full and forthcoming. Get management approval of a preemptive strike. Put in place tough new internal controls that make a repetition of the mistake impossible. Fire, transfer, or demote employees implicated in the problem, depending on their relative culpability. Consider the opportunity to cooperate with the government in the prosecution of someone even more culpable. Then, breathing deeply, head off to visit someone with a view of the Potomac River. Bring out the facts, abjectly. Pray for mercy.

Surprisingly, agencies frequently give special consideration to the penitent, even if the disclosure is not entirely "voluntary." The IRS, for example, used to have a policy that explicitly protected from prosecution those who confessed their sins voluntarily. While the policy is no

---

[8] *United States v. Parrott*, 248 F.Supp. 196 (D.D.C. 1965).

[9] *United States v. Kordel*, 297 U.S. at 11.

[10] See e.g., *SEC v. Drucker*, [1979] CCH Fed. Sec. L. Rep. ¶ 968.21 (SDNY 1971).

longer formal and explicit, even the IRS continues to give significant consideration to the penitent. And if an agency does continue doggedly to press on criminally, the defendant's approach is so candid and forthcoming that it is sure to impress court and jury later—especially where the outcome is inevitable in any case.

3. *A hybrid approach, somewhere between obduracy and confession, is perhaps the most popular, since it permits pursuing two objectives at once.* The company cooperates fully. It provides all documents (as it must anyway). It is friendly and facilitative. In doing so, it has given up nothing, because all the documents are available to the government simply by ratcheting up to a grand jury investigation. There can be no Fifth Amendment claim by a company. This provision of the documents is thus a matter of timing, of when, and not whether.

The corporation then, behaving responsibly, provides counsel at corporate expense for all individuals who have the knowledge that makes the documentation meaningful and who can most likely make a case for the government. The lawyers provided are from the network of lawyers who believe in liberty and equality: the criminal bar. They do nothing without immunity, however cordial they may be personally. In doing so, they are, of course, representing their individual clients well. No individual faced with potential criminal investigation talks without some motivation to do so.

And so, while the corporation is stroking the agency, the pit bulls are biting it in the leg. The corporation is saying, quite truthfully: "We cannot control the individual counsel." The company thus avoids sanctions for lack of cooperation and, with any luck at all, the individuals avoid conviction.

4. *The company is sometimes happy to use an ongoing civil investigation for its own purposes.* If it is clear that the government is going to pursue the company and its officers criminally, the company knows that it will have a difficult time doing discovery. It will get exculpatory information (so-called *Brady* material) at the last possible moment. Usually the government will not find any. It will get witness statements (so-called Jencks Act statements) on the eve of trial, if not on the eve of cross-examination. It will search through the government's "open files" and find nothing of interest.

But if there is an ongoing civil proceeding, more discovery opportunities are available. If the government, for example, is pursuing a civil remedy to enforce an administrative subpoena, the company may be able to get before a hearing officer and have the agent describe what is needed, why it is needed, and the materiality of it, all with reference to some particular regulation. That proceeding can both define the scope of the government inquiry and provide a handy reference to the risks the company faces.

If the government has parallel civil and criminal EPA cases, the company can seek liberal civil discovery, including interrogatories and depositions. In short, a company can take the risk of liberal discovery to get the rewards of liberal discovery, and perhaps find the government willing to suspend its own discovery proceeding.

The company can go a step further. It can launch a civil lawsuit against a party related to the criminal investigation, often the snitch, who is not infrequently a dishonest and disaffected employee who has triggered the criminal investigation. In one major criminal Customs case, the "snitch" was sued prior to the commencement of the grand jury deliberations and in various proceedings (civil lawsuit, unemployment hearings, and the like), and was deposed for eight volumes prior to the criminal trial. At one final hearing on the eve of the trial, the key government witness was so discredited by various contradictions in his voluminous testimony that the federal judge called the U.S. Attorney aside, counseled him not to put the witness on the stand, and referred to the snitch through the balance of the proceeding as a *known perjurer.* The government lost all 26 felony counts before the jury.

5. *Finally, there is the question of what to do when the proceedings are manifestly parallel, not merely potentially so.* The SEC, for example, is free to continue its investigation after conclusion of a major enforcement action.[11] Some courts have even permitted the SEC to continue its investigation after recommending the matter be criminally prosecuted.[12]

The defendant in such a circumstance feels as though he or she is being drawn and quartered—pulled into pieces by investigators heading in different directions. The only choices are the following: seek an injunction or a protective order on the parallel proceeding, "take the fifth" in each of the proceedings, or convince the prosecutors that a civil global resolution is appropriate under the Department of Justice guidelines.

Which of these strategies is chosen depends on a variety of factors. Sometimes a company is willing to take enormous criminal risks to avoid a lethal debarment. On other occasions, management is willing to assume a staunch criminal defense posture to avoid a very small risk that an investigation will go criminal.

[11]See *Suteo Brothers & Co. v. S.E.C.*, 199 F.Supp. 438 (SDNY 1961).

[12]See *United States v. Parrott*, 373 F.2d 649 (2d Cir. 1967).

Some Suggestions

Generally, however, the rules for a business are as follows:

1. *Be risk averse.* The overriding objective in most cases is to avoid criminal prosecution. Avoiding an indictment is the first priority. The next priority is to avoid trial. The final priority is to avoid conviction. All of these suggest risk-averse tactics that do not disclose theories or facts unnecessarily.

2. *Do not rely solely on your own instincts.* Whether you are a rosy optimist or a sullen paranoid, experienced counsel must make a separate assessment of the risks of criminal prosecution and advise a client. It is important to listen to that advice.

3. *If cooperating, make a record of how the cooperation is coerced by civil sanctions.* A conviction may be reversed if cooperation was coerced in a contemporaneous civil case and helped cause a criminal conviction in a subsequent case.[13]

4. *Remind the government of its risks in parallel proceedings.* The government faces a risk of tainting its civil proceeding if a court finds it has used a criminal process to seek a civil settlement. It risks tainting its criminal proceeding under Rule 6(e) if it supplies information to the civil authorities.

5. *Remind the court, if necessary, of your dilemma.* Courts understand the bind parallel proceedings place defendants in. Sometimes they fashion injunctive or other remedies to protect the justifiable interests of both sides. Make sure your counsel is prepared to demonstrate, with practical examples, the difficulty of doing "the parallel proceeding straddle."

---

[13] *United States v. Detroit Vital Foods, Inc.,* 407 F.2d 570 (6th Cir. 1969).

12
Trial by Jury

Are These
Your Peers?

A man sat in the dock. The country was England. The century was the seventeenth. The defendant had been accused of conducting unauthorized religious meetings contrary to a law which recognized only the established church.

England had a state church. To preach, one had to be licensed. To be licensed, one had to be ordained and in good standing with the Church of England. This man viewed the liturgical rituals of the church as a hopeless impediment to true worship. He was a natural icon basher who wanted to clear away the formula prayers of institutional worship and let his own heart be quiet before God. His efforts at freedom of conscience led inexorably to a criminal prosecution.

Now he sat silently, as the jury was being instructed. The jury was composed of twelve men. The judge had two advisers. On one side sat the sheriff of London, on the other the lord mayor. A seventeenth-century body-language consultant would have found no difficulty in reading their feelings. But body-language interpretation was unnecessary in this trial. At one point during the trial, the mayor suggested he would like to cut a co-defendant's throat. All staunch supporters of the Church of England, the panel viewed the trial as a necessary evil, delaying the inevitable imposition of sentence on this refractory defendant.

Give him a fair trial, the thought was, and put him in the tower. Neither the evidentiary rulings nor the instructions were going to go the defendant's way. Because the defendant had tried to take part in the trial and made his own interjections directly to the jury, he now sat mute and motionless, manacled and gagged.

After hearing the instructions, a somber jury filed out of the courtroom. They were sequestered by the bailiff until a ringing bell announced that a verdict had been reached.

In came the jury. The foreman had the verdict in hand. He stood. The judge looked at him momentarily and asked, "Have you reached a verdict?"

"Yes we have, your Honor."

"What is that verdict?"

"We find the defendant—not guilty."

The establishmentarians sharing the judicial bench furrowed their brows in rhythmic succession. The panel, and the recorder sitting in front of them, began to upbraid the jury with profane language.

Regaining their self-control, they then conferred quietly with each other. The judge said, "I would like you, gentlemen of the jury, to retire again into the jury room, to reconsider your verdict, and to come back when you have reached a reasonable verdict." The emotional freight of the sentence rested entirely on the penultimate word: *reasonable.*

The bailiff led the jury out. This time they were sequestered for several hours. Again the bell rang. Again the jury filed into the courtroom.

The court looked increasingly tense.

"Have you now reached a *reasonable* verdict?" he intoned.

"Yes we have, your Honor," the foreman reported.

"And what is that verdict?"

"Not guilty."

The jury had proved far more obdurate than the panel had supposed. The judge and his colleagues conferred with ever greater animation. Finally, the judge decided to put some teeth in his prior direction.

"I'm going to ask you, gentlemen of the jury, to retire again to the jury room, and this time do not come back unless and until you have reached a *reasonable* verdict." The recorder ordered the bailiff to lock the jury up "without meat, drink, fire and tobacco . . . we will have a verdict by the help of God or you shall starve for it."

As the jury was filing out, the distressed defendant had one last interjection for the jury to consider. Crying out in a muffled voice through his gag, the defendant said, "Englishmen, mind your privilege."

The jury deliberated for many more hours. The bailiff faithfully lived up to his charge, allowing the jury no amenities. Soon the bell rang.

The judge was again menacing both in countenance and in tone of voice, "Have you finally reached a reasonable verdict?"

The foreman looked him in the eye. "Yes we have, your Honor."

"And what is that verdict?"

The foreman's mouth was now clenched, and he spit out the verdict. "Not guilty!"

The judge knew nothing of baseball, but he knew when his side was out. He dismissed the jury with no expression of gratitude, and ordered the prisoner to be released. The peers had prevailed over the powers that be.

The defendant, of course, never forgot the scene. When he later emigrated to America in search of expanded freedom for his conscience, he brought with him a profound respect for the jury system. And he insisted that the jury system be transplanted in his territory. The man was William Penn. The territory was Pennsylvania.

The Federalist Papers report that during the Constitutional Convention, there was wide agreement that the jury trial system was important for criminal cases. There was somewhat more debate about the utility of jury trials for civil cases, something unknown on the Continent and elsewhere throughout the world. But even there, the convention was swayed by forces from Pennsylvania carrying the banner of William Penn, who argued—as Madison records in Federalist Papers, No. 83—that a liberal jury trial right was "the very palladium of free government."

Business executives are frequently afraid of the jury trial system. Newspapers carry accounts of runaway juries, eager to pull off any silk stocking they see, hammering hapless corporations with million-dollar punitive damage awards. Rational managers suspect that juries are generally more susceptible to emotional rather than cognitive appeals.

The Defendant's Best Friend?

But in white-collar crime trials, as in civil cases, the jury can be the defendant's best friend. Very few people charged with a crime will waive the jury. The reason goes far beyond the feeling that judges are more difficult to bamboozle. The jury is the first forum in which a defendant can fairly make his case and have real confidence in an objective hearing. If one traces the development of criminal prosecution, one can see why.

A federal criminal case starts with an investigation by an agent. It may be an FBI agent, an IRS special agent, a representative of the Inspector General's office, a Department of Agriculture special agent, an EPA special agent, some other agency representative, or some combination of them.

The agent has opened a file. There is a reason he or she has done so. A competitor has made a complaint. A "snitch" has reported some violation. An industrywide practice has come to public attention. There is enough smoke to infer the existence of a fire. A presupposition is formed.

Agents will certainly be willing to talk with anyone who has information including one representing the target's point of view. The problem is, of course, that they are hardly impartial. Investigators are generally honest, hard working, and, despite feeling overworked and underpaid, loyal government employees. They are, nonetheless, government employees. Their task is to root out, expose, and successfully prosecute misconduct.

The fact that they have taken the time to begin an investigation means that they think there is probably some wrongdoing to be found. Their very calling shows a cast of mind, an interest in prosecution, that would surely lead lawyers to strike them if they were to emerge on a jury panel in an unrelated case. And in cases they are investigating, failing to come up with a prosecutable offense is just that—a failure, either in their initial judgment in opening the file or in their inability to gather enough facts to catch the wrongdoer. Talking to them, in a very real sense, is talking to adversaries.

They report to their boss in Washington, D.C. That boss will generally be in charge of a penalties unit or an office of compliance. The boss will be assisted by a lawyer in the general counsel's office of the agency, or some other lawyer on staff who can give legal guidance to the investigation. If one goes to that level, one is still dealing with a person who is charged with finding and prosecuting crime.

As the FBI quite naturally points to increased prosecutions, increased convictions, and increased fines rolling into the federal treasury as hallmarks of its success, so the agency people in Washington will point to the same thing to justify their budgets for criminal investigations. Few annual agency reports point proudly to the number of people cleared. Statistics do not claim credit for exonerating executives who were initially suspected of wrongdoing or for giving busy middle-class businesspeople the benefit of a doubt in suspicious circumstances.

The widgets produced by these factories are prosecutions. And the more widgets produced and the higher priced to the consumer, the better.

If the agency accepts and approves the special agent's report, it refers the matter to a U.S. Attorney for prosecution. The office of the U.S. Attorney is a government office. It attracts excellent lawyers who are interested in justice, prosecution of criminals, and trial experience, not necessarily in that order.

U.S. Attorneys are pleasant people to play tennis with. They have good war stories of elusive or devious criminals they have masterminded into penitentiaries. But they are hardly empathetic listeners to the accounts (rationalizations? excuses?) of the accused. Their view of the case is largely without form and void until enlightened by the agent. Their first impressions are formed by the agent, and their first impressions, like the first impressions of most of us, do not change easily.

In addition to having heard the agent's side first, an Assistant U.S. Attorney is not without career aspirations. A good white-collar crime case increases the likelihood of promotion and enhances one's professional reputation. And, of course, every attorney has a client. The client is the agency. No lawyer wishes to appear to be a wimp or a lapdog before his or her client. When a defense lawyer seeks to persuade the Assistant U.S. Attorney that no criminal misconduct has occurred, the assistant normally has the agent present. When the defense leaves, the offense takes over. The agent gives the agency rebuttal. Faced with a choice of believing the outsider, or the client, the assistant usually does not need to agonize long.

If one has not convinced the agent, the Washington agency, or the Assistant U.S. Attorney, one can go to the U.S. Attorney. The U.S. Attorney is politically appointed and runs the U.S. Attorney's office in a federal district. The most important skill required for the job, some have suggested, is winning the friendship of a U.S. Senator. Taking on a hopelessly quixotic campaign against an entrenched incumbent, for the sake of the party, is sometimes the best preparation for the office.

As a person chosen more often for political contributions than for trial skills, the U.S. Attorney is sensitive to doing anything as unpolitical as overriding one of the minions. "Support your local police" is the bumper sticker of choice. Prosecution is a discretionary matter, and prosecutorial discretion is something every U.S. Attorney wants to preserve. The prosecutor knows all about—and, in the abstract, agrees with—the axioms laid out by the appellate courts. "A prosecutor must pursue justice, not convictions," dozens of different decisions have intoned. But justice is a protean concept, given form by sound discretion. U.S. Attorneys almost never countermand their assistants.

The next step up the ladder toward a place of fair hearing is the Department of Justice. The Department of Justice must oversee the prosecution of justice in the federal court system throughout the country. Its lawyers will do a "review" of prosecutorial decisions made by local U.S. Attorney's offices. They occasionally lay down rules that require U.S. Department of Justice approval for certain sensitive investigations. If a prominent public official is to be prosecuted, or if some new theory is to be propounded as a base of criminal prosecution, if some political mine field is to be ventured into, whether pornography or foreign corruption, the Justice Department will sometimes require prior approval. It does not want bad law being created by local prosecutors who are over-zealous or insufficiently mindful of the policy interests of the Department of Justice. The Department of Justice will, therefore, politely listen to those seeking to avert or divert imminent prosecutions.

The Justice Department lawyers who convene to hear this internal appeal will generally be intelligent and, if the word may be used in this context, civil. In an important case, they may even have the head of the criminal division sitting in. In other cases, they will have people who know something about the area relating to the prosecution. They will have some administrative authority. On occasion, they may derail or limit the prosecution that the local U.S. Attorney intends to commence. But such interventions are rare. More often than not, they too will support the discretionary decisions made in the field. The local U.S. Attorney, after all, typically still has his or her political friends after assuming office. There is no sense in ruffling feathers by unnecessarily interfering with the decisions of locals on the scene.

Where then will long-suffering Job find his judge? The grand jury gives little promise. How about with the judge or the local federal court? Judges are learned in the law. And the federal bench is probably more immune to the diseases of political appointment than are some state judicial selection processes. Most federal judges are competent and take their job to do justice seriously.

But like the rest of us, they have their own life experiences, values, and perceptions. Few federal judges are ex–public defenders. Indeed, one frequent route to promotion is by serving a tour of duty as a United States Attorney. Many judges are graduates of that elite school, Prosecutors' U. The judge has thought like a prosecutor, mingled and supped with prosecutors, groused like a prosecutor, and prosecuted people like a prosecutor. Now the judge puts on black robes and sees two lawyers haggling before the bench, one a defense lawyer with a private firm, and one the judge recognizes as a graduate from the alma mater, a successor prosecutor. Where will one's normal inclinations lie?

However cynical it sounds, prosecutors and judges are paid by the same employer, share many benefits packages, have offices in the same building, park in the same parking lot, eat in the same government cafeteria, walk down the same halls, and regret the same inadequate compensation. They both have consciously made decisions to sacrifice private positions and pecuniary emoluments to be public servants.

This is not to say that judges are biased or inevitably antidefense. But they are not truly "peers" of the defendant. Their life experiences and cast of mind give them a greater inclination toward the prosecution. Prosecutors will not generally be required to live up to the same standard of briefing as the defense lawyers—they are "understaffed." Prosecutors will win nearly all pretrial motions. Criticism of a prosecutor's actions will draw stinging judicial rebuke far more quickly than criticism of some civil lawyer's actions. Those are the facts of life.

Where then will a fair hearing be found? The best hope for a white-collar defendant is in a jury of twelve. Once they lose their awe of the high-walled federal courthouse, with its paneling and rituals, they will settle down and try to understand the case and correctly decide it. If they are instructed that the defendant is presumed innocent, they will take that instruction seriously. If they are told that the prosecution must prove its case beyond a reasonable doubt, and if they think it is only "probable" that the defendant did the act he was charged with, they will acquit. They should. Juries are fallible. The panel may have its own biases. But those who regularly practice before juries come away with a great respect for how hard they work at doing the right thing.

The juries in federal court are more likely to convict than juries in state court for a number of reasons. Prosecutors invariably get the first and last word, both in the trial and in the order of closing argument. In state courts, defense lawyers sometimes argue last. A federal prosecutor makes the first argument, then saves one or two devastating arguments for rebuttal when the defense has no opportunity to respond. The defendant feels "sandwiched." Jurors cannot generally be questioned by defense lawyers before being selected in federal court as they can through the *voir dire* procedures in state courts. They are more likely to come from a broader geographical area than the city's core. Some of them come in from the hinterlands with rustic presumptions of the rightness of government activity. But they are smarter than the lawyers think, and often smarter than the lawyers themselves. They provide the ultimate bastion of justice for one accused of crime.

Persuading the Peers

The warrior who goes to battle before this group of judges must make sure of three things.

1. *The jury members must know their solemn duty.* No appeal is so strong as an appeal to conscience. The typical jury may believe that the prosecutor wants them to do the right thing, while the defense lawyer wants to appeal to their sympathies and excuse the defendant's wrongdoing. It is important to show the jury that the defendant is asking the jury to do its duty.

Doing the *right* thing in a criminal trial means following the rules that the framers of the Constitution laid down for these proceedings, rather than doing one's *own* thing. Two critical duties are required.

The jurors must first presume that this business defendant is innocent. That means that they are not starting out the case as neutral arbiters. The jury is not in limbo. The jury should already have a mind-set. The mind-set is a presumption: this defendant has done nothing wrong. I presume the defendant is absolutely innocent. The reason for this is clear. No one sounds good when accused of wrongdoing. The mother confronting the child about the broken window realizes that every protestation of innocence seems strained. It is hard to prove a negative. Trying to prove that one did not do something is seldom easy or convincing.

I once had a client who was a sophisticated business executive. He was a well-known figure in his industry, and the chief executive officer of a successful company. But he had a peculiar trait. He could not talk about anything personal.

In normal business settings, he was worldly, witty, and informed. But if he had to talk about the subjective—his past, his parents, his marriage, the accusations against him—he looked reticent, tongue-tied, and guilty. While the conventional wisdom is that a defendant should always testify when his or her state of mind is at issue (the jury will certainly want to hear the defendant's side of the story, the story goes), I decided that this defendant looked terrible when discussing the details of this case. The night before he was to go on, I decided he would not testify. The jury came back with an acquittal on all counts, retroactively justifying the decision.

Two years later, I used him as an expert witness in a securities case. He was the star of the show. Self-confident, credible, he laid in testimony like an expert mason, building a foundation on which the ultimate verdict would rest.

The difference between the two people was understandable. In the second case, the witness was not accused of anything. The same witness giving truthful testimony in two proceedings may be overwhelmingly convincing in one setting and overwhelmingly unconvincing in another. For that reason, the jurors have to understand that their initial presumptions must all be with the defendant, and that when they swore an oath to do right, they were swearing to take that presumption seriously.

The second principle is proof beyond reasonable doubt. The jury must understand that nearly anyone can be accused of wrongdoing. And because of the great potential for injustice, the law makes clear that a defendant can only be convicted if he or she is proved to be guilty beyond a reasonable doubt. That is why there is no such thing as an *innocent* verdict. The verdict is *not guilty*. *Not guilty* only means that the government could not prove its case beyond a reasonable doubt. It does not necessarily mean that the defendant is *innocent.* One can believe the defendant is guilty as charged, without having a "conviction amounting to a moral certainty" that he or she did it beyond any reasonable doubt. The will of the jury must be reached by persistent appeal to that moral obligation. To be a genuine follower of the law, one must do what the law commands in assessing the evidence.

2. *Jury members must believe your metaphor.* Jurors will also want their minds satisfied. To that end, what is important is not only the details that come forward from the witness stand, but how those details are organized.

The poet Edna St. Vincent Millay wrote

> Facts fall like meteors
> They lie, unquestioned, uncontradicted
> Like so many threads . . .
> Wisdom enough to leech us of our ill
> Is daily spun but there exists no loom
> To weave it into fabric.[1]

Jurors will be deluged with meteors of fact. There will be witnesses out of order, thousands of documents, a chaos of competing factual assertions for their attention. How they organize those facts into fabric and whose loom they use will determine how they decide the case. Juries seldom convict because "the defense was too complicated for them." They convict because the defense lawyers did not give them a credible metaphor that explained the big picture of the case.

Few things in life are as powerful as a metaphor. Once, on a dark afternoon in college, a few weeks before the winter solstice, attendees of a small seminar in existentialism were examining a passage from Camus. My boredom was interrupted only temporarily by watching the French-born assistant professor smoking her Salem cigarettes with deep gasping inhales, cigarettes smoked only after laboriously cutting off the filters.

To dispel the boredom, I interjected in the midst of a colloquy about angst, "But what does all of this mean if the Russians choose to lob the big one?"

The question was fraught with existential absurdity, and thus it was taken seriously.

"A good point," said the professor. "Is that the ultimate existential Tat?"

---

[1] E. St. Vincent Millay, "Upon this age that never speaks its mind," in the anthology, *Huntsman, What Quarry?* (1939).

One student offered, "Well it depends in part on what we mean by 'the big one.'"

"Or what we mean by lobbing," said another analytical student.

The remaining 45 minutes of the class brought us to the brink of a nuclear holocaust and its relationship to Camus, Sartre, and Heidegger. But the lesson I drew from the exchange was hardly existential. It was essential. Metaphors are like prisons. People find it hard to fight their way out of them. If one can imprison a fact-finder with the appropriate metaphor, one has generally won the day, especially if the government finds the metaphor so strong that it adopts it as its own.

The metaphor may be a bullying government agency coming after a small business executive who will not play ball. It may be a disenchanted ex-employee who is a "tour guide" for the government, leading a good-hearted but gullible government agent on a tour of unfamiliar territory and getting the agent to believe his or her description of the topography.

Or it may be the description for the jury of the strength of initial presumption. Juries like to learn facts about constitutional history or science or economics from lawyers who view them as equals and refuse to condescend to them. One useful approach a jury can understand is how different presuppositions can lead to quite different pictures of what occurs.

In the *Copernican Revolution,* Thomas Kuhn wrote of the long-time dominance of the Ptolemaic world view which ruled western cosmogony for a millennium. Ptolemy believed that the earth was the center of the solar system. He wrote of the music of the spheres and pointed out how harmoniously all the planets circled in their orbits around the earth. His presumption made sense. It squared with normal perceptions: the sun did seem to rise and set; the earth did seem to remain still.

The problem came when astronomers tried to calculated where various planets or stars would be. Increasingly complicated planetary orbits had to be constructed for astronomers to figure out where they would be at any one moment, given Ptolemy's theory. The orbits of some planets appeared to be rectangles. Others appeared to be like starbursts. One planet's orbit had the appearance of a figure eight. With enough computations and serpentine depictions, one could indeed figure out where everything was. But new facts kept intervening, requiring even more jagged additions.

Notwithstanding the calculations that had to be made, no one really doubted the underlying presupposition. It was too self-evident. The question was simply refining the facts of observation to fit within that presupposition.

Then came Copernicus, Galileo, and Tycho Brahe. With the invention of the telescope, further observations could be made. Suddenly, almost simultaneously, it dawned on the astronomers. If only one change were made, everything else would fall into place. If one simply assumed that the sun was at the center of the solar system, rather than the earth, it was far simpler to determine the orbits of the planets. They became nice, smooth ellipses. But that change could be made only by overcoming the entrenched resistance of those authorities still in love with the earlier presupposition.

So it is with the jury. The prosecutor has constructed a system with a criminal mind at the center. The defense lawyers have put in substantial evidence with respect to motive, method, or character of the accused that tend to negate that presupposition. The prosecutor can still rationalize the case, explaining away all the different defenses with somewhat peculiar twists and turns. But it is far easier to change the basic presupposition that has blinded the government and its investigators. If one assumes simply that there is no criminal mind, but some honest mistakes, all the other facts of the case will be seen with greater simplicity.

If the jury understands this metaphor and adopts it, the case is won. Pictures are far easier to remember than lists, and going before the jury gives an opportunity for the defendant to paint the picture no one else would really look at, the big picture. There is always some foible or failing that led to the prosecution, to be sure, but it is the big picture that ultimately determines guilt or innocence.

3. *The jury must want to decide for the defendants.* The classical philosophers referred to the human personality as the soul, composed of the mind, the will, and the affections. The duty theme is directed to the will. The metaphor is designed to capture the mind. But both of those appeals will be more persuasive if the defendants have captured the affections of the jury. And here, character counts.

The jury will be examining carefully the character of the defendants, both as it is described in past actions and as it appears to them in person. Good legal representation when the problem arises will help with the past acts. Good legal representation during the trial will help with present perception of character.

Juries are repelled by bad moral character. It is often the attitudes of the defendants that infuriate a jury, as much as any of the actions which they have allegedly committed. Most trial lawyers have seen cases where one of the parties has noisy skeletons clattering in the closet that can easily be pulled out and shown in a prosecutorial "show and tell." The opposing lawyers await an opportunity to cross-examine the witnesses and tear them apart. Unfortunately, the defendant refuses to cooperate and confesses forthrightly to his or her bad behavior. Such confessions are no fun for the cross-examiner.

QUESTION: Did you do it?

ANSWER: Yes.

QUESTION: And it was wrong?

ANSWER: Yes, absolutely.

QUESTION: And you knew it was wrong when you did it?

ANSWER: I'm ashamed to say I did.

Instead of having the chance to beat the truth out of a reluctant witness, the skeletons are all out in a matter of seconds and somehow the liar on the stand seems like the most honest person in the courtroom. The actions were appalling, but the defendant's attitude in owning up to them is attractive.

Bad Attitudes and "Be-Attitudes"

There are several attitudes that a jury reacts to with special vehemence.

1. *Pride.* A minor prophet told how angry God was with the land of Edom, a nation with whom God is angry forever. The principal sin of Edom was pride in its own wisdom. "Though thou set thyself a throne in the heavens, I will bring thee down from thence, saith the Lord." There is something about the self-exalting personality that rubs everyone the wrong way.

Lawyers who take themselves too seriously before the jury and talk down to it are usually in for a rude surprise. Business executives may have cultivated a clipped, authoritative, perhaps authoritarian, manner and may have seen how well it works when barking out orders from the bridge, but if they come across as proud and powerful, the jurors may find feelings welling within them that will cause them to want to knock the executives down a peg or more. Before honor goes humility.

2. *Bitterness and blame.* Those who are accused and especially those who feel some compunction of guilt, since there is an element of truth in almost every allegation, can easily become bitter. They blame an overreaching government. They blame subordinates or others. And an acidic bitterness always lies just under the surface of their testimony.

Training a person not to have, or at least not to manifest, bitterness is not easy. It is like the old club fighter under a new manager who promises to turn the fighter into a stand-up boxer. For two or three rounds, the boxer looks like Sugar Ray Robinson, but then a clubbing right upside the head turns the boxer into a brawling club fighter again.

Those who feel oppressed sometimes get bitter about it. But a jury will not sympathize with the oppressed but the oppressor when it sees a venomous bitterness come out under examination. A business or professional person must be generous, assume the best of the adversaries, and let the facts speak for themselves.

3. *Game players.* Trials are forms of ritualized play. They have rules, a playing field, winners, and losers.

Some who get into the combat get so excited about the game that they forget the umpires. The umpires are not amused by tricks and tactical surprises that send lawyers back to their hotel rooms gloating about how they shamed the adversary. They prefer even a stumbling, methodical person they can trust to a slick advocate who is proved to be pulling the wool over their eyes or using fancy footwork.

To bring it all together, no one is harder to convict than a person who has the "be attitudes" of the beatitudes. Being poor in spirit, mourning mistakes (not crimes) that were made, meekly abandoning any attempt to make an oppressive use of personal rights, giving a sense of hungering after justice, showing mercy to others who could have been blamed, appearing to be pure at heart or sincere about putting one's fate into the hands of the jury, trying to be a peacemaker, and rejoicing in the apparent persecution are all attitudes the jury will appreciate, and take as a true measure of the character of the actor and acts in question.

Speak English

If the accused has a defense and the right attitude, it does not matter what color his or her collar. He or she simply needs to communicate with people who will be impartial and take the case seriously. Such communication requires a return to rugged old Anglo-Saxon communication, not the lawyer's Latinisms.

One of the great communicators of the eighteenth century was John Wesley. Wesley could command a crowd of 10,000 people in a meadow at an hour's notice. His preaching was powerful. It was not uncommon for thousands to make decisions that radically changed their way of living because of him.

Once an apprentice preacher summoned up the courage to ask John Wesley whether he could have an hour of his time to learn how to preach. Wesley was a methodical man, as his later adherents testified to by adopting his "methodist" ways. But he made time for the earnest young student of preaching. When the young man came to his house on Bunhill road, Wesley greeted him at the door and quickly walked with his young apprentice down to Billingsgate.

There was the famous Billingsgate fish market. Sea-worn fishermen would bring their wares there to be hawked in the marketplace by the fishwives whose salty speech was the most effective marketing tool in the hurly burly of old London. The fish were fungible: they looked alike. But the barking saleswomen were not alike. Some used their sharp speech to gain the advantage in competing for a place in the market. From that fish market was to come the catchword for political invective, *billingsgate*.

The student was surprised by Wesley's apparent fascination with the fish market, but was too intimidated to ask any substantive questions about the art of preaching. He and Wesley stood silently watching the goings on when the market was in full throat. When the young preacher knew that his hour had nearly passed, he could wait no longer.

"I really don't want to take too much of your time, Mr. Wesley, and you did promise me an hour instruction on preaching. I'm wondering if I could presently have your instruction?"

Wesley paused for a moment, looked the young preacher in the eye and said, "You've had it. Come to Billingsgate and learn to preach." Wesley strode off home.

The advice applies to law as well as to grace. As Seneca, the "great lawgiver," said, "Let the language which is devoted to truth be plain and simple."

Despite the overwhelming number of convictions of white-collar criminals, many do find vindication from the jury of twelve. While newspaper readers are sometimes surprised when DeLorean or Donovan goes free, notwithstanding terrible publicity and scandalous allegations, the readers generally would not be so surprised if they had been at the trial and heard the strong and simple appeal, made in the right way, to do the duty that has been the juror's privilege since the days of William Penn.

To Plead or Not to Plead

Prosecutors will frequently give inducements to avoid a jury trial. *Plea bargains* appeal to a commercial sale mentality. For a limited time only, it will be possible to pay a reduced price. The crime is temporarily marked down from three felonies to two. There will be a cap on the sentence—a savings of three years! Inexpensive visits to the probation office will be offered rather than expensive banishment to distant prisons. Once the trial begins, of course, all these slashed prices are forgotten. Defendants will be punished for seizing the jury trial right by exposing themselves to enormous additional penalties.

Such "bargains" are reminiscent of St. Thomas More's reaction when informed that his sentence of drawing and quartering had been mercifully commuted to a beheading: "God forbid the King should use any more such mercy to any of my friends, and God bless all my posterity from such pardons." They do make sense on occasion, or they would not be so popular. They save the government money. They buy the defendant certainty, a certainty he or she will not experience the worst conceivable outcome.

But they also induce some defendants to violate their conviction they are innocent by falsely admitting they are guilty and by waiving their most precious right in exchange for a brokered compromise. Many times, criminal defendants genuinely feel they have done nothing wrong. But the plea is too good to turn down. Prosecutors will then put the executives on the stand and question them, as will judges, to determine if there is a factual basis for the plea. They will be forced to admit that they knowingly violated the law.

But if they do not believe that they did, they will be faced with two unsatisfying options: perjure yourself and get the deal, or mealymouth your answer and risk losing the deal. Many such defendants, I sense, do a "Milli Vanilli" plea. They lip-synch the "correct" responses their lawyer gives them and do the deal, possibly with fingers crossed under their French cuffs. Only a few have the courage to act out the conviction of Milton:

> I cannot praise a fugitive and cloistered virtue, unexercised and unbreathed, that never sallies out and sees her adversary, but slinks out of the race, where that immortal garland is to be run for, not without dust and heat. (T)hat which purifies is trial, and trial is by what is contrary.[2]

When faced with the choice of exercising that virtue—at the possible cost of self-destruction—the defendant may well respond, "That's easy for you to say."

There is another side to the story. A victory in the criminal proceeding may be Pyrrhic.

In approximately 280 B.C., a coalition of Hellenistic nations was called upon to resist the naked aggression of an expansionist, Pan-Italian fighting force from Rome. One of the local kings invited to the alliance was Pyrrhus. A ruler since he was 12 years old, Pyrrhus wrote one of the great military treatises of all time, and his cunning strategies and tactics were praised by prominent politicians and philosophers, including Cicero.

---

[2]Milton, *Areopagitica.*

Pyrrhus rose up to the task of defending Hellenistic Sicily and contiguous areas. In one great battle at Asculum, Pyrrhus won the day in a bloody battle, by intelligent use of soldiers and combat elephants. In winning, however, Pyrrhus later found the victory had been expensive. He gave the conclusion of many a successful trial warrior when he said, "Another victory like this and all is lost." The same is true of the client who, when advised by a fax message of a successful verdict, faxed back, "Congratulations. The greatest victory since World War II. Albeit at somewhat greater expense."

Unfortunately for Pyrrhus, there were other victories like that in his future, and ultimately a stealthy spear found him one dark night at Argos, where he was putting down an insurrection at Sparta, and cost him his life. Choosing to win the criminal skirmish, rather than enter into a global settlement, may, indeed, be a Pyrrhic victory.

13
Crime and Punishment

Do White-Collar "Criminals" Get Lenient Sentences?

The *New Yorker* cartoon captures well the common perception. A businessman, looking fat and prosperous in a three-piece suit, stands before an addled judge. The judge says, "The defendant will now step forward for the ceremonial tap on the wrists."

White-collar crime does no time, according to popular mythology. Everyone has heard the stories of "Club Fed," that archipelago of minimum-security prisons stretching across the country from Danbury, Connecticut, to Lompoc, California, prisons without walls where the pop of tennis balls being volleyed by well-groomed inmates in Puma warm-up jackets competes with the chirping of songbirds as the only sounds heard. Nowhere is heard the sound of hammer on rock.

There is, of course, an element of truth to all this. When I visited Lompoc to take a civil deposition of one of the prisoners, a prominent banker and one-time owner of the Tropicana nightclub in Las Vegas, I was impressed by the facility. A few miles outside of Santa Barbara, Lompoc was enjoying the bright spring sunshine of southern California. The grass was green. Residents were busying themselves playing softball on a well-groomed field, lifting weights outside under a cloudless sky, or jogging slowly around the palm trees. As I came to the desk to check in, two of the inmates rushed by me for an appointment involving rackets and courts of a more congenial kind. The night before there had been the launch of a satellite from Vandenberg Air Force Base brightening the sky over the nearby foothills.

Ivan Boesky called it home, as had some Watergate and other assorted white-collar crime celebrities. While the necessity of making one's bed and sweeping the room gave the residents some annoyance, it was hardly Devil's Island. About the only thing one could not do was go into town for a pizza.

The element of truth in mythology is not lost on its judges, who periodically punctuate their solemn remarks at sentencing with the ritual commonplace. "If I send poor people to jail for stealing a thousand dollars, I would be remiss if. . . ."

Judges want to be perceived as "tough" on white-collar crime. They want to dispel the notion that class distinction affects their sentencing decisions. As one judge put it at a symposium on crime in the 1990s, held at Loyola University of Chicago, "We will need to get the public *mad* about white-collar crime. . . ." This has the equivalent appeal for judges that the "fairness" issue in taxation has for Congress. Statistics may show that 5 percent of the population pays in 72 percent of all tax revenues, but the popular perception is that the rich get off scot-free while the poor pay the bills. Perceptions may be more important than realities.

With respect to white-collar crime disposition, the reality is far more complicated than the popular mythology of white-collar privilege suggests. In fact, a strong argument can be made that white-collar criminals are given harsher sentences than the street criminal, whose acts are more terrifying—and certainly more dangerous—than the business crimes we are summoned to get people "mad" about.

Compare the treatment given to two criminal violations in New York City in 1989. In one incident, a group of "wilding" toughs brutalized, raped, and sodomized a young professional woman whose only "wrong" was to be running in Central Park at the wrong time and in the wrong location. Leaving her raped, naked, bloodied, and permanently brain damaged, the perpetrators of the brutal assault were given a minimum of five years in prison. The attitude the youths had toward the assault was represented by the reported comment of one of them afterward. "She weren't nothing, man."

At about the same time Michael Milken was standing before a federal judge, accused of various federal crimes, including insider trading. Milken, it was thought, would have had a difficult time defending himself on some of the counts. But on many others, Milken's ingenious maneuvers might not be regarded by a jury as criminal. No one had even been criminally prosecuted for doing what Milken did, and the defense would have had many arguments, legal and economic, to suggest that while Milken may have been inventive, and uncommonly resourceful, he was not criminal. Called to impose sentence on Milken for his plea of guilty to conspiracy and securities frauds counts, the court sentenced him to ten years in prison and ordered him to pay $600 million in fines and restitution.

The pattern is similar elsewhere. Under some state sentencing guidelines, a person has to commit enough burglaries to get convicted three times, before facing a serious risk of jail. For each burglary bungled, there are hundreds that are successful. The idea of someone sneaking into a home while the family sleeps and skulking about in the dark is frightening. It is certainly both more terrifying and more dangerous than a breach of some regulatory provision of the Code of Federal Regulations. But the white-collar criminal finds that the meter generally starts at a year and a day in prison and works up from there, even for a first offense.

Life sentences for first-degree murder are almost universal in states that do not have capital punishment. But a murder sentence usually is reduced to 17 years if there is good behavior, and in some cases as little as 8 years of actual time. Meanwhile, it is not uncommon for some white-collar crime defendants to be sentenced to many years in prison for offenses that would have been handled not so many years ago as civil fraud litigation.

There is, to be sure, randomness in sentencing as much as charging. Drexel Burnham agreed to pay $650 million to settle a securities fraud case brought by federal prosecutors. On the other hand, a sentencing commission recently found that nearly half of the convicted corporations were fined $5000 or less. In two similar cases of tampering with odometers, one company was sentenced to pay full restitution and a fine which essentially was twice the amount of loss to consumers; the other paid no restitution and only ⅓ of the loss.[1] But the general trend is undeniable.

Throwing Away the Key

Bearing in mind the 8 to 17 years served by first-degree murderers, let's take a tally of some recent convictions reported by *The Wall Street Journal.*

- *Jim Bakker.* The prominent televangelist was convicted of fraud in 1989. There was evidence that he diverted funds intended for his PTL

---

[1]"The Case of the Criminal Corporation," *The New York Times* (January 15, 1989).

(Praise the Lord) ministry to his own uses and defrauded investors in his Heritage Theme Park by selling more space than was available. Bakker was sentenced in October 1989 to 45 years in prison and ordered to pay a fine of $500,000. The judge made a prejudgment comment at sentencing that required resentencing. But for the malaprop, the sentence would have stood. On resentencing, the sentence was reduced to 18 years.

- *W. F. Lemons.* Lemons was a savings and loan executive in Dallas. As the noose tightened around chief executive officers of savings and loans associations generally, Lemons was convicted of 13 counts of bank fraud and of accepting a kickback. Lemons was sentenced to 30 years in the federal penitentiary in April 1990.

- *Barry Minkow.* ZZZZ Best's Barry Minkow got 25 years. That is to be followed by five years of probation and restitution of $26 million.

- *Paulo Bilzerian.* Bilzerian was one of the most successful takeover artists of the 1980s. Because he was so successful in taking "green mail" profits on a number of his business investments, some observers were surprised when he actually took over and operated Singer, once a sewing machine company, now a diversified conglomerate. He sold off various parts of the company to pay the purchase price, and was left with several hundred million dollars of residual value as a reward for his risk-taking, entrepreneurial skills. He was ultimately convicted of nine felony counts for securities fraud, conspiracy, and materially false filings before the SEC. While the case against Bilzerian was hardly overwhelming, he was sentenced to four years in prison on September 1989 and fined $1.5 million.

- *Henry Gherman.* An ex–financial planner, Gherman was sentenced to 30 years in prison on fraud charges and fined $12.5 million.

- *James Sherwin.* GAF Corporation lost its vice-chairman, Sherwin, to a six-month prison term for fraud, and itself paid $2 million for its involvement in a scheme to defraud. The conviction was later reversed.

- *Jake Butcher.* Another bank executive, Butcher pleaded guilty to bank fraud, tax fraud, and conspiracy. In June of 1985, he was ordered to serve two concurrent 20-year prison terms.

- *Michael Senft.* Senft was convicted of using his Sentinel Government Securities and Sentinel Financial Instruments entities to dummy up phony tax deductions for his investors, by concocting fraudulent security trades. In July 1984, he was sentenced to 15 years in prison.

- *Edwin L. Cox, Jr.* Mr. Cox was accused of improper conduct in connection with an $80 million loan he received from a bank on whose board he served as a director. Cox paid back the $80 million loan to

First Republic Bank in full. Notwithstanding the repayment, Cox was
sentenced to six months in prison, a $250,000 fine, and 1000 hours of
community service.[2]

As *The Wall Street Journal* put it in its headline description of some
recent sentencings: "Hard time: White-collar offender . . . finds little
mercy, gets sentenced to tough prison."

These harsh sentences, frequently much harsher than those imposed
on armed robbers, rapists, and those convicted of aggravated assault,
reveal another distressing feature of the system mentioned in another
chapter: randomness.

Consider the case of Richard Cannisgraro, whose story was described
in *The Wall Street Journal*.[3] Professor Allen Dershowitz of the Harvard
Law School cited evidence that "we still live in an age of roulette
justice."

Cannisgraro was accused of stock manipulation. Cannisgraro and a
partner, Richard Brotoli, participated in business ventures which Cannisgraro touted through favorable research reports. The government
alleged that the companies were really shams, and that Cannisgraro's
research reports were intended to manipulate the stock price, which
did in fact rise after the publication of the Cannisgraro reports.

Although Cannisgraro did not get rich from his efforts, his life
quickly turned sour. An intelligent man who had earned college and
graduate degrees by the age of 20 from the Massachusetts Institute of
Technology, Cannisgraro had been a prosperous vice president at the
New York office of Wood Gundy, Inc. When the SEC began its investigation, he was terminated from his job with Wood Gundy, fled, and ultimately was convicted. One need not trivialize the serious allegations
against Mr. Cannisgraro to find his sentence, which might bring him up
to 45 years, once pending RICO charges are finally concluded, a bit
harsh.

Cannisgraro ran into a hard-as-nails prosecutor and a law-and-order
judge, Alfred Lechner, Jr. As the judge sentenced Cannisgraro, he compared him to a bank robber. "You took money out of the pockets of the
very people who could not afford it, the small investor, the person who
looks to the noncompromised, market analyst for help." In addition to
an eight-year sentence, Mr. Cannisgraro was ordered to pay restitution
of $725,000, the entire amount of his life savings not already eaten up
by payment to attorneys. The judge denied Cannisgraro's attempt to be

[2] *The Wall Street Journal* (September 8, 1988).

[3] *The Wall Street Journal* (December 18, 1990).

free on bail so he could get his affairs together before going to jail. He left the courtroom in handcuffs (no doubt the result, in part, of his prior attempt to seclude himself in California). The last few years for Mr. Cannisgraro have been characterized by frequent moves from prison to prison, strip searches, hard time in metropolitan correctional facilities, and the other indignities of being a federal prisoner. He would most certainly have done far better if he had chosen to be a bank robber.

Boyd L. Jefferies was a creative force for innovation in the securities industry. His company, Jefferies and Company, facilitated the efforts of institutional investors to be able to trade stocks anywhere in the world and at any time. Jefferies knew the arbitrageurs; they knew his customers. His work habits were the subject of frequent commentary. He rose each day at 1:00 a.m. and was at his office by 3:00 a.m. The logo of his company was a lion standing on its hind legs, its paws ready to do battle. Jefferies ultimately pled guilty to two criminal violations of federal securities laws, resigned as Chairman and CEO of Jefferies and Company, the firm he founded 25 years earlier, and agreed to be barred from the securities business for at least five years.[4]

Things Could Be Worse

If the sentences described above can result from "paper" crimes, one can imagine the kinds of sentences that may be handed down in the future for negligence in providing safe environments for employees. Illinois state's highest court ruled in 1990 that state prosecutors can file criminal charges, including murder and assault, against employers for injuring their employees at work.[5] And there is a growing trend around the country to prosecute "crimes" in the workplace.

The best known case was the prosecution of three management-level employees of Elk Grove Village, Ill. Film Recovery Systems, Inc. A court in Chicago in 1985 found the three executives guilty of murder in the poisoning death of an employee who was exposed to toxic substances at his workplace. After the Elk Grove case, it is increasingly apparent that business executives might find themselves exposed to the most serious criminal charges solely for negligent behavior in not measuring up to appropriate standards of due care in the protection of employees.

Some of these cases are, to be sure, gripping and abhorrent. In one

[4]See *New Times* (March 20, 1987).

[5]*The New York Times* (October 17, 1990).

case in New York, inspectors were intentionally kept away from a mercury reclamation operation in the company's basement which the court found to be "clandestine." Employees worked without adequate ventilation and were exposed to mercury oozing from broken thermometers. One of the employees, Vidal Rodriguez, suffered permanent brain damage due to his working, sometimes without a respirator, feeding a glass crusher with broken thermometers. Such facts, especially the sad reality of permanent physical damage, make a court willing to impose serious sentences. From 1970 to 1988, the first 18 years of OSHA, only 14 people had been prosecuted for safety violations. None went to jail. Now prosecutions are increasing across the country. The standards to which the employers are held are far from clear. The tendency to impose criminal prosecution for negligently failing to live up to that ambiguous standard is troubling. As one New York lawyer, in favor of the trend, points out, "If a corporate executive is in fear of going to jail, he's much more likely to be careful than if it's merely a civil fine which could be seen as a cost of doing business."

Business people face consequences other than prison. The criminal investigation division of the Internal Revenue Service, for example, began some 6000 criminal investigations in 1984.[6] Each one had a variety of potential consequences on conviction of tax fraud beyond fines, penalties, and prison:

1. possible loss of professional and business licenses, or of a government job;

2. loss of the right to possess firearms;

3. potential deportation of aliens or ineligibility to obtain citizenship;

4. loss of civil rights (such as the right to vote, to serve on a jury or as a fiduciary, etc.); and

5. harm to business through adverse publicity.[7]

These consequences are in addition to the possibility of five years in jail for each offense and fines of $100,000 a year (for individuals) or $500,000 a year (for corporations), to say nothing of interest, underlying taxes, civil fraud penalties, the cost of prosecution, and the like.

In short, the trend in penalties is going the same direction as the trend in prosecutions. Penalties for white-collar crime are regularly enhanced. Take, for example, the Insider Trading and Securities Fraud

---

[6]See *Annual Report of the Commissioner of Internal Revenue* (1985) at 18.

[7]See § 13.01 of *White Collar Crime: Business and Regulatory Offenses,* Obermaier and Morvillo (Law Journal Seminars–Press, 1990), at 13-3.

Enforcement Act of 1988, signed by President Reagan shortly after the presidential election in 1988. Maximum jail terms for securities fraud went from five to ten years. Fines went from $100,000 to $1,000,000 for individuals and from $500,000 to $2,500,000 for corporations. And, among other things, the law gave the SEC the right to reward "snitches" with 10 percent of the ultimate penalty imposed on the offender.[8]

The penalties for corporate entities became even more severe when the guidelines of the U.S. Sentencing Commission were enacted into law in October, 1991. When the points are calculated and the multipliers are applied, a corporation may find itself required to pay in fines and penalties four to five times what damages in civil lawsuit might have been. The adoption of those guidelines constitute the most dramatic increase in penalties for corporate crime ever.

Every company executive would do well to read the statute carefully (it wonderfully focuses the mind) and begin to implement immediately the compliance program described in the law, containing the elements described generally in Chapter 8. Such a program may do more than mitigate criminal penalties and show "present responsibility" to administrators contemplating debarment. It may encourage a prosecutor to use discretion and not prosecute in the first place.

At Whose Discretion?

These examples of white-collar punishment reflect the great amount of discretion resident in the criminal justice system. What one prosecutor views as unworthy of his or her attention or refers out for quick civil resolution, another views as a heinous offense. A hostile prosecutor can multiply counts, oppose normal requests for pretrial bail release, stretch the resources of the most wealthy of defendants, and seek the full panoply of criminal sanctions.

As Ira Reiner, a prosecutor in Los Angeles, was quoted as saying in *The Washington Post,*

> A fine, no matter how substantial, is simply a cost of doing business for a corporation. But a jail term for executives is different. What we are trying to do is to change the corporate culture.[9]

Even more frightening is the almost universal policy that some individual target must plead guilty to something and must do some time.

---

[8]"The Case of the Criminal Corporation," *The New York Times* (January 15, 1989).

[9]*The Washington Post*, p. A1 (March 2, 1990).

Corporate pleas are hardly harmless. But no one worries about the corporate seal being sent to jail.

The public policy requiring individuals to plead and serve long sentences is not self-evident. Several penalogical studies suggest that white-collar criminals respond about equally to two months, two years, or for that matter, twenty years in jail, assuming one also takes all their ill-gotten gains away. Indeed, short jail terms seem to have more deterrent effect, if anything.

It is hard to see what other purposes are served, certainly not rehabilitative or the protection of society from these generally skilled, nonviolent professions, by long prison terms for white-collar convicts. Society needs no special protection from a white-collar criminal, whose reputation is ruined and who is not prone to violence. But nonetheless the staggering sentences continue.

The real answer lies in a sophisticated form of social vengeance. White-collar defendants are easy targets for both judicial rhetoric and judicial action. They have commanded an inordinate number of societal privileges in their homes and estates, automobiles, clubs, travel, and wardrobes. The deals they do are large and beyond the common person's immediate ken. When they abuse these privileges, there is an understandable sense of outrage which translates into serious punishment.

The meaning for all of this for the business executive is clear: Stay way away from the gray. Any intentional straying into the gray areas of government regulations are an increasingly great risk. Using a safe but unauthorized ingredient, taking an "aggressive" position with the IRS, or making a representation that used to be called *normal puffery*, can land one in serious jeopardy. Given the declining respect of the public for business people generally, a prosecutor may choose to indict, a jury may choose to convict, and a judge may find that a single decision netted millions of dollars of ill-gotten gains. The result? A large steel door may open slowly and welcome you to a lengthy, rent-free stay at a government prison.

14

The Public Relations Problem

What Does One Say?

The "just spell my name right" theory of public relations needs serious footnoting when the front page story announces a criminal indictment of your company. "No news is good news" becomes the more trustworthy axiom.

In a day when U.S. Attorneys have public relations officers, celebrated defendants can expect a well-constructed detailed account of the government's allegations against them. While federal prosecutors are not subject to election, their ultimate boss is. They remember the one who brought them to the dance. And they hope the President remembers them when he is considering appointments to lifetime tenure on the prestigious federal bench.

The result is an increasing inclination to deliver press releases to the local newspaper and television stations, *The Wall Street Journal,* even remote cities with a corporate headquarters or plant in the area, that announce the misbehavior of the alleged white-collar criminal. For major cases, the Attorney General of the United States will fly in. At a news conference with cameras whirring and clicking, the Attorney General, the U.S. Attorney, and an entourage of assistants and agents will applaud themselves for convincing a grand jury to indict the company.

Those present will, of course, want the other side of the story. And by the time of this indictment, the story may be old news. The media may already have been tipped off to a search warrant to be served on the company or may be told plainly by prosecutors that a company or individual is "under investigation." Such a public statement by a prosecutor may raise ethical questions relating to the need for grand jury secrecy, but it is done. And the media will want to hear from the investigator.

The executive may get conflicting advice. The public relations expert says some comment is absolutely necessary. A conservative white-collar crime lawyer says "no comment" is absolutely necessary. What is the executive supposed to do?

The issue is the same whether the government has tipped off the newspapers to criminal investigation, a mysterious fire in a losing subsidiary, or a revelation about an improper export of sensitive material abroad. The insistent media shove microphones in the faces of corporate personnel and leave demanding messages at the offices of corporate spokespersons. If you answer the request, the press may mangle it. If you say "no comment," you must have done something wrong. If you don't return the call, you will hear, "Despite repeated efforts to reach Mr. Smith, he refused to return our calls."

Consider first the conventional wisdom. The reflexive response of most lawyers is to put a tight lid on all communications. "We cannot comment while this matter is under investigation." Or, "We do not try our cases in the newspapers." Or, "It would be highly improper for us to comment at this time." Or, "The company believes that it has a meritorious defense, and it will become apparent in due course." While many a corporate executive chafes under this kind of advice—wanting to confront the criticism or suspicion directly—there are both principled and practical reasons underlying it.

One principled reason is that lawyers themselves can get into trouble from excessive comments on pending litigation. Lawyers properly must avoid violating the ethical rules of their profession in such circumstances. The American Bar Association (ABA) Code of Professional Responsibility has been adopted in most states. The ABA Code 3.6 applies to statements in any adjudicated proceeding. It prohibits statements which relate to the following:

1. the character credibility reputation or criminal record of a party, criminal suspect, or witness;

2. in a criminal case, the possibility of a guilty plea or the contents of any confession;

3. the results of any examination or test or refusal to take such a test;

4. any opinion as to the guilt or innocence of a defendant;

5. any information the lawyer knows would be inadmissible as evidence at trial;

6. the fact that a defendant has been charged with a crime unless there is included a statement explaining that one is innocent until proven guilty.

Some states, to be sure, are more liberal. In Minnesota, for example, the Minnesota Rules of Professional Conduct have the following restrictions in Rule 3.6:

Rule 3.6 Trial Publicity.
A lawyer shall not make an extra judicial statement that a reasonable person would expect to be disseminated by means of public communication if the lawyer knows or reasonably should know that it will have a substantial likelihood of materially prejudicing a pending criminal jury trial.

Such a rule provides great latitude for comments in the public record. But even such a rule is not without its risks.

Notwithstanding risks inherent in these rules, some lawyers seek to use the press as a weapon in contested criminal matters. Howard Weitzman, in his successful defense of John DeLorean, was holding press conferences almost daily about the trial, commenting on evidence included and excluded, tactics, and rulings. He served almost as a color commentator on the proceeding. The strategy was effective in creating the picture of a defendant who was the subject of government persecution and overreaching. DeLorean's double acquittals may have occurred anyway, without the public relations effort, but it is hard to argue that Weitzman's skillful use of the press hurt the cause. Most lawyers, however, are neither particularly competent for nor comfortable with the use of the media to advance their cause.

There are also practical reasons for restricting the flow of information about the case. The first has to do with a basic rule of warfare: *don't tell the enemy anything.* Criminal proceedings proceed by ambush. The government has a vast arsenal of information that it does not willingly share with defendants, except when statutes or judges force them to disclose it. Defense lawyers also want to shield facts they know about (as well as their strategy and tactics) behind an impenetrable curtain. They don't want potential defendants or an agent of the potential defendant to be revealing battle plans or other secrets when fielding extemporaneous answers to media questions.

Few executives have the ability to fence with the press like an experienced politician and not make mistakes or give up secrets. I recall one press conference where an executive, in a show of frankness and candor, was handling every question, often without knowledge of the underlying facts. As the answers became more speculative and conjectural, the executive sensed he was getting in trouble. He sensed he was shooting from the hip or flying by the seat of his pants. He decided to proceed anyway. Unfortunately, he was not a smooth extemporaneous speaker, and mixed his metaphors. He concluded, "I know on some of these key questions I'm just shooting from the seat of my pants."

Talk in Haste; Repent at Leisure

The second consideration is also an age old rule: *what you say today may not be what you want to have said after full examination tomorrow.* Let's suppose, for example, that the executive comes out with a ringing denial. He issues a release to *The Wall Street Journal* that lampoons the government for its overreaching, its obscure regulations, and its persecution of an innocent company. The *Journal,* suspicious of the government's white-collar crime efforts, prints the story, prominently. What can occur?

- A government agency looking at whether or not to debar the company reads the bold reaction of the corporate official and puts it in the file, as proof that the company has done wrong and has acted irresponsibly and unrepentantly. When the company later seeks to demonstrate present responsibility before its chief regulator, company counsel will see that clipping again, and the present talk of "owning up" and "taking responsibility" will look strangely hollow.

- The prosecutor reads the press release and sees red. Few things in life have the fury of a government employee scorned. And now the prosecutor begins laying elaborate plans not to cooperate with the defense in any endeavor. The U.S. Attorney's office may issue its own releases, campaign for a high sentence, and attempt to ensure that any civil or administrative penalties are exacted in full from the corporate hide, writing "over the back fence" secret letters to the government agency in question.

- The judge reads the *Journal* and concludes that the corporation is challenging a prosecutor the judge knows well. The judge also was likely a prosecutor at one time. The article is filed away in memory when the judge is called up to exercise discretion on behalf of the corporation during the criminal proceeding.

- Competitors read the article and gain new knowledge of the corporation's problems. The press release, with its ringing denial, is news. It has a tendency to highlight the investigation. The competitor begins to get copies of the indictment. Mysteriously, they turn up in the hands of the defendant's customers.

- Six months later there is a plea in which the corporation, on advice of counsel, admits to each element in the indictment, and acknowledges that the behavior was criminal. The U.S. Attorney issues its own release to *The Wall Street Journal,* detailing the plea and the enormous fine.

The executive has succeeded in venting his anger at the government. He has won some public relations points from readers of the *Journal,* who nod knowingly and say, "just like the government." But later he may wish the press release had never happened. Act in haste; repent at leisure.

Things can be even more complicated. The defense can take a firm position on one critical fact. "We have no evidence that the ingredients came from abroad." Two days later, the company may find such evidence. And now the defense is, "We do not believe this regulation bars ingredients that come from abroad." Such shifting assertions create an almost irrebuttable presumption in the public mind: *guilty as charged.* I have never, in some 45 jury trials, ever presented the case to the jury precisely as I initially thought I would when doing my initial interview of witnesses. There is always substantial refinement. More often than not, the case is far different from the one I thought I had. Why pin yourself down in public print if you don't have to?

Gasoline on the Fire

Comments also continue to rivet public attention on a corporate embarrassment. If the local stringer for the newspaper picks up the indictment, or there's a press release from the prosecutor announcing it, you may get lucky and find only two or three paragraphs on the indictment buried in the business section. If you have a press conference or issue a colorful or combative release, you are guaranteed two more stories, the one covering the release, and the one giving the government response. The press, as we all know, can be insatiable. The more it is fed, the more its interest in the controversy grows. In one investigation of a U.S. senator, the senator issued a lengthy release, containing some 35 facts, all of which he believed in good faith to be true. Nearly all of them later became inoperative. In the release, he referred to a document filed with the local registrar of titles. The press had no prior knowledge of the document. When they found it, there was clear evidence that that public filing had been back-dated, which led to further reports, investigations, and ultimately the suspension of the senator's right to practice law in his home state. Arguably, some or all of those things might not have happened but for the press release that the senator felt was "absolutely necessary" for public relations.

Such principled and practical objections to comment suggest a relatively clear strategy: *don't comment unless you have to.* Alas, however, such decisions in a day of expanding white-collar crime litigation is not so simple. There are other things to consider than merely the ethical constraints and litigation tactics of company counsel. Refusal to comment, the classic *stonewall* approach, may have costs that outweigh any benefits in litigation. Reactions to a corporate crisis may have a devastating impact on the business which outweighs even the seriousness of a criminal investigation. How many nuclear power plants, for example, have been built after the Three-Mile Island event?

Take the case of the Exxon *Valdez,* which John Holusha rightly called "Exxon's public relations problem" in *The New York Times.*[1] Some think the headline could have been more descriptive. Many would have called Exxon's handling of the oil spill into Prince William's Sound as a public relations disaster.

There are, of course, no great options when an oil tanker spews millions of gallons of heavy lubricant into pristine wilderness waters. Exxon decided to play it safe. For a week after the disaster Exxon had "no comment." Refusals to comment on such a nightmare suggest to many corporate insouciance, if not downright corporate irresponsibility. It is like Cain responding to God after murdering his brother, "Am I my brother's keeper?" Exxon's "no comment" approach seemed to signal a hard-shelled corporate disinterest: "It's not our problem."

Next, Exxon changed its game plan and began to comment. It made a variety of statements explaining how the accident occurred. These defensive comments appeared self-justifying. No one looks good as a judge in its own cause, and Exxon seemed to be acquitting itself prematurely. Worse yet, its factual assertions were contradicted by other companies in the industry. Now the image went from irresponsibility to self-righteous abnegation of responsibility to pernicious misrepresentation.

---

[1] *The New York Times* (April 21, 1989).

Finally, Exxon held a press conference for a more complete "hang-out." But it chose to do so in Valdez, Alaska, somewhat off the normal beat of the major American media. Such a venue was hardly likely to trigger an outpouring of warm commentary from uncomfortable reporters trying to find a free phone in Valdez. And when Exxon finally did run a series of newspaper advertisements, they still did not accept responsibility. Their regrets were perceived as "too little, too late."

Whatever the results of the criminal and civil proceedings, could they do worse damage to the company than the public relations disaster Exxon created in the aftermath of the spill? Indeed, as Holusha points out, some have speculated that the Valdez spill ultimately would convince the government not to permit the oil industry to carry out its dream of drilling in the Arctic National Wildlife Refuge.

The decision not to make a comment may reflect on the individuals investigated as well. For example, the Chicago Mercantile Exchange formed a special study group to consider what trading changes might be necessary: "Much to the disappointment of many members," *The New York Times* reported, "the Board said it would stick to its position of not commenting on the inquiry unless formal charges were brought. Many traders and brokers say the Exchange should be more aggressive in rebutting even the suggestion that cheating is all too common at the Exchange."[2]

A contrasting case is the Ashland Oil spill. Ashland Oil had to deal with a collapse of an oil tank. The collapse spilled enormous amounts of oil into the Monongahela River in Pennsylvania. Ashland's president, John Hall, initially said, "no comment," heeding the advice of his lawyers. But as the oil worked its way down river, threatening drinking water, Hall flew down the river to examine the site. He was appalled. He came to the conclusion that he must speak out. Lawyers counseled him against doing so. His statements might well be admissions used against the company in litigation. The potential liabilities for the company, quite obviously, were enormous. But Hall ignored the advice. "Our company had inconvenienced the lives of a lot of people, and I felt it was only right to apologize." He went before the press and took questions about sensitive matters head on. He admitted that the company did not have a written permit for the tank and said that while the company had conducted tests which complied with federal standards, they were less extensive than Ashland liked to do. "If we made mistakes, we have to stand up and admit them. I would have preferred that we had done

---

[2] *The New York Times* (February 1, 1989).

some things differently—like (not) using 40 year old steel."[3] The general impression was that Ashland Oil was not a group of corporate outlaws but "pretty good guys."

A similar strategy worked effectively in Chrysler's indictment for selling some 60,000 cars and trucks that were driven by employees with odometers detached. Chrysler had sold the cars as new, notwithstanding the employee use. Lee Iacocca again disregarded the "no comment" advice of his lawyers. He said Chrysler's behavior "went beyond dumb and reached all the way out to stupid . . . the only law we broke was the law of common sense." He went on to say that Chrysler would make anyone whole who bought one of the cars, "This is not a product recall. The only thing we are recalling here is our integrity. Did we screw up? You bet we did. I am damn sorry it happened and you can bet it won't happen again, and that's a promise."[4] After the press conference, the price of Chrysler stock rose, and Chrysler ultimately settled the class action lawsuit and pled nolo contendere to a criminal action.

A similar public relations technique was chosen by Honeywell. The problem was apparent. Honeywell had mistakenly permitted technical data to be exported. There was evidence that it had found its way into the hands of the Iraqis. The timing of the revelation was particularly painful. It came just as the Gulf War was beginning and American troops were risking their lives in a foreign theater. The president of Honeywell announced that the company had been wrong, and apologized, but nonetheless suggested that there had been no criminal wrongdoing. The revelation, though front page news in several newspapers, blew over quickly and, from a public relations standpoint, the *confession and avoidance* appeared to work well.

Neither the talk nor the "keep the lid on" strategies are without perils. There is no universally right strategy when disaster occurs. But some rules make sense, across the board.

Manager or Managee?

Corporations ought to manage crises and not let crises manage them. A company ought to seek to control the flow and accuracy of information. A crisis is, after all, a double-edged sword. The word *crisis* in Chinese has

---

[3]Clare Ansberry, "Oil Spill in Midwest Provides Case Study in Crisis Management," *The Wall Street Journal* (January 8, 1988).

[4]John Bussey, "Lee Iacocca Calls Odometer Policy Dumb," *The Wall Street Journal* (July 2, 1987).

two characters, *danger* and *opportunity*. In Greek, *krisis* means judgment to acquittal or conviction and comes from a root word that means to divide in two. A crisis point in illness is when the patient hovers at an intersection between life and death. At such moments, companies at a critical fork in the road must seize the opportunity to choose a path and make the best of it.

Every company should, therefore, prepare plans to deal with corporate crime. Such crisis planning has several elements. First, management should define and categorize potential crises. The kinds of crises will range from takeover rumors, to termination of key officers, to shareholder suits, to the corporation as victim of computer crime, of embezzlement, or extortion. There may be crises from layoffs difficult to explain in the local community, recalls, problems with corporate products, union battles, and a host of other problems. Among the possible crises, however, should be included the potential for a criminal or regulatory investigation against the company.

Once the crises are laid out, the company should form a team. The irreducible minimum of such a team is the president, the public relations officer, and company counsel. A corporation may want to engage an outside consultant. Good outside consultants can bring a dispassionate, thoroughly objective view different from those who have actually lived through the problem.

As Gilbert Osnos put it in *Business Management Skills*, "The arrival of a crisis manager in the company means you have a relationship which creates the classic good news/bad news situation. You already know the bad news, because the company was already in trouble. The good news is that corrective measures will follow shortly."

That team can then proceed to deal with the crisis when it occurs, absent any member—whether crisis manager or lawyer—who may be inappropriate because he or she is tarnished personally by the nature of the allegations.

This team should have one spokesperson through whom all information passes. No one else on the team should be speaking to the media, absent special circumstances.

There is nothing more attractive to a reporter in search of a story than to get apparently conflicting accounts from different corporate representatives. The choice of the speaker is critical. Using the chief executive officer is often a tour de force. It underscores the importance of the matter to the company, and negates the feeling that delegation ultimately represents shuffling off responsibility to somebody else. When the corporate executive is quick on his or her feet, tough, smart, and sincere, the strategy works well.

Sometimes, however, there is a more suitable speaker. The chief executive officer must, after all, look after the day-to-day interests of the company, and it is understandable when someone else is used as liaison with the media. When the latter person is chosen, he or she may know reporters personally and have accumulated goodwill over several years of contact with the people who will actually be doing the reporting.

The team should also consider how the information will be gathered when crisis occurs. The speaker will hear the question, "What happened?" And that question will be followed by another, "What are you doing about it?" The team will need to know how information will be collected before disseminating it to the media. Team members need phone numbers, business and home, of other members of the team, as well as the identity and telephone numbers of the necessary support staff. The rule seems almost inviolate. A criminal investigation will occur when you least expect it. Like a good military assault at night, an investigation often appears suddenly, like a Stealth Bomber at 12 o'clock high.

Some Guidelines

As important as any of these recommendations, however, is the proper care and feeding of members of the press. They will determine how the cold facts are portrayed. Those reporters will have almost untrammeled discretion on how the facts are organized and presented. As one politician used to say, "Never get into a war of words with people who buy ink by the barrel." That suggests the following rules:

1. *Treat the reporters with dignity.*   Reporters like to view themselves as professionals. They have antennae highly sensitized to detect disrespect or irreverence directed at their social status by business people. Even if media representatives are obnoxious or insistent, they should be treated as people who are only doing their job. Everything should be done for their creature and ego comforts. They should be extended every courtesy and given the benefit of every doubt.

2. *Don't play favorites.*   There is a temptation to ignore the local media and to play to the national media, or to slip out information to favorite reporters. That strategy tends to create one friendly and many hostile accounts of the same information.

3. *Choose words carefully.*   "No comment" has generally lost its usefulness. Some words do not age well. The word *stink* used to be neutral. *Smell* is on the way to meaning *stink*. In a few years, *fragrant* will probably be in the same category, with someone rushing to the window, with

wrinkled nose saying, "There seems to be a fragrance in here." In the same vein, "no comment" has lost its usefulness. It is better to say, "I'm sorry, I'd like to help you out, but I just can't tell you."

4. *Think carefully before seeking a correction.* The account that ultimately comes out in the press, or on television, will contain many errors. Some of them will be a major source of irritation to corporate insiders. Good outside consultants can sometimes calm vexed executives before they launch a major assault that looks like nit-picking to the public and like a personal offense to the media. Battling public presses, with their barrels of ink, is unwise. If there is a major misstatement, it may be sensible to correct it. Seeking to correct some minor tidbit will add further gasoline to the flames, and may have the paradoxical effect of hurting the image of the corrector.

5. *Tell the truth, the whole truth, and nothing but the truth.* Cover-ups are more damaging than the facts which they seek to cover up. The textbook example on that is Watergate. The investigative reporter loves to catch someone in a lie. Don't be a risk taker. If a statement is subject to question, don't say it. Better to suffer in silence than to suffer as an exposed liar.

6. *Never assume that you are "off the record."* Those who do not deal often with the media are sometimes shocked to find things reported that they thought were "off the record." Some reporters, probably most reporters, are quite scrupulous about living up to promises about keeping things off the record. But that promise must be explicit. And even if explicit, the matter will likely ultimately appear in some form. The best rule is also a simple one. If you don't want it to appear in print, don't say it.

7. *Never comment in anger.* When one's viscera are rumbling in controversy, one's mouth ought to be shut. Many misstatements come from anger or bitterness. Even if the statements are true, the statements sound bitter and defensive. And angry comments are generally not sensible comments. Wait until the emotion subsides before exposing one's indignation to the media.

For Further Reading

Aronson Ward, Inc., *The Leadership Advantage in Crisis Communications*, 1988.
Donald W. Blohowiak, *No Comment! An Executive's Essential Guide to the News Media*, Praeger, 1987.
Warren Brown, "Thriving on Corporate Trouble: Public Relations Firms Con-

sultants Helping Put Out Bad News," *The Washington Post* (November 13, 1990).

Robert L. Dilenschneider, *Power and Influence: Mastering the Art of Persuasion*, Prentice Hall Press, 1990.

Fred J. Evans, *Managing the Media: Proactive Strategy for Better Business—Press Relations*, Quorum Books, 1987.

Dennis Cole Hill, *Power PR: A Street Fighter's Handbook of Winning Public Relations*, Fell Publishers, 1990.

Nancy Jeffrey, "Preparing for the Worst, Firms Set Up Plans to Help Deal With Corporate Crises," *The Wall Street Journal* (December 7, 1989).

15

The Race Is Not Always to the Swift

Judge Solomon, having tried his share of difficult cases, gives us his reflections using the persona of the preacher in the Book of Ecclesiastes. Among his many quotable conclusions from a lifetime of observation is this one:

> I returned and saw under the sun that the race is not to the swift, nor the battle to the strong, neither yet bread to the wise, nor yet riches to men of understanding, nor yet favour to men of skill, but time and chance happeneth to them all.[1]

Those who defend white-collar crime cases find Solomon's axiom resonating with their own experience. Predicting the outcome of any criminal case is dicey. An overwhelming defense may not persuade a jury. Evidence of guilt so substantial that the prosecutor refuses even to discuss a plea bargain may result in a full acquittal. The element of fate and chance enters into every prosecution.

The legendary litigator, Henry Halladay (whose accomplishments included winning the famous patent case testing who had prior claim to the invention of the computer, Honeywell or Univac), was once asked by an aspiring trial lawyer what was the most important trait in an effective litigator. Halladay thought for a moment, inhaling his ever-present

---

[1] *The Bible*, "The Book of Ecclesiastes," chapter 9, verse 11.

cigarette, "Given the luck of this business," he said finally, "eternal insecurity."

The randomness factor is, of course, a double-edged sword. To defendants embarrassed by the weakness of their cause, it offers hope. To defendants righteously indignant about the weakness of the charge, it awakens fear. There are no reliable handicappers in the white-collar crime business. Fate and chance happen across the board, popping up in jury selection, judicial attitude toward the case, and the twists and turns of trial itself.

As a recent law school graduate newly hired by a large law firm, I was given the opportunity to become Chief Public Defender in the county for nine months. The firm paid me but I administered the office, taking trials for myself that I thought might improve my experience. The Monday after being sworn in as a lawyer before the Supreme Court in my state, I was defending misdemeanants against criminal charges. One of my first jury trials had an intimidating set of facts. The defendant was 18 years old. He had been clocked at 110 mph on a local highway. He had exited by driving across three lanes without signaling. When the police began to pursue him, giving admonitions by loudspeaker, Mars lights flashing, and sirens wailing, it took approximately one mile for the defendant to recognize and respond to the policeman's appeals to pull over.

When the policeman opened the door to get his license, he fell out of the car. There were six bottles of strong beer (beer with alcohol content greater than 3.2 percent) by his feet, three of them empty, two of them full, one of them half and half. A breathalyzer put his blood alcohol content at 0.18 percent, nearly double the Minnesota standard for drunk driving of 0.10 percent. He was charged with two counts of drunk driving, one count of reckless driving, one count of hazardous speeding, and one count of open bottle.

He wore a soiled T-shirt to court the morning of the trial, half tucked into his faded jeans. His face was puffy and his eyes bloodshot at 9:00 a.m. in the morning. His father sat in the back of the courtroom to follow the trial. He later confided in me that he came in hopes that his son would be convicted. The case was not without its challenges.

During the voir dire, in which a lawyer interviews the jury panel, it became apparent that the jurors were relatively nondescript. After one disqualified himself, a new member was added to the panel. The clerk read the name, "Rose Wipley." Rose came from the back of the courtroom wearing a purple print dress, black schoolmarm shoes, and a black hat covering silver hair that appeared to be tightly knotted in a bun. She took her seat in the jury box and sat there primly. In response to questions, she responded that she had been a lifelong school teacher, was 67 years old, and was now retired. She had never had a driver's license nor driven a car. She was unmarried and had been single all her life.

As I tracked her responses, I quickly concluded that she was everything a prospective juror should not be for the case at hand. The treatises on jury selection with their boldface *practice pointers* would point her the way off the panel. I had a peremptory strike left. But with an increasing sense of resignation and gloom at the case presenting itself to me, I could not exercise the strike. I left Rose on the panel.

The trial went as anticipated. I hammered on the test and its extrapolation of data from microscopic samples. I produced, as was my ethical duty, every argument I could think of for my client. The prosecutor, meanwhile, was also a lawyer in private practice, whose firm contracted with the suburb to undertake these criminal prosecutions. He did a commendable job. After two days of trial, the jury was sent out. When it came back an hour and a half later, the foreman articulated the words no one expected to hear. "Not guilty on every charge."

I turned around quickly, expecting a handshake from my client, but his nerve impulses were not traveling at normal speed. He still looked benumbed by the process—at least I hoped it was the process. His father made a gesture of regret at the back of the courtroom and walked out quickly. The prosecutor charged after the jury, inquiring with scarcely concealed frustration about the logic of their verdict. I ascribed it, as trial lawyers are wont to do, to good advocacy.

Two weeks later, I was defending a group of Minneapolis citizens accused of brawling in a bar on Franklin Avenue. A number of other long-time defense counsel represented other individuals. The witnesses were sequestered. In the "trial by ambush" setting so typical in criminal proceedings, none of the defense lawyers knew whom the city was going to call. After the normal pretrial skirmishing, the prosecutor rose to call his first sequestered witness. "Rose Wipley, please."

The name sounded dimly familiar, but it was lost in the fog of two dozen trials since that last drunk driving case. I looked with some curiosity toward the double doors at the back of the courtroom to see if I could recall how or where I had heard the name before. Into the courtroom, with self-demeaning grace, strode a women in black schoolmarm shoes, a purple print dress, and a black hat with a hint of a veil, covering silver hair tightly wrapped in a bun. It was my juror in the DWI (driving while intoxicated) case. What could she be doing here?

Rose took the stand, was sworn, and began to answer questions. She confirmed that she was 67, a retired school teacher, and had lived a single life, all of it in Minneapolis. Then the questioning got somewhat more specific:

QUESTION: Directing your attention to the night of June 23rd, where were you at that time?

ANSWER: At the Poodle Dog Bar.

QUESTION: Is that the one on Franklin and 13th?

ANSWER: Yes, sir.

QUESTION: When did you arrive at the Poodle Dog?

ANSWER: About 9:30 a.m.

QUESTION: How long were you there that day?

ANSWER: Until approximately closing time.

QUESTION: At approximately 10:00 at night did you observe a scuffle on the premises?

ANSWER: Yes, sir, I did.

QUESTION: What had you been doing at the bar prior to that time?

ANSWER: Just what I normally do most days. Playing poker, and talking with my friends.

QUESTION: Prior to getting to what occurred here, did you have anything to drink during that day?

ANSWER: Not much.

QUESTION: How much is "not much"?

ANSWER: Seven or eight strong beers.

Rose went on to give a detailed description of the bar brawl, fortunately distancing my client from the combat, and ultimately leading to his acquittal.

It turned out that Rose had been the stubborn juror in the DWI case who insisted that the modest quantity of alcohol consumed by the 18 year old was hardly enough to have had an impact on his driving. She had been the iron lady who won the acquittal for which my client had not been duly grateful. The race had not gone to the swift. Providence had overruled. Or put another way, it showed again the truth of another axiom: *it is better to be lucky than good.*

Experienced trial lawyers have their own unscientific hunches about jurors. The more famous the lawyer, of course, the more such hunches become dogma. Clarence Darrow wrote a classic description of jury selection in a 1936 issue of *Esquire Magazine.* Interstrewn among his tips were highly specific rules:

An Englishman is not so good as an Irishman. . . . If a Presbyterian enters the box, let him go . . . if possible, the Baptists are more hopeless than the Presbyterians . . . beware of the Lutherans especially the Scandinavians . . . especially [keep] Jews and agnostics. I formed a fixed opinion that [women jurors] were absolutely dependable, but I did not want them.[2]

Such casual stereotypy may have some basis. But it is not long in a criminal practice before Rose makes her way into the box and one's theories have to be adjusted.

Lawyers read jury reactions in different ways. During voir dire of one panel, a juror smilingly acknowledged she knew me. As the strikes were made, I noticed the other lawyer was not striking her. I figured he was saving her for last. But in his last strike he struck the woman next to her, not her.

I leaned over and whispered to my client, "I can't believe he didn't strike her. He must have forgotten that she knew me."

My client grinned wryly, "I wouldn't be so sure," he said. "Maybe her knowing you is what he's banking on."

The same holds true with judges. Those who deal with judges in criminal proceedings know that the quality of their judgment is not necessarily better, and is sometimes far worse, than that administered by juries. It is subject to unpredictable twists and turns as well.

Al Dobbins was a successful dealer in private planes. Indeed, he was the top salesman of Ballanca Aircraft in the early 1970s. But the oil crunch hit. His business got in trouble and soon thereafter, he did too.

He sought to supplement his dealership income by hiring himself out as a pilot. His clientele hired him to make business trips around the country, and sometimes even to the Caribbean. He asked no questions. He simply flew the plane.

He flew a plane on this occasion to the Bahamas. His mission was to pick up some businessmen and bring them back to the United States. He was then to leave the plane at an airport in the Georgia countryside. His client supplied the plan and the plane. When he arrived in the Bahamas, he was advised that the trip was off and he should fly back to the United States. Before he could do so, he was arrested by Bahamian police at the airport. The local Bahamian officials said that the plane he was flying had been reported stolen from the United States. The police told him that he would not be released until the FBI arrived from the United States and had time to question him.

But after several hours the FBI had not arrived and then, mysteriously, the Bahamians let him go. He decided to fly the airplane back to the United States and put it back just where he got it. He took off a few hours before the FBI arrived to find him and the airplane missing. He

---

[2]Clarence Darrow, "Attorney for the Defense," *Esquire*, p. 36 (May 1936).

flew the airplane back to the airport in St. Paul, left the keys in it, and hoped the incident would go away.

Dobbins knew there were risks in supplementing his income by hiring himself out as a pilot. When he transported business executives out of the country, especially to the Caribbean, he was troubled. Dobbins knew the reputation of Grand Cayman and other Caribbean stops, like the Bahamas. They were the bankers of those who wanted to keep their affairs confidential, often from U.S. taxing authorities. The Bahamas and Grand Caymans were Switzerland-like in their banking secrecy laws. And the Caribbean was also known as a source of marijuana for the United States. But Dobbins felt that what he did not know would not hurt him. And so he transported business people without questioning the nature of their business or why they needed to fly there.

On this particular occasion, he had not known the businessmen who had hired him to pick up two businessmen in the Bahamas and fly them back to Georgia. That man supplied the airplane by giving him the keys to a Beechcraft twin engine aircraft at the St. Paul airport. According to Dobbins, his introduction to Bahamian police, coming shortly after the phone call that the businessmen were not coming and that he should fly back, was his first indication that something might be wrong with the aircraft.

But soon the federal government was in tough with him and his Georgia lawyer. At the advice of his counsel, who thought he could get a quick nolo contendere plea, he had an interview with the U.S. Attorney. Unknown to him, the U.S. Attorney believed none of the Dobbins story, but he did have a crucial defect in his case, a problem of proof. He could prove that Al Dobbins had been in the Bahamas in possession of an aircraft that had been reported stolen. He could prove that the plane had been returned. But he had no way of proving that Dobbins had transported it across state lines. Neither Dobbins nor his counsel were sensitive to this point of federal jurisdiction. The U.S. Attorney asked him, innocently enough, whether he had indeed flown the plane either to or from the Bahamas. Dobbins, seeing no inconsistency with his story, confirmed that he had. In doing so, he gave the government the last fact they needed to frame an indictment.

In due course the indictment came down. The prosecutor ruled out any plea bargain. The trial went forward.

During the course of the voir dire, it turned out that one of the jurors was a well-known local reporter who covered the court beat for *The Minneapolis Tribune*. The judge trying the case, Miles Lord, had a reputation for enjoying publicity. He sometimes called reporters over when sentencing a business or a prominent personality so that his sermon at sentencing could be duly recorded. He relished his high-profile position within the federal judiciary. The stories about him were legion. And his eyes twinkled at the prospect of a journalist on the panel.

Before the questioning of the jury was completed, he summoned both me and the prosecutor into his chambers. "I think it would be very helpful to the people of this state and the city if Mr. Sorensen were permitted to sit on this case. Do you know what I mean?"

Both the prosecutor and I sat in silence. I was afraid that the reporter had heard my closing argument before and was therefore inoculated to its appeal. The prosecutor was afraid that he might be politically liberal, and antiprosecution.

Hearing no response, the judge went on. "Let me strongly encourage you not to exercise your peremptory challenge on this one. I know you both have the right to represent your respective clients. I am certainly not telling you what you have to do. But I want to make it very clear what I think should be done. I would be very disappointed if you did not leave this man, who I am sure is utterly fair and impartial, on this jury panel."

This was no time for talk. I sat mute. The prosecutor was more forthcoming. "I'm afraid I may have to strike him, your Honor. I apologize, but I have to represent the government in the best way I know how."

The judge's countenance fell. "I think you should think hard before doing that, Counsel," the judge said through pursed lips, "think very hard."

When we got back into the courtroom and completed the voir dire, it was time to make our strikes. Making peremptory strikes happens in a "Ping-Pong" fashion. Jurors are struck one by one, alternately. The prosecutor had the last strike. Suspecting that my endorsement of the judge's opinion on the reporter-juror was not sincere, he refused to strike the reporter. Prior to my making my last strike, I thought hard, as the judge had admonished me, and played my hunch, that the prosecutor would strike the reporter on his last strike. I struck somebody else. The prosecutor fulfilled my expectations. I tried not to look relieved.

The clerk then brought the record of our strikes to the judge. His eyes looked quickly down the slash marks striking certain names on the sheet. When he saw the last strike, his fingers squeezed the paper more tightly. He looked up, fastened the prosecutor with a frightening stare which seemed to last for minutes, then called a recess.

When the testimony began, for whatever reason, nearly all the evidentiary rulings went for the defense. It was critical that they do so. My factual investigation has revealed some peculiarities in the title of the aircraft. It had been owned by a local leasing firm, then sold to an individual without apparent financial wherewithal to afford such a luxury. When that buyer defaulted, it was turned back to the leasing company. But substantial moneys were still owed on the aircraft.

As it turned out, both the individual and the company knew each other well. The individual had worked for the company, was a close friend of the officer of the company who had approved the sale, and knew well where the keys were kept for company aircraft. When I traced down the individual, I found that his last known address was the Golden Egg Gold Mine in Las Vegas, Nevada. His most recent job was a shill in a gambling casino, while also purporting to be the operator of a gold mine. While casting about trying to figure out who the gentleman was, I got an important piece of information. One acquaintance said that he had heard that the fellow was now in jail in Mexico on drug smuggling charges.

A likely scenario suggested itself. The owner had bought the Beechcraft airplane from this friend at the leasing company to use it for drug running from the Caribbean. When payments could not be made and there was no visible means of support, both the individual and the officer who approved the deal saw how they were heading for trouble. Could it be that this airplane was insured? And if so, to whose benefit? Research into the insurance papers revealed that it was jointly insured by the individual and by the officer of the leasing company. The possible plan? Get some desperate pilot to fly the plane to the Bahamas. Bring back some drugs. Ditch the plane in an obscure Georgia airport. Collect money for the missing plane from insurance. If things go awry, you have a pilot who does not know who he's picking up or anything about the underlying transaction, and you are insulated.

To make this claim, one needed discretionary rulings from the court to go our way. We got them. When the officer of the leasing company took the stand, he was expecting a 15-minute appearance to put in papers showing a technical but necessary element of the government case. He had to show ownership of the airplane, so the government could prove that my client was not entitled to be in possession of it.

But on cross-examination, I began to explore the officer's relationship with the operator of the Golden Egg Gold Mine. One could see the helpful effect of the examination on the witness even at its introductory stages.

Before long, the U.S. Attorney was smelling a rat. He asked for the jury to be excused. With some indignation, he accused me of a "fishing expedition" into "irrelevancies." The judge looked at him with the same severity as he did at the beginning of the case, "Mr. Vosepca, if you want to get down in the dirt, you've got to expect that you will be dirtied up a bit yourself." Looking at me, the judge said, "You may proceed, Counsel."

The interrogation proceeded.

QUESTION: So you knew Joe Leoso?
ANSWER: Yes, I did.

QUESTION: Was he a friend of yours?

ANSWER: Yes.

QUESTION: He was quite a close friend, wasn't he?

ANSWER: He was over at my house.

QUESTION: He worked for you?

ANSWER: For a while.

QUESTION: What did he do?

ANSWER: He was a leasing agent.

QUESTION: He leased out airplanes?

ANSWER: Yes.

QUESTION: He leased out this particular airplane from time to time?

ANSWER: I think so.

QUESTION: He was sort of like the person who works at the front desk of a hotel, right?

ANSWER: That's right.

QUESTION: So he determined who got the plane?

ANSWER: That's right.

QUESTION: He made sure it was paid for?

ANSWER: Yes, of course.

QUESTION: And he also gave out the key?

ANSWER: Yes.

QUESTION: He knew where the keys were to all these airplanes?

ANSWER: Of course.

QUESTION: And he knew what keys fit what planes?

ANSWER: That's what he did.

QUESTION: At some point in time, you also had a social relationship with him?

ANSWER: Yes, he came over for dinner, as I said, a good deal.

QUESTION: Your wife knew him?

ANSWER: Yes, we all knew him.

QUESTION: And at some point, he bought the airplane from your company, correct?

ANSWER: At some point, yes.

QUESTION: How much did he pay for the airplane?

ANSWER: I don't recall.

QUESTION: (Showing him the title and additional papers) Does this refresh your recollection that he was to pay $227,000?

ANSWER: That looks right.

QUESTION: How was he employed at the time he entered into this agreement with you?

ANSWER: I don't have the foggiest idea.

QUESTION: He was no longer employed by you?

ANSWER: That's right.

QUESTION: Well, what generally did you think he did for a living?

ANSWER: I told you I don't know.

QUESTION: You decided to sell a plane to a person and you didn't know what his employment was?

ANSWER: That's right.

QUESTION: Did you know whether he was employed?

ANSWER: I assumed that he was employed, but I didn't know.

QUESTION: Did you ever discuss his employment when you had him over for dinner during this period of time?

ANSWER: Not that I recall.

QUESTION: Did he tell you what he was going to be using the plane for?

ANSWER: We never discussed it.

QUESTION: He remained a good friend of yours?

ANSWER: Yes.

QUESTION: And you never asked him what he was going to be doing with the plane?

ANSWER: I thought that was none of my business.

QUESTION: Within months he began defaulting on payments, is that right?

ANSWER: As I recall, he couldn't make all the payments.

QUESTION: And that was an embarrassment to you, was it not?

ANSWER: It happens.

QUESTION: Well, it was embarrassing that you sold an airplane to someone with no visible means of support, and now he was defaulting on his obligation, isn't that right?

ANSWER: I suppose you could say that.

QUESTION: As to the time of the incident we are talking about here, was the plane insured?

ANSWER: Yes.

QUESTION: Of course, part of the insurance was against theft?

ANSWER: Yes, that's in the standard insurance agreement.

QUESTION: Who was the beneficiary if the plane were to be stolen?

ANSWER: Joe and I jointly.

QUESTION: By the way, Mr. Smith, where is Joe Leoso, now?

ANSWER: I don't know.

QUESTION: Do you have any idea where he is?

PROSECUTOR: Objection, your Honor! Absolutely irrelevant!

THE COURT: He may answer.

ANSWER: I honestly don't know.

QUESTION: At the present time, he is in jail in Mexico for drug smuggling, isn't he?

PROSECUTOR: Objection! Your Honor, could we dismiss the jury momentarily?

THE COURT: Ladies and Gentlemen, you may be excused while counsel and court discuss a matter that has come up.

The jury walked quietly out of the courtroom, leaving the edge of the chair where they had been perched over the last ten minutes of the interrogation.

Again the prosecutor, now out of the jury's hearing, waged bitter war to exclude the line of examination. The judge repeated his description of dirt and dirtying, and he repeated his ruling. The jury filed back in with a sense of anticipation. The judge informed them that he had overruled the prosecutor's objections. The question was repeated.

QUESTION: Isn't he now in jail in Mexico for drug smuggling charges?

ANSWER: That's what I've heard.

QUESTION: And you knew he was a drug smuggler when you sold him this plane, didn't you?

ANSWER: I had no reason to know that.

QUESTION: Did you discuss his drug smuggling activities prior to entering into this agreement?

ANSWER: I don't recall doing that.

QUESTION: On the many occasions that you had him over for dinner, did you discuss what role, if any, this airplane would serve in his drug smuggling operations?

ANSWER: I don't think that ever came up.

The interrogation went on, and the jury seemed transfixed at how quickly a dull piece of testimony on title turned into a mesmerizing account of dealings with a drug smuggler.

The trial was not without its normal setbacks. But when the verdict came in, after six and a half hours, it was an acquittal. Notwithstanding

Al Dobbins' seat in the cockpit of a stolen airplane in the Bahamas, the jury did not believe that he knew it was stolen or knew the purposes of those who hired him to fly it. The circumstances were prejudicial, at the least suspicious, for Dobbins. But the defense seemed plausible. The judge easily could have denied critical testimony for the defense, however, without ever being second-guessed by the Eighth Circuit. And the judge, a former U.S. Attorney, might well have done so, but for a curious coincidence in the voir dire. The race is not always to the swift.

After years of involvement in the criminal justice system, some judges feel like they too are a part of the *prosecution team*. As a public defender, I once represented Robert Altimus. Altimus was accused of driving a stolen car, running head on into a police vehicle while making an illegal left turn, fleeing from the scene notwithstanding two punctured tires and a radiator spewing smoke, ditching the vehicle two blocks later, only to take refuge in a local church where, bursting out of the men's room to surprise a pursuing officer, he broke three of the officer's teeth. The case was complicated somewhat by the fact that Altimus was away without leave from a federal penitentiary for interstate car theft at the time of the incident.

His defense was that he had been given Valium for back problems and that it triggered a paradoxical reaction. Valium calms most patients who take it. But a few have a reaction with Valium that causes hysteria and a frantic hyperactivity. He claimed he was in the latter group. When given the tablet, he did not know it was Valium. The strategy of the case was not to put Altimus on the stand and expose his prior record to jury view. Dr. Humberto Ortiz, who gave him the Valium, and who was an expert in his own right on its paradoxical impact for some patients, was to come in and testify that he personally gave Altimus the Valium and also describe the impact of the Valium on some people.

Judge C. William Sykora saw that Dr. Ortiz's personal contact with Altimus might enable the defense to keep Mr. Altimus from the stand. He refused to permit Dr. Ortiz to testify unless Mr. Altimus himself personally testified that he took the Valium tablet. The ruling was questionable, but its effect was not. Altimus had to take the stand.

After direction examination, the local city attorney undertook the cross-examination. Not expecting to see Altimus, he had no prepared examination. He jumped here and there, and finally, not finding his place readily in the batch of yellow sheets in front of him, he said, "no further questions."

I interjected, as quickly as I could while remaining calm, "no questions." The prosecutor had forgotten or chosen not to inquire about Altimus' past record. Judge Sykora, looking exercised, immediately called a recess and told counsel he wanted to see them in chambers.

When I got back to chambers, Sykora was fuming, walking back and forth across his chambers with black robes flowing behind him. He fastened his eyes on the prosecutor, as a laser fixes itself on a target, "I can't believe you. I can't believe you did it."

The prosecutor answered somewhat meekly, "Your Honor?"

"Here I get this crook on the stand for you and you don't ask him about his prior felonies. I can't believe it. How could you be so stupid? This guy might get off!" I detected at that point some potential prejudgment in the judge's attitude. Next, the judge sat down and telephoned another senior member of the district bench. "I've got a guy up here with a cockamamie defense based on involuntary intoxication. Do you have instruction that might prevent the jury from being confused on it?" he said in my presence. His attitude was further punctuated by turning his chair around, swiveling to look at the wall, putting his feet up on the railing, while I was giving my closing argument. Altimus was ultimately acquitted.

The fortuities sometimes arise from "evidence" that does not come from the witness stand. Consider the case of Mack Sitensky. Mr. Sitensky was 44 years old. Extraordinarily bright, he had lustrous academic credentials and was president of three companies and president of a major national trade association. He was personally charming, conservative in his tastes, honest to a fault. But now he was faced with utter destruction. He was accused of tax fraud, a felony charge, along with failure to file income tax returns for other years. What could lead such a successful businessman to file no income tax returns or to file an inaccurate return?

To know why, one had to know Mack's father. His father had built a multi-million-dollar fortune through hard work and a stubborn will to succeed. He viewed his son as somewhat soft, despite his greater education and sophistication. He had abused the boy from childhood for not being tough enough. He made promises to take him camping and would renege on them without even advising the child. In one classic example, my client reported that he had planned to go fishing with his father one Saturday in the summer, based on his father's promise. He had packed a little suitcase and boasted to his friends about what his father was going to do for him. Saturday morning came. His father did not even remember the promise. When his son began to cry, his father told him he was a sissy to cry, and that he was ashamed of him. As he drove off down the elm-lined street in his Cadillac automobile, his son ran after him, suitcase in hand, crying.

His father was a picture of the ancient Roman paterfamilias, the father who controlled every detail of his children's lives, even into adulthood, the monarch who brooked no interference with his authority until he died. Mack Sitensky, Sr., had built a fortune out of cunning business decisions and an intimidating manner. His life had been given over to being the richest man in town. He had little time for his family generally or his son particularly.

When Mack got out of college, his father continued to dominate the financial side of his life. He told him that he would have to work at a "social security minimum" wage. His father continued to criticize his performance and make him totally dependent on him for money.

At the end of the year, his father would give him a small slip of paper, indicating how much he had made in one of several partnerships. He would then make his son beg for money to pay the taxes on the partnership distribution that he had never received. When the son could not tolerate the confrontations with his father anymore, he stopped asking his father for money to pay taxes. Paralyzed, Mack refused to include such partnership income on his tax return, and ultimately failed to file his tax returns altogether.

For those who knew Mack outside of the context of his relationship with his father, that this could happen was inconceivable. He was confident, humorous, and generally at ease in social relationships. There was only one dimension of his life where he was utterly dependent and helpless. That was in the relationship with his father. His father viewed him as a parasite. When his father gave him a wedding gift, he took the money to pay for it out of his son's trust. When he gave him a birthday present, he charged his son's trust. On other occasions, he gave him money beyond the social security minimum only when he pled for it.

When the indictments came down, all of the problems Mack had with his father crystallized. I met with his father. He tried to sympathize with his son's predicament ("well, of course, like everybody else, I myself keep a second set of books for Uncle Sugar," he chuckled). Basically, his attitude was severe. His son was weak, incompetent, and stupidly got himself in trouble with "Uncle Sugar." In all these matters, he was unlike his father who was omnicompetent and able to keep a step ahead of the government.

But how was a jury to understand this psycho-history? Would this peculiar and eccentric relationship look like a desperate or deceptive defense tactic? After all, Mack had not filed his returns. Those charges were true. And the other returns were not accurate. That was true, too. Was this focus on the father just a devious device to confuse?

Various witnesses confirmed the son's terror in the presence of his father. One described a particularly frightening confrontation, where Mack's poise melted, his face went white, his posture slumped, and he went off like a whipped dog under the domination of his father. The problem with such testimony was its vagueness and its inconsistency with the picture of a knowledgeable and successful business executive. And when the prime witness of these confrontations, a long-time employee of the family business, took the stand, he looked like a deer frozen in the headlight beams. His answers were yes and no, scarcely audible. "Yes," he said, "I have seen many confrontations between Mack and his father, some friendly, and some not so friendly." The *Sturm und Drang* of the confrontation as he related it in private could never be successfully communicated to the jury. The jury looked impatiently over at his questioner, wondering why he had been put on the stand.

But when the time came, Mack Sr. was ready for his starring role. He marched confidently to the witness stand. It soon became apparent what his strategy was. He would kill the defense by kindness. Despite his protestations that he supported his son, it became clear that one by one he was attempting to destroy any of his son's defenses to the charges.

The graying man on the stand was hardly the monster that appeared from interviews or from Mack Jr.'s own accounts, Kindly, soft-spoken, expressing warm sentiments toward his son, his manner obscured his true designs. And his testimony was lethal.

On cross-examination, after a bit of fencing, I decided to take the risk of confronting him.

QUESTION: You love your son?

ANSWER: Of course.

QUESTION: You give him presents, is that correct?

ANSWER: Yes, as any father would do.

QUESTION: You tried to remember special days?

ANSWER: Why, yes I do.

QUESTION: And when you do give him a present, do you pay that money out yourself?

ANSWER: (Laughing) Yes, I give that money out myself.

QUESTION: Could I show you a statement of your son's trust (showing exhibit in evidence)? Do you recognize this as a trust account that you have set up for your son?

ANSWER: Yes.

QUESTION: And that's your son's money that you are supervising for him as trustee?

ANSWER: Yes, I am the trustee of this account.

QUESTION: Reviewing entry for June 4, 1967, do you see a withdrawal for $250.00?

ANSWER: Yes, I do.

QUESTION: That was money you withdrew from your son's account to pay for his wedding present, isn't that right?

ANSWER: (Flushing) I don't recall, but I suppose it could have been.

QUESTION: And if you look at the ten following years, would you agree that there is a withdrawal annually from your son's account to pay for his own birthday present?

ANSWER: (Somewhat irritably) I don't remember. I don't personally keep all these books.

QUESTION: In fact, you keep two sets of books, don't you?

ANSWER: I don't know what you're talking about.

QUESTION: Don't you keep one set of books for yourself, and one set of books for the IRS?

ANSWER: All business people keep various records for various purposes.

QUESTION: But don't you keep special books solely to satisfy the IRS?

ANSWER: I don't know what you're talking about.

QUESTION: Do you recall telling me on February 14 of last year that you kept two sets of books, that one was solely for "Uncle Sugar," and that "what Uncle Sugar doesn't know, doesn't hurt me?"

ANSWER: As I said, I do keep various sets of records, Counsel, for various purposes.

His eyes looked nervously to the back of the courtroom, where there sat an IRS special agent with whom he was familiar and who was, he knew, monitoring the trial of his son. His father's face was now fully flushed. But the insistent cross-examination was also having a peculiar effect on his son. Mack Jr. began to breathe heavily, burst into tears, and rushed from the courtroom to the shock of the jury. Judge Edward Devitt, the dignified, white-haired prototype of all federal judges, and chief judge of the district, called a recess.

As the jury went out the side door of the courtroom, I went out to look for Mack Jr. I did not know how the jury was taking this confrontational cross-examination of an elderly man. Was I beating up on a kindly old gentleman? Was I, as a U.S. Attorney was later to complain, representing "a young wolf biting at the flanks of an aging stag?" I was not at all sure of the wisdom of the attack. But as I walked to the main corridor, one of those unplanned and unexpected serendipities happened before my eyes. I heard loud talk as I came around the corner. There was Mack Sr., enraged, leaning over his son, whose face was thrust into the palms of his hands, sobbing uncontrollably. "You're a weakling, you'll never be anything in life. You should be ashamed of yourself and your lawyer. You're not a man and you never will be." The insistent browbeating went on furiously when, suddenly, the jury of 12, led by the bailiff, came around the same corner. There the jury had, right in front of them, the picture that could not be described by any witness. They deflected their eyes in embarrassment and went on to the jury room.

Later, a key fraud charge was dismissed by the judge. The "failure to file" counts (income tax returns had clearly not been filed) went before the jury. Believing his claim of diminished capacity resulting from his relationship with his father, the jury acquitted on all counts. Mack was free.

But without that confrontation in the hallway, would the result have been different? Again, the lesson is clear. The race is not always to the swift, nor the battle to the strong, but fate and chance happeneth to all.

16

"How I Love the Law"

Lon Fuller was a wise and gentle legal philosopher. He was for years a dominant thinker in jurisprudence. Through many fruitful years of enlightening classes at the Harvard Law School, he sought to stretch his students' frame of reference for analyzing issues of law and justice.

Professor Fuller used to speak of two metaphors which can form a person's perspective of the law: the law may be seen either as a *guidepost* or a *harness*. For some, the law is a harness, a continuing chafing threat to their autonomy. It is the means by which the will of the government is imposed on and rudely communicated to the individual, restraining one's liberty, hampering one's creativity, coercing one with punishments. For others, however, the law is a guidepost, pointing the way to right behavior, facilitating the realization of good ends, encouraging the full realization of potential. Either metaphor can frame the perspective one has toward the legal system. Sometimes the dominating metaphor can change rapidly.

My client and I sat in the high-walled federal courtroom. The closing arguments had been concluded that morning. Now we sat in the huge courtroom alone at the counsel table, back early from lunch with 30 minutes on our hands before the U.S. Attorney returned with his FBI agents, the jury of 12 filed back into the jury box, and the judge gave his final instructions.

The client was an unlikely defendant in a federal criminal trial. Well-dressed and prosperous, he had been one of the most successful figures in his business in the United States. But that was now of little comfort. Even the fact that the trial had gone well did not remove the terrors of the trial for the businessman defendant. As I saw him gradually transformed from the smiling and self-confident salesman to a haunted and haggard defendant, I again thought of the comment of Judge Learned Hand:

> After now some dozens of years of experience I must say that as a litigant I should dread a lawsuit beyond almost anything else short of sickness and death.

The fairness of the system, the due process of law, and the jury trial right that the writers of the Constitution viewed as the "very palladium of free government" seemed to him only so much window dressing, a conspiracy of forces to destroy him and bring him down. The law to him was a whip and a harness. That perspective was soon to change.

I could not stay in town for the verdict. When I called back to the office the next afternoon from San Francisco, an associate who had taken the verdict had good news. The verdict had come in after eight hours. It had been a complete acquittal, not guilty on all counts. My client was now suddenly celebrating the fairness of the legal system. He was gracious to the prosecutor, smiling at the jury, giving handshakes all around. He had immediately called an Atlanta friend who later told me the acquitted defendant was "as happy as a pig in slop." Suddenly, the law was viewed from a different point of view. Our system of criminal justice was now "the greatest system on earth."

Table 16-1 depicts the difference between the two perspectives of law.

Each of these metaphors has had its supporters in jurisprudence. One group sees the law as an agency of punishment, the other as an agency of instruction. An inability to distinguish these or to see the validity of both models has led to a confusion that results either in legalism or lawlessness, in a Pharisee or a libertine.

Many legal scholars have focused on the law's punishment of bad men. The great jurist, Oliver Wendell Holmes, for example, made popular the "bad man" theory of law. If you want to know the vitality of a law, ask the bad man. Does he comply with it? If so, the sanction must be adequate. Do you want to know if you have a good contract? Ask what the sanctions are for breaking it—its value is limited to what you can recover if the bad man breaks it. The purpose of the law is to ensure that such "bad men" don't commit crimes, break contracts, or swindle poor widows. This view, though pessimistic, is ancient. Paul takes this view in I Timothy 1:9,10:

> Knowing this, that the law is not made for a righteous man, but for the lawless and disobedient, for the ungodly and for sinners, for unholy and profane, for murderers of fathers and murderers of moth-

Table 16-1. Two Views of Law

	Harness	Guidepost
Focus	Punishment of law	Purpose of law
Function	Restrain evil works of bad man	Facilitate good works of confused man
Motive for compliance	Fear (of punishment)	Love (of law's purpose)
Extent of compliance	Minimum (to avoid punishment)	Perfect (to accomplish God's purpose)
Approach of actor	Negative (seeks to avoid obvious "don'ts" to avoid punishment)	Positive (not only avoids "don'ts" but seeks positive "do's" to accomplish purpose)
Nature of obligation	Duty (▼) Imposed	Aspiration (▲) Beckoning
Actor's will	Chafes under harness	Positive desire to follow guidepost (one will)
Actor's relation with others	Judge (seeks to punish breach of duty)	Guide (seeks to call others to higher aspiration)
Actor's attitude	Pride (accomplishes minimal compliance, avoids punishment)	Humility (strives for perfection)
Location of law	External (on tables of stone)	Internal (written on the heart)

ers, for manslayers, For whoremongers, for them that defile themselves with mankind, for menstealers, for liars, for perjured persons, and if there be any other thing that is contrary to sound doctrine . . .

This bad man theory of law naturally focuses on punishment, because that is what it takes to get a bad man to do right. This focus leads to the *fearful defendant.*

There is another side of law, however, that goes more directly to the purpose of law. Law is not only a harness on people's activity; it is also a guidepost. This view is equally ancient. The law, the psalmist says, is meant to be "a lamp unto my feet and a light unto my path."

Although laws are made for the bad man, they are also made for the good man, or at least for the confused man. They have an important function in directing a confused man of good will to the right end. The confused father wants to know how to pass on his property to his heir, and the law frees him to accomplish that purpose by defining a valid will. The suitor wants to share life with his beloved, and the law enables him to do so by providing a contractual form of marriage. The law instructs people how to carry out their good intentions successfully. They do not think of the law as threatening punishment if they do not properly negotiate and execute a contract. The only "punishment" for disobedience is the nullification of their hoped-for agreement; the threat is that they fall short of accomplishing their purposes.

One who has successfully represented white-collar crime defendants has seen both perspectives. From investigation through trial, the defendant sees nothing but the overwhelming force of the law, compelling, forbidding, accusing. To the defendant facing the bar of justice, the process seems to be a horrible mismatch, the governmental advantages overwhelming. It is a time of terror. But if a verdict of acquittal is rendered, the perspective changes. "What a great system," says the defendant, "what a great country." The defendant leaves the courtroom with a new love for the law and its due process.

After many jury trials, it is clear to me that this conversion of perspective happens with less pain before—rather than after—questionable behavior has led to a criminal investigation. When corporate executives view the law not as a harness (requiring minimal compliance) but a guidepost (leading to an aspiration of perfect compliance), they will so manage their affairs such that the pains reflected in this book will usually not be visited on them. And they will be expressing love for both the law and for themselves.

Index